Booker T. Washington in American Memory

THE NEW BLACK STUDIES SERIES

Edited by Darlene Clark Hine and Dwight A. McBride

A list of books in the series appears at the end of this book.

Booker T. Washington
in American Memory

KENNETH M. HAMILTON

UNIVERSITY OF ILLINOIS PRESS
Urbana, Chicago, and Springfield

To the Memory of my Sister
Ava Benita Hamilton and
Brother-in-law, Curtis Embry Anderson

Publication of this book was supported by the
William P. Clements Department of History at
Southern Methodist University.

Library of Congress Cataloging-in-Publication Data
Names: Hamilton, Kenneth Marvin, 1947– author.
Title: Booker T. Washington in American memory /
    Kenneth M. Hamilton.
Description: Urbana : University of Illinois Press, [2017]
    | Series: The new Black studies series | Includes
    bibliographical references and index.
Identifiers: LCCN 2016042453 (print) | LCCN 2016045181
    (ebook) | ISBN 9780252040771 (cloth : alk. paper) |
    ISBN 9780252082283 (pbk. : alk. paper) |
    ISBN 9780252099229 (E-book)
Subjects: LCSH: Washington, Booker T., 1856–1915—
    Influence. | Washington, Booker T., 1856–1915—
    Death & burial. | Eulogies—United States. | Culture
    conflict—United States—History—20th century.
    | Collective memory—United States. | Protestant
    work ethic. | Southern States—Moral conditions. |
    Northeastern States—Moral conditions. | Civil rights
    movements—United States—History. | African
    Americans—Intellectual life.
Classification: LCC E185.97.W4 H355 2017 (print) | LCC
    E185.97.W4 (ebook) | DDC 370.92—dc23
LC record available at https://lccn.loc.gov/2016042453

Contents

Illustrations follow page 124

Acknowledgments

As a teenager living in Wichita, Kansas, during the early and mid-1960s, I spent most of my wonderful leisure time either playing basketball or hanging out with my lively, and sometimes mischievous, friends. They included Dale Diggs Jr., Eric Hutcherson, James Leroy Johnson, Charles Duane Stovall, Warren Wigley, as well as the late Cletus Crowley, Harold Peter Daley, Donald Diggs, William Oliver Hamilton Jr., Gary Jones, Gary Mills, and Roy Walker. Since Wichita, like most towns and cities during those years, did not provide many activities for working-class black males, we often congregated in and outside of the Dunbar Drug Store at the corner of Ninth and Cleveland Streets, or at some other public place, like McKinney (now McAdams) Park, or at one of the fellows' home. During those gatherings we joked, lied, signified, and theorized. From these seasons emerged a group consensus concerning the first and most important question that we should ask ourselves before making a decision concerning any perceived significant event in our respective lives. More so than any other member of the crowd, Harold—we called him Peter—would challenge himself and the other members of the group with the all-important question: *"What does it mean?"* That is the primary question I have attempted to answer in this book concerning the letters of solace sent to the survivors of Booker T. Washington and about his obituaries, his funeral, his eulogies, and his commemorations.

Over the quarter century that I have researched and written about the memorization of Washington, numerous persons have assisted me, and I am most grateful for their assistance. I must acknowledge the invaluable contribution of the late Tuskegee University archivist Daniel Williams, who in 1990 introduced me to a massive collection of National Negro Business League papers that the university had recently acquired. Those papers inspired me to ask what Americans thought of Washington at his death, how they memorialized him, and what their commemoration meant. After Daniel retired, his successor, Cynthia Wilson, not only allowed me to continue accessing the Washington collection, she provided me with many fruitful research suggestions. I must also thank Deborah Dandridge at the University of Kansas Kenneth Spencer Research Library. Other helpful archivists included the staffs at the Columbia University Rare Book and Manuscript Library, the Fisk University Special Collections and Archives, the Howard University Moorland-Spingarn Research Center, the Hampton University Harvey Library, the Library of Congress, the New York Public Library, the Rockefeller Archive Center, and the Schomburg Center for Research in Black Culture. I extend a special thank-you to the Southern Methodist University Library research staff who helped me to locate more than a few obscured sources.

I am grateful for assistance from a number of other people. Dorthea Wilson Caldwell helped with the copying at the Tuskegee University. Professors Ernest Allen, Shubha Ghosh, Timothy Davis, James Dormon, Joe Hawes, and Willison Moses displayed true friendship, as did Merline Anderson, Bian Beverly, Telana Hicks, Adriane Livingston, and Judy Nobie, when they read and edited all or parts of the manuscript. I must extend a special thank-you to Shawn Alexandra. I am extremely grateful to Stephanie J. Shaw, who went far beyond her professional responsibilities in sharing her editorial suggestions with me—a very gracious deed. Other charitable persons include my Southern Methodist University colleagues, Bradley Carter, Charles Curran, David Hanes, John Lewis, Kenneth Shields, Dennis Simon, and Theodore Walker Jr.: they too read one or more chapters of the manuscript. Over the years I received considerable encouragement from Edward Biehl, Dennis C. Dickerson, Robert Gregory, and James Quick, Southern Methodist University colleagues who teach outside of the History Department. I very much appreciate the members of Southern Methodist University's William P. Clements Department of History. They each took time out of their respective busy lives to read and provide oral and written responses to drafts of chapters. While Daniel Orlovsky suggested readings regarding historical memory, Edward Countryman frequently provided recommendations concerning my research, conclusions, and prose. Displaying true friendship, Kenneth Andrien, as he did for my previous book, meticulously read the full manuscript several times. It is hard to image a collection of more benevolent colleagues.

I must acknowledge the assistance of Charlotte Brewster, the former Southern Methodist University Ethnic Studies administrative assistant. No one worked as long or as hard with me on this study. For more years than I care to count, she helped with research, exchanged ideas with me, organized materials, and edited my prose. I am indebted to her for her invaluable help.

Also deserving of thanks are student research assistants Angelica Alaniz, Joe Louis Bryant, Corey Capers, Jeremy Claybrook, Jeremy Milhouse, Tony Pedote, and Shereka Derrick.

My family's support was crucial. I thank my sister, Carolyn Anderson, my brother, Timothy M. Hamilton, my daughters, Kelley and Kristy Hamilton, and my son, Kenneth II. At an early age, Kenneth accompanied my lovely, brilliant, generous, and devoted wife, Deborah Lee Hamilton, to the Howard University archive for me. Deborah also joined me on research road trips to Tuskegee, Alabama, Washington, D.C., New York City, and other locales. She unstintingly supported me throughout this long and tedious process. She too read several drafts of the manuscript and provided me with valued suggestions. I am deeply grateful for her assistance.

I appreciate the generous financial support for this study that I received from the Southern Methodist University through its William P. Clements Department of History, as well as for assistance from the University of Illinois Press and its editor-in-chief, Laurie Matheson, and acquisitions editor, Dawn Durante.

Finally, I must thank John Manning for allowing me to accompany him to hear a lecture that Playthell Benjamin gave on the campus of Wichita State University on August 20, 1968. On that day, Benjamin's amazing oration inspired me to become a historian of the African American experience.

Note to the Reader

Readers should note that my analysis of printed accounts of the eulogies of Washington considered reporters' possible mistakes as well as their biases and those of their editors and publishers. While it is true that occasionally periodicals have misconstrued or misquoted assertions in order to secure wider circulation, there is no evidence that one or more persons deliberately misstated or mischaracterized a tribute to Washington. A majority of the cited published accounts concerning Washington, eulogists, and his commemorations are from articles that are compiled in collections of clippings either at the Hampton University Library, the Library of Congress, or the Tuskegee University Archive. The remaining ones acknowledge articles I found in copies of journals. These articles often provided the race and sex of the named commemorators. Moreover, I have not altered the spelling or the punctuation of quotations from journals, articles, or other sources.

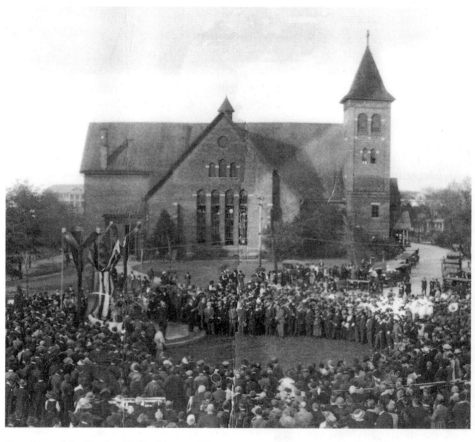

Unveiling of the Booker T. Washington Monument on April 5, 1922. Tuskegee University Archives, Tuskegee University

Prologue

This account examines how, when, who, where, and why Americans, blacks and whites alike, commemorated the life of Booker T. Washington in the period shortly after his death. For months, tens of thousands of Americans, especially blacks, honored his memory. Their memorials revealed that Washington enjoyed widespread national support for his vision of America and the programs he sponsored to achieve his aspirations. Their actions and articulations provide an unmatched rich insight into how a wide cross section of Washington's contemporaries viewed him. In private messages of solace, and in public pronouncements, countless Americans portrayed him as a revered national icon. Among other characteristics, commemorators voiced their appreciation of his humanitarianism, humility, nationalism, perseverance, philanthropy, progressivism, spirituality and wisdom.

Hence, their view of Washington strongly challenges many of the prevailing negative assessments that latter-day scholars hold of him. Louis R. Harlan's two-volume biography of the Tuskegean, one of which won a Pulitzer Prize, has become the point of reference for most assessments of Washington. Harlan alleges that Washington accepted segregation and that pursuit of power motivated him more than anything else. Harlan joined a list of scholars who had vilified Washington before the 1972 publication of his first volume. Scholars like Benjamin Quarles, who asserted that Washington "seemed to view things from the point of view of the whites," and Lerone Bennett Jr., who stated, "by implication anyway, he (Washington) accepted segregation," preceded Harlan's biography.[1]

Not all of the pre-Harlan scholarship concerning Washington presents an overwhelmingly negative appraisal. Among the exceptions are August Meier's

1957 "Toward a Reinterpretation of Booker T. Washington" and Samuel R. Spencer Jr.'s 1955 biography. Meier asserts, "Washington was surreptitiously engaged in undermining the American race system by a direct attack upon disfranchisement and segregation." Presenting an assessment similar to what many of Washington's contemporaries articulated after his death, Spencer alleged that the Tuskegean "fired the imagination of even the poorest tenant farmer by offering him an active role in a creative, dynamic program which affected him personally and directly. By setting tangible goals and demonstrating how they could be reached, he pointed the way to a better life for the Negro in his own home and community."[2]

Spencer's study discussed the life of an African American man who, by the time of his death, had become the most prominent and effective evangelists of the Yankee Protestant ethic. Born and reared in the South, Booker Taliaferro Washington died at 4:45 A.M. on November 14, 1915, at the age of fifty-nine. For approximately twenty years he had commanded a large and diverse group of culture warriors in their individual and collective efforts to transform southerners, particularly African Americans, into adherents of the Yankee Protestant ethic. Although he promoted both the religious and secular aspects of Yankee Protestantism, Washington placed the greatest emphasis on the latter. This precept included asceticism, calling, charity, cleanliness, education, efficiency, honesty, humility, orderliness, perseverance, pragmatism, promptness, service, steadiness, systematic work, thrift, and the dignity of labor. Years of exposure to teachers trained within the evangelical Yankee Protestant tradition inspired Washington to embrace and champion their doctrines. He and his teachers participated in a movement that consisted of a cadre of Yankee Protestant missionaries, philanthropists, and other like-minded whites, along with northern and southern black allies. This movement, like most others, included individuals, groups, and organizations who created a collective identity in the process of transforming "private troubles into public problems" and engaged in a combined sustained effort to solve them. Historically, participants in this movement perceived much of the southern secular society as a problem.[3]

For over forty years, members of the Yankee Protestant evangelical movement had viewed the majority of southerners (specifically, those residing in states that sanctioned slavery in 1860) as a people who embraced a profane ethic that undermined the glory of the nation. In the minds of evangelical northern Protestants, southerners refused to embrace the godly calling of labor, service, self-denial, economy, humility, and other aspects of the Yankee Protestant ethic. Movement members tended to view white southern elites as narcissistic, arrogant, individualistic, self-indulgent, hierarchical aristocrats, with little commitment to the common good. They generally perceived all southerners—whether prosperous or poor, black or white—as inefficient, lazy, leisure-seeking spendthrifts who grossly undervalued education for the masses. The movement therefore engaged in a long-term culture war to win the hearts and minds of the southern population in its quest to transform the former land of slavery into a southern New England. This movement employed a multiplicity of educational and evangelical agencies in its efforts to persuade southerners to cast off their perceived depraved characteristics and embrace the values and behaviors of the Yankee Protestant ethic.[4]

Over time, the face of the movement changed. During the antebellum era, temperance societies, free-soilers (persons who fought the spread of slavery but did not seek to abolish it) and abolitionists, including John Brown and his fellow terrorists who violently fought to end slavery, became the prevalent images of the movement. Throughout the Civil War, Union troops, and freedmen's aid societies, including the multitudes of teachers they respectively sponsored, prevailed. Federal governmental agencies, particularly the Bureau of Refugees, Freedmen, and Abandoned Lands (Freedmen's Bureau), assisted northern businessmen and aid societies with their successful combined efforts to control the movement during Reconstruction. Whereas the aid societies engaged in philanthropy and the entrepreneurs sought profits, both groups, for a variety of reasons, sought a more enlightened and productive southern population.[5]

During his pre-Tuskegee years, Booker T. Washington encountered numerous persons who, simultaneously and sequentially, helped to shape his Yankee Protestant worldview. Although many of these people had no contacts with each other, they all supported the Yankee Protestant evangelical movement to remake the South into the image of New England. Washington met several of these people during particularly vulnerable periods of his life. Perhaps his state of mind during those times increased his susceptibility to the evangelicals' proselytization. Their efforts and his life circumstances combined to produce a southern black advocate of the Yankee Protestant ethic, and they produced the ideological foundation that helped shape and direct the adult Booker T. Washington throughout his life.

Washington first encountered a systematic exposure to the Yankee Protestant ethic from Viola Ruffner, a transplanted former teacher from New England. She hired him as her family's houseboy "about 1865." A few months earlier, Washington and his mother, Jane Ferguson, brother John Washington, and sister Amanda Ferguson, had moved to Malden, West Virginia, from their place of enslavement in western Virginia to live with his stepfather, Washington Ferguson. Three years before his mother's death in 1871,

Washington had worked and lived, off and on, with the Ruffners. During the years that he labored for the family, he quit them "a dozen times to try his hand at different occupations." After Jane's death, however, Washington resided with Viola Ruffner for an additional year. For several years she became the most important adult in his life. While in the employment of Viola, Washington received regular tutoring from her as well as the inspiration to embrace the tenets of Yankee Protestantism. For most of his adult life Washington endorsed these principles, especially education, service, thrift, and the veneration of work. More than once, Washington declared that aside from the training he received at the Hampton Institute, Viola Ruffner gave him "the most valuable part of" his education. From her, he declared, "I received my first training in thrift and industry; from her I learned that the difference in social conditions is principally the result of intelligent energy."[6]

He left the Ruffners in the fall of 1872 at the age of sixteen to attend Hampton Normal and Agricultural Institute. With substantial financial assistance from the Freedmen's Bureau, the American Missionary Association (AMA)—a society consisting primarily of northern Congregationalists and Presbyterians—established the institute to academically enlighten and transform the secular mores of the South's African American population. Within a few years of its founding, in 1870, the AMA provided the institute's board of trustees with the deed to the school with the stipulation that "its religious teaching should forever be evangelical." Even though the Congregational and Presbyterian denominations dominated the AMA and founded the institute, instructors taught nondenominational Yankee Protestant values. Presenting Christian values free of denominational content avoided alienating large numbers of southern black students who, as a group, overwhelmingly embraced either the Baptist or the Methodist faith. Unlike white southerners, who as a group overwhelmingly rejected the northerners' religion and their ethic, many African Americans displayed receptiveness to these nondenominational tenets.[7]

The students' responsiveness and eagerness for an education allowed movement members to utilize schools as the primary means of converting southern African Americans into the type of citizens white Yankees preferred. In pursuing their objectives, by 1870 Hampton Institute's founders, along with the other freedmen's aid societies, had provided approximately $8 million, or the equivalent of $145.5 million in 2014 dollars, to support the education of the former slaves. They donated almost $2.75 million more than the Freedmen's Bureau spent altogether on teaching blacks, and almost as much as southern African Americans contributed. Members of the freedmen's aid organizations understood that, next to churches, schools could influence the lives of blacks more than any other public institutions.[8]

Samuel Chapman Armstrong, a former Civil War general, Freedmen's Bureau agent, and founding principal of the Hampton Institute, possessed a clear understanding of the ability of schools to mold the minds of children. As a child living in Hawai'i with his Protestant missionary parents, he initially became aware of the power of education to alter the character of students. Although the indigenous people practiced Christianity, young Armstrong viewed them as immoral uncivilized "grownup children," but educable. After commanding African Americans during the Civil War and interacting with them as a Freedmen's Bureau agent, his assessment of blacks mirrored his views of Hawaiians. Armstrong, who proclaimed African enslavement "the greatest missionary enterprise of the century," expressed a racist, paternalistic view of African Americans. In 1872, the year that Washington enrolled at the Hampton Institute, he wrote that "the colored student does not come to us bred in the atmosphere of a Christian home and community, but too often with the inheritance of a debased nature, and with all his wrong tendencies unchecked either by innate moral sense or by good domestic influence." A proper education changed the values of some of the Hawaiian students, and he augured it would do the same for a selected group of freedmen. Such instruction, Armstrong suggested, would successfully counter such undesirable traits as "improvidence, low ideas of honor, and morality, and a lack of directive energy, judgment and foresight."[9]

Industrial training is what he sought to provide at Hampton Institute to a cadre of preferred African American students. He borrowed the concept from the Hilo Boy's Boarding School that evangelical Yankee Protestants had established on Hawai'i. Its students experienced a curriculum that encompassed a combination of academics, morality instruction, and intense manual labor. This course of study, Armstrong concluded, produced "the best teachers and workers for their people." He proclaimed that he wanted to "train selected negro [sic] youth who should go out and teach and lead the people first by example, by getting land and homes; to give them not a dollar—they could earn for themselves; to teach respect for labor, to replace stupid drudgery with skilled hands, and in this way to build up industrial system for the sake not only of self-support and intelligent labor, but also for sake [of] character."[10]

He therefore requested and received a charter from the state of Virginia to operate the Hampton Institute as a normal school. Neither high schools nor colleges, normal schools at first enrolled elementary-school graduates and ultimately instructed them in the art of teaching common-school pupils. To enhance the process of generating the type of African American teacher that Armstrong desired, he insisted that its coed student body board on campus. Armstrong strongly believed that students should reside under the control of the institution during the academic year. He claimed that in such an environment the Hampton Institute could more thoroughly shape its students' character. Armstrong proclaimed that because "the darky is an ugly thing to manage," teachers needed to control each hour of black students' lives so that they could eradicate "old ideas and ways," replacing them with new ones. He alleged that when a black student's "whole routine of life is controlled, the . . . pupil is like clay in the potter's hands."[11]

Reflecting this precept, Hampton Institute offered a peculiar course of study. Armstrong and his teachers designed it to produce graduates markedly different from those who attended other predominately black–populated schools in the South. Hampton Institute offered its extensively managed student body the standard academic disciplines of the era: civics, history, language, mathematics, and science along with Bible study. It also presented the pupils with several nontraditional courses of studies, such as agriculture, commerce, and vocations. Similar to the Hilo school, manual labor augmented the boarding of the students and their class work. As a pedagogical instrument, school officials demanded that students toil at a physically demanding job. Armstrong asserted that hard labor helped students adopt the preferred characteristics while inspiring them to intensify their efforts at mastering the school's curriculum. He attempted to create methodically indoctrinated culture warriors, a small army of intensely dedicated black disciples who understood the "vital precepts of the Christian faith." With their behaviors and words, they would teach African Americans to accept his concept of their place and role in a reconstructed South. He conceptualized a black population that deemphasized political activism until white men deemed them fit for it, and that embraced efficient manual industrial and agricultural laborers.[12]

The institute exposed Washington to approximately five years of systematic proselytization of the Yankee Protestant ethic: he took classes for three years and worked another two at the institute. Between his time as a student and his employment years, Washington spent several months studying at the Wayland Seminary and College in Washington, D.C. During his three years at the institute, 1872–75, missionary teachers and administrators methodically advocated Yankee Protestant tenets. He imparted those values to students at a Malden common school, where he taught for a couple of years after graduating from Hampton. He quit teaching to attend Wayland Seminary. The New York–based American Baptist Home Mission Society established

Wayland in 1865 to train African American preachers and teachers. George Mellen Prentiss King, a native of Maine and graduate of Colby College, served as its president. It is easy to imagine that Wayland's instructors inspired Washington to continue embracing the Yankee Protestant values that both Mrs. Ruffner and the teachers at the Hampton Institute taught him. Like Armstrong, King "demanded work of his students of head and hands."[13]

After Washington left Wayland in 1879, Armstrong hired him to teach and perform other nonspecific duties at the Hampton Institute. He replaced James C. Robbins, who had served as Armstrong's personal secretary. Washington transitioned from that position to a night-school teacher and finally "housefather of the Indian boys' dormitory." Armstrong rightly believed that Washington could resolve "a difficult and delicate race question" concerning the institute's ability to educate blacks and American Indians together. He asserted that Washington "settled the whole question most satisfactorily." Washington's successes as a night-school teacher and housefather may have inspired Armstrong to select and strongly endorse him for the job of principal at Tuskegee, Alabama. Perhaps Armstrong really believed, as he wrote in his letter of recommendation, that Washington, of all the persons he knew, manifested the desired traits and possessed the greatest ability to succeed in the Black Belt of the Deep South.[14]

In addition to Armstrong, Washington established beneficial relationships with teachers at the Hampton Institute and the Wayland Seminary. Although some accounts claimed that seminary administrators expelled Washington for smoking, he helped King obtain a teacher's pension from Andrew Carnegie. More importantly, Washington credited the seminary's president with teaching him the English grammar and elocution that enhanced his public speaking. During his time at Hampton, Washington developed a special rapport with Helen W. Ludlow, an English teacher and the daughter of a New England Presbyterian minister. Ludlow, who for thirty-eight years edited the institute's official newsletter, the *Southern Workman*, published letters in the journal that Washington wrote to the periodical before and after he moved to Tuskegee. She also wrote the 1884 Tuskegee Institute promotional pamphlet *Tuskegee Normal and Industrial School for Training Colored Teachers, at Tuskegee, Alabama, Its Story and Its Songs*.[15]

Washington also received special attention from Elizabeth H. Brewer. Washington wrote that he owed her a debt for helping him in his "spiritual life," which led to a love and understanding of the Bible. Brewer taught natural philosophy at Hampton. A Phi Beta Kappa, and known throughout her professional life as a religious and warm masterful teacher, Brewer spent almost all of her adult life as an unmarried missionary educator. Born in

New Haven, Connecticut, and a graduate of Vassar College, she belonged to a prominent New England family. It included her father, Josiah Brewer, a renowned Congregationalist minister, and two U.S. Supreme Court justices, her brother, David Josiah Brewer, and a maternal uncle, Stephen Johnson Field.[16]

While not a native New Englander like Brewer, the Reverend Hollis Burke Frissell, to whom Washington ingratiated himself after returning to Hampton as an employee, actively advocated the theology and secularism of Yankee Protestantism. A son of Amasa Frissell, a Presbyterian minister from Massachusetts, Hollis hailed from South Amenia, New York, a border town with Connecticut. Amasa had served as the secretary of the American Tract Society, an organization dedicated to the distribution of pamphlets that proclaimed conservative Yankee Protestant evangelical theology. Hollis, who graduated from Yale College and the Union Theological Seminary, worked as an assistant pastor at the New York Madison Avenue Presbyterian Church and for the AMA before taking the chaplain's position at Hampton. Although he arrived in 1880, just a year before the departure of Washington, the two bonded. Frissell provided Washington with postgraduate instruction. What started as a mere relationship between a student and his teacher evolved into a long-term association that benefited them both. They became very close coworkers in pursuing funds for their respective institutes and promoting educational opportunities for African American students.[17]

Of all of his Hampton Institute teachers, Washington established his most enduring and intimate relationship with Nathalie Lord. From his second year as a Hampton Institute student until his death, Washington sought and received occasional advice from her. Along with Brewer, he credited Lord with assisting him in achieving a greater spirituality, knowledge and fondness of biblical scriptures. Washington attended Lord's Sunday school classes and received biblical lessons from her every day for fifteen minutes before lunch. A reading teacher, Lord provided Washington with "many extra lessons in elocution," the art of formal speech. She assisted and rehearsed with him his Hampton Institute postgraduation speech. He once proclaimed, "whatever ability I may have as a public speaker I owe in a measure to Miss Lord." A daughter of a New England editor of a religious periodical and a Congregational minister, she developed a swift and deep affection for Washington. Lord declared that she "was much interested in him from the first. His quiet, unassuming manner, his earnestness of purpose and faithfulness greatly impressed me. I saw in him one whom you could completely trust." Perhaps those attributes inspired her to offer Washington individualized tutoring as well as employment as her personal boat rower. Lord stated that he took "the necessary care of my boat" and he went "out rowing with me, whenever I needed help at the oars, in this way earning a few more dollars to meet his school expenses."[18]

Washington needed a considerable amount of money and faith to successfully establish and operate a normal school at Tuskegee. For the most part, blacks residing near the school lived in abject poverty, and most whites inhabiting the area did not possess the financial means or interest in contributing to the education of African Americans. Hence, the local residents did not prepare adequately for the opening and operation of a school. Tuskegeans resided in the Black Belt of Alabama. Like most residents of the cotton-producing South, persons living in the Black Belt, regardless of their race, experienced a depressed economy. Their financial distress resulted from a combination of factors that encompassed the legacy of the Civil War, including the emancipation of slaves, postwar labor arrangements, single-crop dependence, limited access to capital, inefficient farming techniques, depleted farm lands, low crop prices, along with the enforcement, sometimes violently, of racial hierarchy. Other than employment in agriculture in 1881, southerners could not find many jobs anywhere in the South and fewer still in the cotton-growing region. Racial prejudice, in general, prohibited African Americans from competing for the rare nonfarming occupations. From the era of slavery, whites in the area had restricted, many times violently, all financial opportunities for African Americans. Consequently, four-fifths of all black southern workers depended on farming for their livelihood, but only about 10 percent owned the land they cultivated. These landless agrarians mostly cultivated cotton, a commodity that commanded low prices through most of the late nineteenth century. As a group, black and white people who lived in the "major cotton-producing states in 1900, for example, made just 50 percent of the per capita income earned by non-southerners." On the average, black men earned between eight and twelve dollars a week. The interest that a majority of African American renters and owners paid to holders of mortgages on their respective crops effectively reduced even this paltry compensation.[19]

Poverty created and aggravated many of the problems that blacks in the Tuskegee area suffered. In describing the material condition of blacks around the town when he arrived, Washington asserted, "as a rule, the colored people all through this section are very poor and ignorant." Many, if not most, of the African Americans in the vicinity, experienced various forms of degradation common to rural southern blacks during the late 1800s. Their housing, as much or more so than any other factor, revealed their deprivation. Similar to slave quarters, they typically lived in a small one-room log cabin with either dirt or plank flooring. They generally possessed few changes of clothes. In numerous cases, children wore no shoes for much of the year and many of them as old as teenagers wore only a long-tail nightshirt or nothing at all. Washington revealed that on a visit through the Tuskegee hinterlands he saw at one African American's "house, two boys thirteen or fourteen years old, perfectly nude." He alleged that he saw "many other children five and six years old" wear no clothes at all. Of the children that Washington observed wearing clothes, most wore only a single, very dirty garment. Country children and adults subsisted on a diet not much different from the one they endured during enslavement. Those individuals fortunate enough to enjoy a garden for a few months could supplement the common basic diet of corn and fat meat with vegetables and fruits. Their inadequate diets, coupled with dilapidated housing and little clothing, greatly increased their susceptibility to a wide range of sicknesses. Much more often than southern whites, African Americans suffered with "typhoid, malaria, smallpox, scarlet fever, diphtheria, yellow fever, measles, tuberculosis, and pneumonia."[20]

Washington could not reasonably hope to develop the institute that he envisioned just from the financial support that African Americans in the Black Belt could provide and the funds the school received for the state of Alabama. Unlike the generous financial support that the organizers of the Hampton Institute received from both the United States government and the AMA, the state of Alabama appropriated only $2,000 to the institute for teachers' salaries. (A month after Washington died, state lawmakers increased the contribution to $4,500; until then, they had not provided money for either facilities or equipment.) Washington had to raise needed funds from students and donors. In response to this reality, he quickly transformed himself into a money-raising sensation. As the *New York Tribune* asserted, "as a money raiser Washington stood without a peer." No black person had ever solicited as much money as had Washington in his role as the principal of the Tuskegee Institute. These contributions allowed him to increase the institute's student body, lands, faculty, facilities, and operations. It permitted the waiver of tuition for all of the institute's students during his lifetime. Other than a small enrollment fee that the school implemented during the late 1890s, students needed only to pay for their books, room, board, and personal upkeep.[21]

After two months of teaching, Washington expressed a desire to provide the students with employment that would enable them to pay for their personal needs. He alleged, "as a rule, the colored people in the South are not and will not be able for years to board their children in school at ten or twelve dollars per month, hence my object is, as soon as possible, to get the school on a labor basis, so that earnest students can help themselves and at the same time learn the true dignity of labor." Within a few years of the institute's establishment, he had raised enough money from donors and the institute's moneymaking enterprises, like brick making, to compensate students for working on campus. Their pay provided them with some or all of the money needed for books, food, and lodging.[22]

The Tuskegee Institute's curriculum included a requirement to work. In addition to creating a course of study that reflected his educational experiences and his Yankee Protestant evangelical enculturation, Washington put in place a curriculum that revealed his clear understanding of the financial realities of southern black people, his students, as well as the financial needs of the institute. The institute offered a four-year course of study. It included traditional normal-school subjects, such as English, history, and speech. It also offered instruction in several vocations, such as blacksmithing, brick making, carpentry, dressmaking, farming, laundering, masonry, printing, sewing, and training as a wheelwright. Vocational training enabled the institute to employ relatively inexpensive skilled student workers to construct the desired campus buildings and infrastructures, manufacture clothes, as well as to produce the food to feed both the students and the staff. Washington asserted that the skills the students utilized in developing the institute's physical plant "would make its graduates successful and self-supporting" after they completed school. As a former southern common-school teacher, Washington knew firsthand about the inadequate pay that teaching commanded. Lessons in salable vocations, he asserted, would enable graduates to subsidize their annual incomes. Washington hoped, moreover, that graduates and other former students would become living models of the Yankee Protestant ethic. He wanted them to inspire other blacks to embrace those preferred values.[23]

Although Washington looked to Hampton as a model for his academy, he did not fashion it as a mere carbon copy of the Virginia school. He did adopt some of the institute's characteristics, including coed education, dress codes, student boarding, teacher education, and vocational training, as well as intensely encouraging students to embrace the Protestant ethic. Some very noteworthy distinctions between the two, however, did exist. Armstrong employed no African American teachers when he opened his school. He subsequently hired several to teach military discipline and vocational academic subjects, but rarely did he employ any for the institute's academic classes. By contrast, with the exception of Henry Romeyn, who helped with military instruction in 1897, Washington did not hire white instructors. Whereas students at the Tuskegee Institute took classes such as the Negro in Africa and the Negro in America, no such courses existed at the Hampton Institute, and perhaps no other predominately African American–populated school in the nation. Tuskegee Institute offered a four-year course of study, a year longer than that offered at the Hampton Institute. Armstrong and his successor, Hollis Burke Frissell, sought to graduate annually a small cadre of intensely indoctrinated ideologues. Washington wanted to expose the greatest number of black students possible to the ideas promoted at the Tuskegee Institute. Armstrong and Frissell sought indirect access to the black masses; Washington wanted an unfiltered connection with them.[24]

More so than any other factor, Hampton and Tuskegee Institutes differed on their approaches to public service. Both schools required their students to engage in community service. Washington, however, placed far more emphasis on what he called extension work, than did either Armstrong or Frissell. He gave community service almost as much attention as he did the teaching of his students and the physical development of the campus. He promoted it as an integral part of the school. Washington initiated public outreach programs years before his renowned 1895 Cotton States and International Exposition speech in Atlanta. During 1893, the Tuskegee Institute offered fourteen extension activities. Sixteen years later, these public outreach activities had interacted annually with 213,000 people. Several of these programs, like the National Negro Business League, and its affiliated organizations, possessed a national constituency. Most of Tuskegee Institute's extension work sought to improve meaningfully black people's material status. Although as a Yankee Protestant evangelist, Washington sought to inspire the conversion of as many nonbelievers as possible to Christianity, he understood that "it is pretty hard thing to make a good Christian of a hungry man." For more than thirty years, Washington argued that adopting the Yankee Protestant ethic would help black people secure more wealth and greater local and national esteem while becoming "good Christians."[25]

Extension work along with Washington's public presentations and publications had a much greater influence upon the nation, especially African Americans, than did graduates and other former students of the Tuskegee Institute. By the time of his death, Washington had spoken to millions of people. In 1909 alone, he claimed to have addressed 130,000 people. He published numerous books and articles that advocated his philosophy. These reinforced the influence that his former students, his speeches, and the Tuskegee Institute's outreach programs provided him. The institute, though, provided Washington with the enormous base of support that allowed him to enjoy more political influence than any other black man in the United States did. With it, he appropriated control of the Yankee Protestant evangelical battle for the hearts and minds of black America. Between 1895 and his death in 1915, with the Tuskegee Institute as his wealthy and prestigious center of operation,

Washington became the dominant southern advocate of the Yankee Protestant ethic. Under his leadership, the movement to transform southerners, particularly African Americans, into the image of Yankee Protestants, metamorphosed into the Tuskegee movement. Washington commanded and controlled the refocused transfigured movement at the Tuskegee Institute.[26]

After his death, leading supporters of the movement wanted to perpetuate it. They used obituaries, burial rites, memorials, and eulogies as weapons of choice in their efforts to continue a culture war between a supposedly democratic North and a seemingly aristocratic South. Within days following his passing, prominent black members of the movement poured their perspectives into public presentations that rallied and inspired black masses to construct a shared preferred memory of the Tuskegean. This portrayal helped to motivate members of the movement to continue the culture war. Important white supporters of the movement, moreover, reassured African Americans that they would not abandon the cause. They too wrote obituaries, sponsored memorials, and delivered eulogies that enthusiastically encouraged African Americans to embrace the values that Washington exemplified and championed.

1. "A Great Man Fallen"

The Immediate Death Notices

Soon after Booker T. Washington's death, which occurred Sunday, November 14, at 4:45 A.M., sympathizers sent his relatives and close associates messages of solace. These notes provided numerous senders a simple way to individualize memorials for Washington. The notes expressed many of the same sentiments that audiences who attended commemorations for the late educator experienced. Many of the messages indicated that Washington's death traumatized countless number of Americans, especially African Americans. Although newspapers throughout the nation had reported his hospitalization after his collapse in New York City, November 4, 1915, Washington's supporters seemed not to be emotionally prepared for his imminent demise. When Algernon Brashear Jackson, a friend of Washington's widow, Margaret, learned of his death, she proclaimed shock "beyond measure." Jackson claimed not to "know what to say . . . I am," she went on to write, at a "loss for words." Tuskegee instructor William H. Walcott also divulged that words failed him in trying to communicate the intensity of his shock at the news. Washington's death so stunned R. W. Thompson, an African American journalist, that he claimed to be unable to compose graceful prose. Although Louis G. Gregory, a Washington, D.C., African American attorney, could command words, he asserted that Washington's death "left him somewhat dazed."[1]

Gregory and many other devotees viewed Washington as a significant contributor to the formation of a desired American society. His death forced them to realize that they now needed to construct a vision of a new future without him. Many of them wrote notes describing various mixtures of fear, disappointment, loss, and depression. Perhaps they felt like Edythe Williams, a one-time member of the Tuskegee Institute community, who claimed that knowledge of his death so shocked her that she felt that it "effaced all other cares for the time." On the other hand, they might have experienced feelings similar to those that Spencer Patterson, a black man living in Relay, Maryland, expressed. He wrote that after his family and he learned of Washington's passing it seemed as though we "were sitting in a lighted room and suddenly the light goes out."[2]

Washington's death probably did not inspire a majority of sympathizers to experience similar feelings. Hundreds of condolers sent telegrams and letters to people closely affiliated with Washington, with his widow, Margaret James Murray Washington, receiving the bulk of these, although many sympathizers sent communiqués to members of Tuskegee Institute Board of Trustees, administration, and faculty. A few condolers directed their notes to persons closely associated with Washington who did not enjoy an official connection with the institute. Sympathizers began sending notes of solace as early as the Sunday morning that Washington died. Many of them learned of the late educator's demise through telegrams from the secretary of the Tuskegee Institute and Washington's aide-de-camp, Emmett J. Scott. He had wired a short, passionless statement that "Principal Washington died here this morning at four forty five o'clock. Funeral Wednesday morning." A majority of the messages, however, came from people who had read newspaper accounts of the death. The Associated Press, having received confirmation of Washington's passing from Scott, informed affiliated newspapers in time for many to publish a report about it that Sunday.[3]

While a sizable number of the messages conveyed nothing more than the courtesy normally extended to the bereaved, many expressed their veneration for Washington, with a significant portion of the authors declaring that he occupied an important place in their lives. Even though some writers possessed a personal relationship with the late educator, the majority did not. Memories of the real or imagined roles that Washington played in the life of many of the writers helped to shape these messages. For these consolers, Washington had become a symbol of the aspirations that they held for themselves, for African Americans, or for the nation. Their expression of their grief manifested a belief that Washington's death greatly diminished the likelihood that his vision for African Americans, the South, and the nation would materialize. Writers signified that they believed that a desired cultural transformation would occur in the United States if a significant number of African Americans, especially those living in the South, would embrace the tenets of Yankee Protestants.

Along with their grief, well-wishers expressed sympathy and appreciation for Washington and his accomplishments. Shaped by individual and group memories of Washington, the collage of communications portrayed the late educator as one of the most accomplished leaders of his day. Within this comprehensive collective image emerged a picture of the leader of a long-term movement to transform the culture of the people living in the South, especially African Americans. Although the words *Yankee, Protestant,* or *ethic* didn't appear, many of the notes strongly indicated that they believed that Washington sought to inspire southern blacks to embrace and emulate the values and behaviors commonly reflected in early-twentieth-century secularized New England. While these principles included asceticism, call-ing, charity, humility, perseverance, pragmatism, and sobriety, Washington and his supporters placed significant emphasis on cleanliness, education, efficiency, honesty, orderliness, promptness, service, steadiness, thrift, sys-tematic work, and the dignity of labor.[4]

For generations, New Englanders had dispatched religious and secular missionaries of the Protestant ethic throughout North America. During the antebellum years, many of these culture warriors promoted tenets that included a society without enslaved workers, embracing instead free labor. Most proponents of the Yankee Protestant ethic, however, wanted primarily to contain slavery, rather than eliminate it. After the Civil War, thousands of advocates of the ethic relocated to the former Confederacy. Teachers, three-fourths of them women, made up a significant portion of these evan-gelicals. Many of them, blacks as well as whites, left the North with the inten-tion of transforming an intensely race-conscious, manual-labor-despising, aristocrat-dominated population into southern Yankees. During their prepa-ration to teach freedmen, officials at Oberlin College, an institution that promoted the Yankee Protestant ethic, told students that they must convert and puritanize the South.[5]

*   *   *

Although southern whites as a group rejected the missionaries' efforts at transforming them, these agents of the Yankee Protestant ethic did not retreat. They instead concentrated their evangelical efforts toward reshaping the South's African American population. They wanted blacks to internal-ize the principles and become, in their worldview and actions, as much like white middle-class New England Protestants as possible. Schools became the primary means for them to realize their quest. Under the auspices of several freedmen's aid societies, like the Congregational Church–affiliated American Missionary Association (AMA), and with the aid of the federal government, they operated hundreds of schools. Using these institutions as bases of operations, the New England Freedmen's Aid Society sought to recruit "enough teachers to make a New England of the whole South." The society, the AMA, and the several other northern philanthropic associations, sponsored both black and white missionary teachers who taught thousands of former slaves and their children for several decades after the Civil War. W. E. B. Du Bois wrote that these instructors fought "the most wonderful peace-battle of the 19th century." He contended that New England gave "the freed Negro, not alms, but a friend, not cash, but character."[6]

That is what Washington received at the Hampton Institute. As James D. Anderson convincingly argues in his insightful and path-breaking study of southern black education, Armstrong believed in white supremacy. He held that blacks did not possess the moral character to participate on an equal footing with whites in the body politics. There is no extant evidence that Armstrong's students internalized those ideas. Even Washington, Armstrong's alleged foremost disciple, participated in West Virginia conventional politics soon after he graduated from Hampton. Nor did Armstrong's racist world-view inspire Washington not to vote or seek the franchise for all black men while he headed the Tuskegee Institute. Washington associated with both black and white politicians. They assisted him with his efforts to produce a cadre of black culture warriors who would spread, primarily among African American schoolchildren, the tenets of New England.[7]

Teachers at the Hampton Institute also greatly impressed Washington. He once proclaimed, "No one can pass from here [Hampton Institute] without being a better man, a better woman, because of the sweet, strong influence gathered on these grounds." Even though Washington as a student had a relationship with Nathalie Lord that seemed closer than the one he had with Armstrong, he publicly credited the institute's principal with contributing much to his worldview. Along with the residual influence of Ruffner, the Hampton Institute staff successfully converted Washington into a southern black Yankee Protestant evangelist. Their teachings significantly contributed to his desire to become a proponent of middle-class New England values. He became the most effective African American teacher of the tenets, and a large plurality of his mourners praised him for his efforts.[8]

Messages of sympathy to close associates of Washington did not directly promote the late evangelists' objective. Sympathizers, however, wrote notes that provided substantial evidence that Washington and his missionary efforts had positively resonated with a sizable and diverse segment of the nation's population. These notes of solace indicated that Washington had enjoyed a significant reservoir of goodwill and biracial support. Hence, it is easy to imagine that the massive outpouring of sympathy reinforced the commitment of the Tuskegee movement's remaining leadership to continue to fight the culture war that Washington had led for much of the previous twenty years.

Margaret, Emmett, and other individuals closely associated with the late educator received messages from people in every region of the nation. Blacks and whites, rich and poor sent the numerous messages mourning the death of Washington. Well-wishers living as far south as Ocala, Florida, and as far north as Milwaukee, Wisconsin, sent correspondence. They came from the far western regions of the United States, as well as from the most eastern portion of the nation. During the immediate weeks following the passing of Washington, citizens living in every identifiable geographical area of the country sent one or more expressions of solace to someone intimately identified with Washington.[9]

Even a few condolers living abroad contributed to the massive number of sympathy notes. Margaret received letters from Canada as well as the West Indies. In a message from Winnipeg, Canada, E. M. Henderson lamented, "I am very sorry to note, the lost [sic] to us of our Leader The Hon. B. T. Washington." Allerta E. Allwood and several Tuskegee graduates living in Kingston, Jamaica, sent acknowledgments. Other West Indians wrote to Scott, including Jerome B. Peterson, a resident of San Juan, Puerto Rico, and Cuban residents Guillermo Kessel, Jose A. Manroque, and Narciso Nodarsy. Despite Washington's previous visits to Europe and his contacts with Africans, apparently no messages came to the Tuskegee Institute from either of those two quarters. This is noteworthy since Washington visited Europe extensively twice; he had corresponded with a number of Africans, he had over the years enrolled a few students from Africa, and a small number of its African American graduates had relocated to the continent.[10]

Foreign as well as domestic writers used their notes as tools of comfort. Sympathizers sought to reassure Washington's bereaved family and friends that they had recognized his passing and that his death caused them emotional pain. Along with the other death rites, these notes helped reassure Washington's survivors that, despite the man's death, the community at large would continue to embrace them. Although a significant number of the messages declared enduring support for the ideas and objectives that the late educator promoted, the messages primarily provided Washington's loved ones with emotional support during their period of mourning.[11]

Authors informed Margaret, his widow, that they felt sympathy for her loss. The famous songwriter and arranger John Rosamond Johnson and his wife, Nora, offered their "Deepest Sympathy." A similar expression of condolence came to Margaret from Harriette (Hattie) B. Sprague on behalf of her and the other granddaughters of Frederick Douglass. In a telegram to Margaret and family, Sprague extended the granddaughters' sincere sympathy in their "hour of great bereavement." A closer acquaintance, Mary E. Josenburger of

Fort Smith, Arkansas, declared to Margaret that her heart went out to her "in this terrible bereavement." Margaret also received a number of condolences from her husband's associates, including Harold Peabody, who told Margaret that his friendship with Booker T. Washington inspired him to ask her to accept his "sincerest sympathy in" her "great loss."[12]

A group of writers informed Margaret that they shared her pain, wanting to reassure Margaret that she did not grieve alone. While these messages probably did not diminish her grief, they perhaps lessened her sense of loneliness. Lillian V. Ramsey Mines, a resident of Prescott, Arizona, and the daughter of Julius B. Ramsey, the longtime commander of cadets at the Tuskegee Institute, proclaimed that she shared Margaret's "moment" of sorrow. Acting on behalf of the members of the predominately white Newport (NJ) Union Congregational Church, the Reverend Clifford L. Miller conveyed the same message to her. Julius Rosenwald, the president of Sears, Roebuck and Company, reported to Margaret that he felt "too sad to attempt words of consolation for" her.[13]

Emmett Scott received the second greatest number of messages. Many people correctly believed that Scott, as Washington's aide-de-camp and his primary functionary within the movement, had suffered an irreplaceable loss. Perhaps that is what Lyman Beecher Stowe, an author, editor, and grandson of Harriet Beecher Stowe, had in mind in offering Scott his "Keenest Sympathy." R. W. Thompson, the president of the National Negro Press Association, explicitly declared that he knew what the death of Washington meant to the secretary. Charles H. Moore, a renowned North Carolina educator and former National Negro Business League (NNBL) organizer, had firsthand knowledge of the nature of Scott's association with Washington through his duties with the NNBL. His insight into their relationship led Moore to assert that "I am somewhat in a position to sympathize with you. As you were close to him and entered into his soul and thoughts as only a few had the opportunity." That visible relationship also inspired William H. Davis to portray Scott as a child of Washington. This resident of Washington, D.C., praised Scott for being "our honored leader . . . a son so loyal and so helpful."[14]

In their praise of Booker T. Washington, black condolers often recognized him as the paramount leader of black America. According to a note that Cal F. Johnson, a Knoxville, Tennessee, resident penned, Washington achieved the status of African Americans' "most noted leader." Echoing the same sentiment, John M. Gandy, a prominent member of the Negro Organization Society of Virginia and a Petersburg resident, declared Washington the "most distinguished leader" of the race. Energetic is how Henry Plummer Cheatham, an African American former congressman from North Carolina remembered Washington, proclaiming him black peoples' "truest and liveli-est leader." R. C. Hintone, a resident of Thomasville, Arkansas, added the adjective "greates [*sic*]" in his note declaring Washington the "truest Leader of his day."[15]

Margaret and Scott, as well as other members of the Tuskegee Institute community, received notes of condolence from a variety of persons who wrote on behalf of various African American groups. In a message to Mar-garet, troopers of the predominately African American Ninth U.S. Cavalry, one of the famous Buffalo Soldier units, proclaimed Washington the "fore-most leader" of the race. A committee of African Americans in Des Moines, Iowa, made the same declaration in their note. The group included Samuel Joe Brown, a Phi Beta Kappa, and an attorney. He served as both the presi-dent of the local chapter of the National Association for the Advancement of Colored People (NAACP) and as secretary of the local NNBL chapter. Representatives of the Indianapolis Colored YWCA, and the members of the Birmingham, Alabama, chapter of the Knights of Phythias, a predominately black fraternal society, all declared Washington the leader of black America. Members of the United Woodsman Benefit Association of Crystal Springs, Mississippi, called Washington "the greatest leader of our race." A telegram from the members of the Hotel Brotherhood U.S.A. placed Washington within a global context. They proclaimed him the "worlds [*sic*] leader of his race."[16]

Numerous black theologians also declared Washington the leader of Afri-can Americans. More than any other segment of African Americans, preach-ers understood leadership and many of them recognized it in other people. Although Washington alleged in an article published in the August 14, 1890, issue of the *Christian Union* that "three-fourths of the Baptist ministers and two-thirds of the Methodists are unfit," many African American preach-ers seemed not to have allowed his criticism to lessen their assessment of his leadership. While the Reverend S. W. Bacote, a Kansas City, Missouri, resident and the editor of the African American–oriented *National Baptist Yearbook*, proclaimed Washington an "ideal leader" of black people, G. W. Robinson, the pastor of the Second Baptist Church in El Paso, Texas, sug-gested that the late educator had no peers. A communication from the Rev-erend R. S. Stout, the minister of the Colored Methodist Episcopal Church in Houston, Texas, declared that Washington had become black people's "greatest leader." Squire J. Channell, a prominent African Methodist Episco-pal Church preacher, asserted that Washington ranked as one of the world's "greatest leaders."[17]

In addition to African American ministerial groups, several different denominations' laymen associations recognized Washington's leadership of black people. Members of the Southwest Georgia African Methodist Episcopal Church Conference told Margaret that Washington had become one of black people's "ablest leaders." Likewise, attendees at the Washington Conference of the Methodist Episcopal Church, an African American ministerial assemblage, conveyed to the widow that they considered Washington the race's "foremost leader." Members of the Colored Baptist Ministers Conference of Birmingham proclaimed him the "greatest living leader" of black people, and the note from members of the Demopolis (AL) Morning Star First Baptist Church declared Washington "the undisputed leader of our race."[18]

Although belief in the social construct of race seemed to have shaped more than a few messages that numerous whites wrote, many of them made similar proclamations regarding the quality of Washington's leadership. Race consciousness, which preordained that a number of these condolers would limit their praise of Washington to within context of black America, did not stop either southern or northern whites from praising his leadership accomplishments. Even though Washington sought to transform southern blacks into the image of Yankee Protestants, whites living in the South wrote more than a few messages extolling him. Regardless of their location, religious as well as secular white people praised his leadership. That is what W. D. Wetherford, a resident of Nashville, signified in his message by proclaiming Washington "a sane and powerful leader." In his note, L. B. Brooks, the pastor of the First Baptist Church of Waynesboro, Virginia, acknowledged Washington as "a real leader" of black people. Owners of Schloss and Kahn, a Montgomery, Alabama, wholesale grocery and liquor enterprise that likely sold goods to Washington and the Tuskegee Institute, conveyed to Margaret that they considered him the "leader of his race." His leadership, asserted E. S. Shannon, the postmaster for Nashville, Tennessee, "has been a big factor in its development and progress" of African Americans. A northerner, however, offered the strongest endorsement of the Tuskegean's leadership. Andrew Carnegie, the philanthropist who provided Washington, his family, and several of his projects with thousands of dollars, declared to Margaret that "History is to tell of two Washingtons: One the father of his country, the other the leader of his race."[19]

In discussing his leadership, a number of writers labeled Washington a modern-day Moses. They conveyed a message similar to the one that Dr. and Mrs. L. L. Burwell, two African American residents of Selma, Alabama, sent, which referred to Washington as "Moses of the Negroes of America." A white couple, W. S. Schley and his wife, also recalled Washington as "the Moses of his race." Other sympathizers, such as the representatives of the predominately black–populated Asheville (NC) Newspaper Association bemoaned that they "lost the Moses of our race." A self-proclaimed representative of Minnesota, W. T. Francis, wrote from Saint Paul that "the old world and the new . . . utters one voice of sympathy on the death of . . . Washington, the Moses of the Negro race."[20]

A surrogate parent is how another group of sympathizers imagined the late educator. These empathizers venerated and identified with Washington in part for his perceived wise counsel. Like most young sons imagine their fathers, J. I. Washington of Beaufort, South Carolina, alleged that since his boyhood Washington had been his ideal person. Little Rock, Arkansas, resident, Walter R. Nicholson lamented that as "a son personally [I] am most grieved by the shocking news" of the death of Booker T. Washington. Mary Lou Austin of Lawrenceville, Virginia, likewise possessed an imagined relationship with him, writing that to her, Washington's death felt like the loss "of a father."[21]

Some condolers remembered him as royalty, sending messages that memorialized Washington as a benevolent ruler. These writers penned notes that included such terms as *chief, chieftain*, and *king*. Washington's nephew-in-law and Louisville, Kentucky, newspaperman, Roscoe C. Simmons, called his uncle "the Great Chief." Like-minded Cincinnati, Ohio, resident Jos L. Jones wrote that the entire African American race "lost its chieftain." Attendees at the North Carolina African American Baptist State Convention in Wilmington asserted that black people had lost their chieftain, and P. K. Foville, the African Methodist Episcopal Zion pastor in Auburn, New York, alleged that African Americans felt earnestly the death of their "chieftain." A former spy for Washington and an Oklahoma City newspaper editor, Melvin J. Chisum, sent a message that elevated Washington from chief to monarch: the "King is dead . . . Long live the King."[22]

Many more sympathizers recalled Washington as a U.S. citizen, rather than a nobleman. A "patriotic" citizen is how R. C. Huston Jr., the African American president of the Fort Worth (TX) Provident Bank, recalled Washington. Edwina B. Kruse, an African American who worked as the principal of Howard High School in Wilmington, Delaware, declared Washington "the formal American citizen." Neither condoler, nor any of the other writers, mentioned that Washington, as an ex-bondsman, did not become a U.S. citizen until the July 9, 1868, enactment of the Fourteenth Amendment to the U.S. Constitution. In the remaining forty-seven years of his life after that date, however, Washington had evolved from a preteen freedman to, as L. B. Brooks, the white pastor of the First Baptist Church of Waynesboro, Virginia, alleged, "one of the distinguished citizens of the United States." To several black authors, though, no other American possessed national prestige comparable to Washington's. In separate notes, W. C. Chance, the principal of Parmelen (NC) Industrial Institute, and J. W. Tuner, a Columbia, South Carolina, minister, both proclaimed the late educator America's "foremost citizen."[23]

Since notes of solace can reveal much more about the author than the departed, perhaps the ones that proclaimed Washington a citizen manifested the writers' concerns about contemporary issues. Their notes may have reflected worries about major challenges to black peoples' citizenship claims. African Americans throughout the nation suffered discrimination, intimidation, violence, and segregation, acts that undermined their rights as American citizens. During the twenty years prior to Washington's death, blacks, who had never enjoyed full civil privileges, experienced substantial constitutional entitlement restrictions. Conceivably, the authors of these notes wanted to reassure readers, that despite his race, Americans did not question Washington's citizenship status.[24]

Increased constraints on the citizenship rights of African Americans occurred while an unprecedented number of immigrants relocated to the United States from Central, Eastern, and Southern Europe. From 1880 to 1919, over 23,500,000 immigrants arrived. They included a large number of socialists, Roman Catholics, Jews, Catholics, and Muslims. Immigrants' alien ways seemed antithetical to the Yankee Protestant ethic, and a number of prominent persons and influential organizations voiced questions and apprehensions about their loyalty to the United States. Many of these recent arrivals and their children proclaimed dual national loyalty. Writers of notes of solace that declared Washington a U.S. citizen might have harbored a concern about this phenomenon. One author known to have intense feeling about the issue, President Theodore Roosevelt, publicly objected to the "so-called hyphenated Americans" and what he characterized as their divided national loyalties.[25]

Washington taught black people how to become the type of Americans that Roosevelt desired. The late educator's extraordinary proficiency at "Americanizing" blacks—namely, teaching them how to transform themselves into carbon images of middle-class northern white Protestants—substantially helped to propel him into the position of paramount African American leader. Americans, black as well as white, who highly valued civil order, social stability, and unquestionable patriotism very much approved of Washington's teachings. Indeed, former president William H. Taft's telegram to Scott described Washington as "one of the most powerful forces for the proper settlement of the race question that has appeared in his generation[.] His loving candor to his fellow [N]egroes[,] his inspiring encouragement to make themselves individually valuable to the community[,] his urging upon the homely virtues on industry[,] thrift[,] and persistent use of their opportunities with a promise of higher achievements as a reward have done more for the Negro race than any other one factor in their progress."[26]

Although the prevailing public memory of Washington associated him closely with educating African Americans in general, it specifically remembered him as the founder and longtime leader of the Tuskegee Institute. In the minds of countless Americans, Booker T. Washington and Tuskegee Institute, then the most famous academy for African Americans, had become one and the same. Washington had established a symbiotic relationship with the institute. Promoting purposefulness, industry, patience, and resolve enabled Washington to secure unprecedented influence and fame for the school. In turn, the institution provided Washington with the hegemony that he needed to both recast African Americans and improve their relationship with whites. Washington's extraordinarily effective uses of the Tuskegee Institute as a cultural and political tool catapulted him into the role of race leader. In addition to the tens of thousands of students who enrolled in the school during Washington's tenure, officials of the institute conveyed aspects of the movement's tenets to millions of Americans. As early as the 1908–9 school year, officials had personally delivered the movement's messages to more than 212,700 persons. Using the staff, money, space, and other resources that the school provided, Washington evangelized both black and white Americans. The Tuskegee Institute provided Washington with the local, regional, national, and international audiences for his teachings.[27]

Although Washington alleged that the school provided its students with an industrial education, it, however, primarily taught its students how to teach children in the lower grades. The Alabama State Legislature granted the Tuskegee Institute a charter to operate a normal school. Employing a precollegiate curriculum, such academies trained schoolteachers. A need to construct a physical plant and pay the students' board inspired Washington to revise and expand the institute's course of study. Over time, he devised a curriculum that coupled classical academics with teacher training, vocational education, and an overt indoctrination of Yankee Protestant values, especially asceticism, honesty, service, thrift, systematic work, and dignity of labor.

Washington did not originate the concept of "industrial education" or coin the term. Johann Heinrich Pestalozzi and Philipp Emmanuel Von Fellenberg, two Swiss citizens, introduced vocational education to the Western world during the early 1800s. The first such school appeared in the United States in 1819. At the peak of its popularity, Calvinist missionaries merged vocational training with Protestant tenets, labeling this instructional method *industrial education*. By the end of the Civil War, although the concept had largely gone out of fashion, Samuel C. Armstrong, who had witnessed the education model on the Hawaiian islands, introduced the methodology at Hampton Institute. He promoted the concept enthusiastically. In the process of soliciting financial support for Hampton Institute, Armstrong successfully marketed the system. His impressive promotion of the educational model, along with Hampton Institute's successful utilization of it, helped revive its attractiveness.[28]

Washington took what he had learned as a student at the Hampton Institute and made significant additions to the curriculum at Tuskegee. They included teaching students to seek and adopt ways to increase the speed and quality of their work in order to improve their efficiency. Washington, moreover, sought to inspire his students to want to assist ordinary African Americans in their pursuit of enhanced material well-being and citizenship rights. While many people, particularly whites, seemed not to understand his version of industrial education fully, it did win widespread acclaim. A considerable number of condolers noted that Washington did more than anyone else to promote and popularize industrial education. Indeed, members of an association of interdenominational preachers in Houston concurred. They declared Washington the "father of industrialism."[29]

His success at promoting and utilizing industrial education inspired a segment of mourners to venerate Washington. They commemorated him for teaching black people the supposed advantages of employing the philosophy. Black Republican activist, religious magazine editor, and prominent member of the movement John C. Dancey declared that Washington "founded the nation's greatest industrial institution." In a message to Scott, Chicago resident Sylvester Russell asserted that Washington founded "real manual and industrial training." Stanley Yarnall, a white Cheyney Institute trustee, declared that Washington led "his people into new and wise lines of training in their advance in efficiency and character." A group of Macon, Georgia, African Americans forwarded a resolution asserting that black people of that city believed "thoroughly the industrial ideas" that Washington advocated "in his public writings and his speeches."[30]

Washington's influence on education, asserted many condolers, transcended African American communities and attracted multiracial and multinational followings. Wade H. Richardson, a white Milwaukee real

estate broker, contended that Washington "set up new methods of education which others have willingly adopted with great benefit to the world."
Beaufort, South Carolina, black residents, in a commemoration resolution
sent to Scott, asserted that Washington's "scheme of Industrial education has
been copied, not only by the people, white and colored, of this country, but
also by foreign nations." B. W. Allen, the president of Lincoln Institute (now
Lincoln University) in Jefferson City, Missouri, made a similar claim in a note
that purported that Washington established "a system of education which
has influenced education materially not only in this country but in foreign
countries also." The black dean of the Howard University teacher college,
Lewis B. Moore, a University of Pennsylvania PhD, asserted that both the
nation and the world accepted Washington as "the leader and teacher of all
people in the line of industrial education."[31]

Some sympathizers praised the late educator for supporting liberal as
well as industrial education. Despite his latter-day reputation of deprecating
the liberal arts and higher education for African Americans, Washington
helped to raise funds for a number of schools for black students, including
Howard University, which did not offer an industrial education curriculum.
He even assisted with fund-raising for the New York Free Kindergarten for
Colored Children. Washington's support for formal education motivated
heads of literary associations and professional educators to write compli-
mentary depictions of him. They wrote of his Herculean efforts to secure
an education for himself, and later, for countless boys and girls, especially
African Americans. Writing for themselves and on behalf of their respective
schools, representatives of various institutions recalled Washington as one
of the most important promoters of education of his day. Their notes placed
him among the elite of educators.[32]

Members of the Tuskegee Institute community received messages that
memorialized Washington as Africa America's preeminent educator. The
notes indicated that no one contributed as much to the general schooling
of blacks as had Washington. In its condolences, the predominately white
Cheyney Institute Board of Managers asserted that "Negro education has lost
its great national leader" with the death of Washington. The school's black
principal, Leslie Pinckney Hill, claimed in a separate note that he appreciated
the "extraordinary service" Washington "rendered to every Negro school in
the country." That alleged assistance seemed to have inspired members of
the Ninth U.S. Cavalry to declare Washington Africa America's foremost
educator.[33]

Black and white professional educators, as well as lay persons, wrote
notes that recalled Washington as one of the most important promoters of

education during his era. They praised him for his contribution to formal education for all people and not just for African Americans. The white president
of Ohio Wesleyan College, Gordon Nelson Armstrong, asserted that with
the "passing of Washington, the educational profession . . . has lost one of its
wise leaders." Representatives of all-black Shaw University of Raleigh, North
Carolina, made a similar contention; their school's community mourned "the
great loss to the . . . cause of universal education in the death of" Booker
T. Washington. Agreeing that "the cause of education in general has lost a
friend," members of the Eatonville, Florida, predominantly black Hungerford
School community sent a note proclaiming that their own school owed "to
a very large extent its existence and inspirations" to Washington.[34]

*   *   *

With extraordinary effectiveness, Washington taught in and outside of
the classroom. For thirty-four years, he instructed a multitude of formal
and informal students. He instructed them in the classrooms of Tuskegee
Institute, as well as in various venues that hosted his numerous public presentations. Washington spoke to audiences indoors as well as outside. He
gave speeches in churches, schoolhouses, auditoriums, as well as on outdoor
platforms. Washington supplemented his speeches with the large number of
articles and books published under his name. These materials, along with
the publications written about him, supplemented his teaching efforts. They
helped to encourage and guide an array of his followers. Willis Jackson, a
black man living in Rembert, Alabama, who admitted that he had "never met"
Washington, sent a note declaring that he "read a great eale of him all so has a
histre of his Woork and Life." A white New Orleans coffee importer, William
B. Reily, stated that over the years he benefited from reading Washington's
speeches. A. L. Cassidy, from Cheraw, South Carolina, wrote, "I have been
reading Dr. Washington's speeches for many of years and they were all fill
[*sic*] with delight and wisdom."[35]

Washington's speeches, even more than his publications, became the most
successful weapon utilized in the movement's culture war. For years, he spoke
before tens of thousands of people. He gave addresses from the East Coast
of the United States to its western shores.[36]

Although Washington most often shaped his public presentations to both
raise money and promote the Tuskegee movement, he subordinated his solici-
tations during his Southern Education Tours. From 1908 through 1912, he
toured and spoke throughout the South. Members of state and local affiliates
of the National Negro Business League (NNBL) arranged the tours for him.
Washington founded the NNBL in 1900 and served as NNBL president for

its first sixteen years. While presiding over the league, Washington repeatedly asserted that successful African American–owned businesses would substantially increase black people's status, which, he alleged, would inspire whites to allow them to enjoy greater civil rights. Washington located the headquarters of the NNBL at the Tuskegee Institute. Before his death, the organization consisted of six hundred local and state affiliates. The NNBL and its affiliated associations—the National Negro Funeral Directors' Association, the National Negro Press Association, the National Negro Insurance Men's Association, and the National Negro Retail Merchants' Association—provided Washington with a following of no fewer than forty thousand African American entrepreneurs. Adherents of the league met regularly in one of the local chapters. Once a year, chapter delegates gathered at a national convention. At these meetings, Washington addressed representatives of the general membership. His speeches encouraged and guided hundreds of delegates and visitors, many of them NNBL members.[37]

Members of the NNBL accompanied Washington on his southern tours, which he used to assess respective local race relations, as well, as the "progress" of African Americans living in the areas of the South that he visited. Audiences that gathered to listen to Washington while he toured the South became some of his most earnest informal students. Over five thousand persons, for example, attended his 1909 mid-November presentation in the small town of Bristol, Tennessee. A listener to his 1908 speeches in Mississippi declared that "'Washington delivered plain, inspiring, and practical talks which the people warmly received.'"[38]

Tours and the annual national meetings of the league enhanced Washington's ability to promote desired aspects of the Yankee Protestant ethic. In the first speech that he delivered at the initial NNBL meeting, which convened in Boston during late August 1900, Washington espoused such Yankee Protestant tenets as cleanliness, education, efficiency, honesty, steadiness, orderliness, perseverance, promptness, service, thrift, and systematic work. After his NNBL speeches, attendees often conveyed the information they had heard from Washington to African Americans in their respective communities. Indeed, he encouraged listeners to apply the tenets themselves and to relay them to other blacks. Within a short time, devotees of the ethic fashioned an effective nationwide network of articulate African American businesspersons, politicians, and activists. In the process of taking up the cause, adherents became potential culture warriors for the movement. Supporters of the NNBL, along with educators and students who had attended industrial education schools, provided Washington with a large group of potential allies in his struggle to transform the culture of the South.[39]

A much larger and more diverse population than league members, educators, and industrial education students enjoyed and appreciated Washington's informal teachings. A wide cross section of Americans as well as a number of foreigners sent notes recalling Washington as the quintessential teacher, a man who dedicated his life to teaching. Writing from Cuba, Jose A. Manroque described the principal as an "incomparable teacher," and Walter S. Buchanan, president of Alabama Agricultural and Mechanics College in Normal, Illinois, described him as "a paragon in his efforts to guide and instruct his people." Condolers proclaimed him a life model and a major inspiration. W. H. Ellis, the first black stockbroker on Wall Street, who also owned additional offices in Mexico, appraised the impact that Washington's guidance had on the nation's populace, particularly African Americans, when he asserted, "it is an extra awful loss that the black race will suffer and the entire American people will miss the advice given by this great prophet." A note that the "Colored Students of Ohio State University" signed claimed that they would "forever strive to emulate his useful life and to disseminate the doctrines of righteousness and principles of education which our departed leader so zealously emphasized." Washington's admirers embraced his counsel.[40]

*   *   *

Well-wishers appreciated that Washington unambiguously highlighted and taught the Yankee Protestant tenet of serving other people. Washington told audiences that if they really wanted happiness and "a contented life . . . one of genuine pleasure," they had to "do something for somebody else." He instructed them to "go out into the world being helpful." He followed his own advice, and his mourners memorialized him for it. Herschel B. Cashin of Decatur, Alabama, articulating a common turn-of-the-century term for good works, wrote that Washington lived a "life of . . . incomparable usefulness." Along the same lines as Cashin, the Illinois Womans Missionary Auxiliary to the State Baptist Convention, remembered Washington as a person who toiled for years "accomplishing great things for the people." According to W. N. Mixon—an African Methodist Episcopal minister, founder of the Payne Institute of Selma, Alabama, and the first professional black journalist in Alabama—he had "done more for God and humanity than any man in" his day and generation.[41]

Acts of heroic charity attributed to Washington encouraged sympathizers to write testimonies that described the impact of his life story. Charles S. Medbury, the chaplain of Drake University in Des Moines, Iowa, alleged that Washington's "life has been an inspiration to me and I have tried to pass his spirit on to others." Maryville, Missouri, resident, B. T. Smart, asserted that the educator's "life was so worthy and so fruitful in good works that it will be an inspiration to others for all time." Washington's muse would last for hundreds of years according to Scott Bond, an official of the Arkansas Business League, an NNBL affiliate. His message announced that the "spirit of enterprise, frugality, thrift, and forbearance" Washington had "called up" would summon "us and will lead us through the coming centuries."[42]

His benevolence seemed to have inspired authors to remember him as a guardian of the African American race. They suggested that he diligently worked to improve the condition and prestige of black people. Authors applauded Washington for his attempts to enhance black people's reality and status. His efforts encouraged Bishop J. W. Alstork to memorialize him as "a true and self-sacrificing friend" of the race. It motivated two whites, James M. Curley, mayor of Boston, and Charles H. Albert, a Bloomsburg, Pennsylvania, resident, to both declare that Washington had "served his race with ability and fidelity unsurpassed in present American history." Some authors declared Washington the most significant patron of black people in the history of the United States. They seemed more grateful to Washington than to President Abraham Lincoln, the Great Emancipator of enslaved African Americans. Even Sheadrick B. Turner, a black Illinois state representative and publisher of the *Illinois Idea*, wrote to designate Washington the "Negros's [sic] greatest beneficiary."[43]

Notes from a multitude of African American groups articulated similar acknowledgment of Washington's value to the race. Expressing a shared memory of Washington promoted race consciousness. Like the notes from individuals, these too suggested that he diligently worked to improve the condition and prestige of black people. An assembly of African Americans in Sterling, Kentucky, alleged that Washington's "services to his race throughout his brilliant career were inestimable." A group identifying itself as the "Colored Citizens of Alexandria," Louisiana, pronounced his passing "an irreparable loss to the race." A proclamation from Talladega, Alabama, reported that "colored people . . . representing all phases of our business intellectually and spiritual life unite in sincere and hearty expression of the sense of the great loss we all sustain in the passing of" Washington. Condolences from these various assemblages give witness to black people's receptiveness to Washington's teachings.[44]

Many of the writers asserted that Washington assisted not just African Americans but all residents of the South. Several days before his death, Washington's declaration that "I was born in the South, I have lived and labored in the South, and I expect to die and be buried in the South" seemed to grasp firmly the reality of the symbiotic relationship between black and white southerners. He understood that he could not help the vast majority of African Americans improve their material well-being without doing the same for southern whites. In fact, Washington took it upon himself to work as a goodwill ambassador in and for the Southland. J. Y. Joyner, the Raleigh, North Carolina, superintendent of public instruction, wrote that Washington's death deprived not just blacks: it is "a great loss to both races." In a message to Warren A. Logan, the acting principal of the Tuskegee Institute, Wade H. Richardson asserted that since Washington focused his "life and teaching so as to uplift his race, win the respect and admiration of the whites . . . now they mourn his loss as a loss to both races."[45]

To condolers such as W. A. Hunton, the international secretary of the YMCA, Washington had become a highly valued national asset, which made his death a loss to the nation. A sizable number of whites and African Americans wrote notes similar to the one that Thomas Jesse Jones, a black Washington, D.C., resident, penned, alleging that the nation suffered when Washington died. Many more northern whites than southern, however, identified Washington as a national asset. In their respective notes, northern white writers included the chancellor of the University of Pittsburgh, S. B. McCormick, Caroline Hazard, the former president of Wellesley College, and Charles W. Fairbanks, a former Republican U.S. vice president (to President Theodore Roosevelt), referred to the passing of Washington as a "distinctly . . . public loss." Not just a loss, but also an irreparable one to the country is what New York banker Isaac Newton Seligman wrote. Harvard psychologist and philosopher William James declared it "a National Calamity," and former President William H. Taft called the demise an "irretrievable loss to the nation."[46]

A person of such good influence, some writers reasoned, must have acted on God's behalf. They contended that only the divine could have sent to the world a man as wise and effective as Washington. His good works inspired Jerseyville, Illinois, resident H. L. Chapman to write "that God selected him to carry out His wonderful purposes." The Presbyterian Ministers Association of New York and Vicinity recalled Washington as a "true prophet" who "spoke for God. He delivered God's message to man." Such praise from a group of northern black well-educated Calvinist clergy is extraordinary—as believers in the concept of predestination, these Christian leaders signified in their extolling of Washington that they believed God not only placed the Tuskegean among his chosen people but also selected him to lead them. George W. Hays, a Cincinnati, Ohio, resident, similarly declared that God sent Washington "to help his poor, oppressed and despised people." From Boston, members of the African American–populated Peoples Baptist Church asserted that Washington "was a God made golden link which bounds in mutual interest and friendship the white and black races of this country." Members of the Ethiopic Republican Association declared that "God has never given to the human race a more brilliant & learned man . . . he was not only a help to his race, but to all races of civilization."[47]

Some religious condolers asked God for assistance. Authors within this group of sympathizers, like the teachers at Palmer Memorial Institute in Sedalia, North Carolina, sought divine intervention in accepting the anguish they felt. These educators requested that God help them "to bear this great shock to our race and nation." Some writers wanted God to locate a replacement for Washington. Members of the African American Peoples Baptist Church of Boston begged the Lord for "another to complete the work" of Washington. Whereas, A. W. Dewar, the white corporate secretary of the John A. Hertel Company, a Chicago Bible publishing house, implored God to provide black Americans with a "worthy successor." F. B. Hooker and T. J. Elliott jointly penned a note that prayed for the Lord to "give us a strong leader to continue" Washington's "great work." A black man from Rembert, Alabama, Willis Jackson, seemed to have concluded that excellent leadership would produce "great work." Jackson wrote that he wanted God to provide "a nother [sic] great Leader to Lead" his people.[48]

A number of condolers wrote to convey their belief that Washington acted as God's great warrior. These sympathizers referred to an Old Testament verse describing the killing of Abner, a celebrated Jewish soldier. Even though Washington did not engage in or advocate violence, condolers paraphrased or quoted 2 Samuel 3:38, which commended the renowned fighter. That verse is one of only two biblical verses that refer to a person as "great," and both persons awarded this designation had distinguished themselves as warriors, men of very impressive valor, and leadership ability. Abner led the army of Israel's house of Saul. Jo'ab, a military commander in the house of Judah, murdered Abner, who for several years had led the army of Saul against the house of Judah. Shortly before the assassination, Abner had agreed to peace and subordination to King David, the future king of all of Israel. Jo'ab committed the murder to avenge his brother's death at the hands of Abner, but the execution occurred without the approval or knowledge of David. After learning of the death, the king cried and told Abner's mourners that he did not authorize the soldier's murder. Following Abner's burial, David announced to his servants, "Know ye not that there is a prince and a great man fallen this day in Israel?"[49]

A wide spectrum of Booker T. Washington mourners found David's expression of esteem for Abner appropriate to use in their efforts to convey veneration for the Tuskegean. Their paraphrases, which ranged from loose interpretations to close facsimiles of the biblical quote, reflected their memory of Washington as a warrior and commander. Although the Tuskegean did not lead a military force, he commanded an army of Yankee Protestant activists in a war to secure improved material well-being and increased social status for African Americans. In their memory, Washington led his troops to tremendous victories against insurmountable foes during an immense ongoing war. Like Abner's death, Washington's demise occurred prematurely, before his army of social activists achieved ultimate victory.

Some references to the verse revealed the writers' general understanding of the biblical story of Abner, even if they could not quote 2 Samuel exactly—they possessed knowledge sufficient to inspire them to make the analogy between the death of Washington and that of Abner. One such condoler from West Virginia, John C. Gilmer, the African American editor of the *Charleston Advocate*, portrayed Washington's death as the demise of a remarkably strong character: "a mighty oak has fallen." Likewise, President J. S. Clark of Southern University, the state-funded college for black people in Louisiana, took literary liberties in his condolence telegram: "Truly a great man and a true leader has fallen." In addition to loosely restating the biblical verse, the black Birmingham, Alabama, couple, H. C. Bryant and his wife, in their note of sympathy, clearly revealed a perception of Washington as their commander who died while fighting a continuing culture war: "a truly great man has fallen, our general lies prostrated in the heat of battle."[50]

Most of the people who sent messages inspired by the verse from 2 Samuel kept their text much closer to the original passage. Matthew Anderson—a Princeton Theological Seminary graduate, pastor of Berean Presbyterian Church, and founder of the largest black-owned building-and-loan association in Pennsylvania—awarded the status of royalty to Washington in his note: "a prince and a great man has fallen in Israel." W. A. Fountain, an AME preacher, chancellor of the Church's Macon, Georgia, Conference, and president of Morris Brown College, also proclaimed Washington a prince: "a great man has fallen yea a prince." M. Baranton Tule, a white former Christian missionary to South Africa, was among the condolers to likewise replace the word *Israel* in a scriptural paraphrase: "A great man has fallen in the nation." In a second note, this time written on behalf of his wife and himself, W. A. Fountain professed, "A great man has fallen in America." President Susie W. Fountain and Secretary E. F. Gray of the Peninsula Baptist

Women Missionary Union of Hampton, Virginia, used similar phrasing. A few sympathizers—such as the members of the Indianapolis "colored" YWCA who sent a note stating that "a great man in Israel has fallen"—conveyed messages that contain paraphrases closer to the biblical text. W. T. Johnson, self-professed friend of Washington and the pastor of the predominately white First Baptist Church in Richmond, Virginia, ensured the exactness of the text in his note. He asserted that "2 Sam. 3:38," articulated his "estimation of" the dead principal.[51]

*   *   *

But the majority of the notes expressing the writers' memories of Washington's greatness did so without referencing the Bible. Some of them, like the members of the African American ABC Baseball Club of Indianapolis, simply proclaimed Washington a "great man." E. Sutcliffe of Memphis, Tennessee, remembered him as "a great and good man." Other sympathizers placed Washington's eminence within a contemporary international framework, as in W. J. Button's declaration from Glendale, California, that history would record Washington "as one of the greatest and best of the men of his day and generation." Similar sentiments appeared in the note from James H. Dillard, who held membership on the Southern Education Board and the General Education Board while leading both the Jeanes Foundation and the John F. Slater Fund, four organizations that made major contributions to the education of black students. Dillard remembered Washington in his message as "one of the world's great men." To Leo Strassbunger, a white resident of Montgomery, Alabama, Washington's greatness transcended his lifetime. He forecast that Washington would "go down in history as one of the greatest men America has ever produced." A. W. Dewar, an employee of the Hertel Publishing Company, publisher of *Up from Slavery*, believed Washington's esteem would transcend the nation's borders. He prophesied that the Tuskegean would "go down in history among the Great Ones." A former Confederate general and president of Bull Durham Tobacco Company, Julian S. Carr wrote along the same lines: "Worms may destroy" Washington's body, "but [his] name and fame will live as long as the stars shine."[52]

Race consciousness helped shape some white people's assessments of Washington's life. These authors seemed not to write evaluations of it without mentioning his race. St. Joseph, Missouri, resident J. B. James did that when he proclaimed Washington "the greatest of his race." Another white sympathizer, Clarence E. Woods, a former Democratic mayor of Richmond, Kentucky, and chairman of the Executive Committee of the Florida Press Association, wrote that Washington's value transcended place and time, but not race: "[He was the] Greatest member of his race since the Egyptian Kings."[53]

Without declaring his greatness, two important white associates of Washington, John D. Rockefeller Sr. and Thomas W. Bicknell, highly praised the memory of the Tuskegean and his work. One of America's leading industrialists and its wealthiest man, Rockefeller, commented to Mrs. Washington that her husband "rendered invaluable services to his race in a life devoted to their uplift, and he was most highly appreciated by multitudes of the best people in the land." The white New England educator Bicknell assessed the Tuskegean as among the world's immortals. Bicknell had established a relationship with Washington during the late educator's school days at Hampton Institute. A former commissioner of education for Rhode Island and former official of the National Education Association (NEA), Bicknell had invited Washington to speak at the NEA's 1884 annual meeting in Madison, Wisconsin. Having accepted the invitation, Washington subsequently made his first presentation before a cross section of Americans. This speech, as well as Washington's years of work to transform black people, had immensely impressed the white New Englander. Bicknell wrote to Washington's brother, John, stating that he held the late educator in high esteem: "Lincoln emancipated a race of slaves. Booker Washington wrought the slave into a person of marvelous moral and economic values. No other man of any race or age has so far as my knowledge extends, in so brief a period as thirty years, made and left upon his race and generation so lasting an impression for righteous living and acting."[54]

Even though James P. Munroe of Boston asserted that it would take no less than "another generation" to evaluate properly the significance of Washington's charity, several other sympathizers speculated about the long-term results of his benevolence. They believed that the principal's largesse would produce significant benefits during the near future. This alleged enhancement of black people's material well-being and prestige provoked statements extolling the value of Washington to his race. They argued that no persons or entity surpassed the worth of his bequest to the African American community. A resident of Washington, D.C., Julia P. H. Coleman claimed that Washington "left the race a legacy rich and rare." Members of the Atlanta (GA) African Methodist Episcopal Church Ministerial Union predicted that the work and life of Washington would inspire "his race for unnumbered years to come." Wade H. Richardson wrote Washington left black people with an improved ability to financially support themselves while enjoying greater self-esteem and an increased status among whites.[55]

His death, contended a segment of the authors, created a momentous leadership and philanthropy void within the nation, particularly within black America. Mourners tended to understand that no other person had contributed as much directly or indirectly to African Americans' postbellum pursuits of civil rights, education, and material prosperity. Manifesting their knowledge of the precarious position of blacks in the country, these condolers expressed in strong terms the type of loss the nation incurred when Washington died. One of them, mourner Shelby J. Davidson, president of the Howard University Alumni Association, wrote that "the death of Booker T. Washington . . . will be deeply felt by the entire nation." Other African Americans pronounced the passing of the educator an "irreparable loss." William S. Scarborough, president of Wilberforce College, and national representatives of the Kappa Alpha Psi fraternity, a social organization for African American college men, made similar claims. Some writers, like Robert Moton, who would become the second principal of the Tuskegee Institute, contended that "the nation can ill afford the great loss we sustain in the death of Dr. Washington."[56]

Even a few southern whites proclaimed the demise of Washington a national deprivation. Perhaps these condolers recognized Washington's personal accomplishment, or they might have mistakenly believed that the Tuskegean promoted a permanent economic, political, social, and cultural place of subordination for blacks. Regardless of their reasons, they announced the passing of Washington a great loss for the United States. William C. Lloyd, superintendent of the Postal Telegraph-Cable Company Birmingham office, wrote that the "country has lost a splendid citizen" with the death of the Tuskegean. From New Orleans, coffee importer William B. Reily pronounced the passing of Washington a sincere loss to the "whole nation." John C. Anderson, chief justice of the Alabama State Supreme Court, pronounced the late educator's demise a loss to the "entire country" of a "great and good man."[57]

White and black authors residing in the South, including the Auburn Ministers Union, sent a collage of notes that imagined Washington's passing as a particular loss to their region of the country. Nashville, Tennessee, resident W. D. Wetherford alleged that "the Southern white people lost a great friend and helper" when Washington died. His death produced an "irreparable loss" to the South, wrote B. W. Allen, the black president of Lincoln Institute in Jefferson City, Missouri. Southerners mourned his loss because Washington had, asserted Alabama governor Emmett O'Neal, "won the confidence" of southern people and no other "man since the Civil War did more to create harmonious relations between the races."[58]

More than a few condolers stated that his influence extended beyond national borders. Mourners who held this view remembered Washington as a defender and promoter of all humanity. Their notes of solace seemed to have as much or more concern for humankind as they did for the Tuskegean's immediate survivors. Perhaps their awareness of the war already underway in Europe stimulated a concern for planetary peace and harmony. These writers envisioned the realization of Washington's ideas as the desired means of "uplifting" all materially deprived persons while stimulating worldwide interracial friendship. Both black and white condolers wrote notes of solace that called Washington's passing a loss to all humanity. Educator James L. Curtis of New York City bemoaned that the "human race "has lost a benefactor," and Kelly Miller, a Howard University professor, declared that the "human race will feel the loss." In a resolution, members of the Eatonville, Florida, Hungerford School community wrote, "the world humanity at large has lost a true and tried friend." Edyth Williams, a former member of the Tuskegee community and an enthusiastic supporter of Washington, wrote that she could not begin "to imagine what a serious loss this will be to the world in general."[59]

*   *   *

Although the authors' sincerity and motivation are undetermined, they wrote notes of solace that termed Washington a proficient southern black evangelist of Yankee Protestantism. Washington's family, friends, and close associates received letters, notes, resolutions, and telegrams depicting him as a major charitable force for Americans, particularly blacks. Individually and collectively written notes manifested memories of Washington that hailed him as a leading proponent of the Yankee Protestant Ethic, a benevolent masterful educator, a skillful leader of men, and a transnational icon. Many of the authors—black, white, northerners, and southerners—alleged that he had held an important place in their lives and those of many other Americans. A number of the writers sent sympathy messages out of a sense of duty or respect; while adhering to the adage "never say anything bad about the dead," their notes also contributed to the image that "a great man has fallen." That widely held perception seems to have elicited feelings of various degrees of sadness from a number of supporters of Washington and his movement. National expressions of grief, particularly among African Americans inspired W. H. Walcott, a Tuskegee Institute instructor, to allege hyperbolically that "so wide spread is the grief and sorrow among our people that I doubt if they have ever mourned the death of any national character as they are mourning Dr. Washington's."[60]

2. A Symbol of America

Obituaries and Other Published Memorials

Published obituaries of Booker T. Washington helped to shape personal and public memories of him. With few exceptions, Washington's obituaries memorialized him as the foremost leader of African Americans. His leadership, as many of his death notices observed, emerged from his success as a culture warrior. Washington, the articles suggested, relied heavily on the Yankee Protestant Ethic in his effort to lead black people out of poverty and degradation. In the process, he fought to overthrow the southern ethic and replace it with Yankee Protestant tenets. Obituaries stressed, overtly and implicitly, that Washington's esteem stemmed from his embrace of this ethic and his efficient use of it. He employed this system of values to help African Americans enhance both their material well-being and their national prestige. It endorsed, among other beliefs, systematic work, self-denial, steadfastness, conscientiousness, frugality, pragmatism, and education. While taking note of his successful employment of these tenets, obituaries depicted Washington's life as an object lesson, one that not only instructed African Americans but taught all optimistic, ambitious Americans how to achieve success. His death notices reinforced a long-held myth that the nation's bountiful opportunities would allow all persons, regardless of their status at birth or of their sex, race, or ethnicity, to succeed if they adopted the Yankee Protestant ethic paradigm. They portrayed him, moreover, as an optimistic, magnetic, philanthropic leader who endeavored to change the nation's realities for African Americans, particularly in the U.S. South.

Some obituaries, moreover, honored Washington's life as a beacon of hope for the nation as a whole and not just for selected individuals. They posited that his life reinforced U.S. nationalism. These articles implied that

Washington's teachings represented the best opportunity for the nation to achieve racial and political harmony. They asserted that his public policies and activities taught both black and white Americans, especially in the South, how to improve race relations substantially. Many of the death notices claimed that Washington's personality, teachings, and strategy to improve race relations provided the nation with a safe, rational, and beneficial means of securing long-term harmony among blacks and whites, as well as between northerners and southerners.

Although obituaries depicted Washington as a benefactor of the nation, they most often focused on his activities that they believed enhanced the South. Publications around the country alleged that he boosted the prosperity of the South. They argued that Washington, who actively endorsed industrial education, taught the black working class to internalize efficient laboring techniques that helped to increase meaningfully the productivity and wealth of the region. He therefore assisted northern and southern investors, along with black workers and their white employers.

More so than any other group, articulate blacks published remembrances of Washington commemorating him for helping them secure entrée into various types of U.S. marketplaces. They believed that he diligently struggled to increase their access to schools, businesses, and jobs, while assisting their efforts to acquire real estate, especially homes. These blacks believed, moreover, that Washington promoted African Americans in the bazaar of ideas, commerce, politics, and philanthropy. Black obituary writers noted that he wanted to end racial biases. As a dual symbol of hope and success, Washington both represented and voiced the African American community's most treasured desires—to possess equitable rights and privileges.

*　　*　　*

Newspapers and other periodicals throughout the nation reported Washington's death and memorialized his life. They reflected on the importance of his life and conveyed their interpretation of its meaning to a large segment of both black and white America. These journals printed articles, poems, and letters related to both the life and death of Washington. Starting the day after his death and continuing for weeks following it, periodicals published obituaries of Washington.

Newspapers deeming his death front-page news included the *Pittsburgh (PA) Times*: "Booker T. Washington Noted Negro Leader, Dies in Alabama Home." The *Duluth (MN) Tribune* published in large bold type "BOOKER T. WASHINGTON DIES NEAR INSTITUTE HE FOUNDED." That same day the *Augusta (ME) Journal* announced "DEATH OF DR. WASHINGTON

AT TUSKEGEE." At the other end of the country, the headline of the *Oregonian* (Portland, OR) read "FOREMOST NEGRO EDUCATOR IS DEAD." In Houston, Texas, the *Post* proclaimed "NEGRO EDUCATOR CLAIMED BY DEATH." The *Cleveland (OH) Plain Dealer* stated simply and elegantly in bold, "A Great American Gone." Five months after his death, the Pittsburgh (PA) *Methodist Recorder* published an article titled "A Tribute to Booker T. Washington."[1]

The articles under such headlines often provided details about Washington's death: the time, place, and cause of his demise; some even named the persons at his bedside when he died. Although the Tuskegean actually died on November 14, at 4:45 A.M., a number of papers printed times that ranged from 4:30 A.M. to 5:00 A.M. A few, like the *Newton (NC) News* and the *Pueblo (CO) Chieftain*, provided no specific hour. Most of the nation's periodicals correctly placed his death at Tuskegee. A minority of newspapers in both the South (e.g., *Richmond [VA] Planet*) and the North (e.g., *Freeman [OH] Messenger*) revealed arteriosclerosis (hardening of the arteries) as the cause of Washington's death.[2]

*   *   *

Any obituary, Washington's included, fulfills a number of purposes. Notifying the general public that persons have died is their primary purpose but, in the process, they reflect and promote the cultural and political interests of the writers. People who pen obituaries write what is important to them and not necessarily what the deceased valued. By calling attention to past lives, printed commemorations endorse the prevailing cultural and political values of the leaders of a targeted community. Thus writers use a filtered memory of a deceased person's life to promote a particular objective. They habitually tell readers details of the deceased's life that highlight desired characteristics. The writers, moreover, either neglect undesirable aspects of the dead person's life or downplay their significance. This is especially true for obituaries that paid staffers of various news media write. Their writings, however, reflected the values of the journals' management.

Obituaries attempt to legitimize the esteem and authority of the deceased. Writers, directly and indirectly, inform readers of the important role that the dead person's values and objectives played in securing the extraordinary esteem extended to them. Obituaries written for these persons serve as self-help guides for the living who seek veneration. Therefore, the life of the dead person becomes a role model for the living.[3]

As a nationally known culture warrior and a very important teacher of Yankee Protestant values, Washington's obituaries often provided synopses and insights into his life while promoting a certain worldview. Readers of these death notices could easily interpret many as implicit praises of the United States and its Yankee Protestant values. Washington obituaries frequently conveyed the message that the nation possessed a vast number of opportunities that allowed a lowly born slave to achieve substantial accomplishments. Obituary crafters retold the stories of how Washington began life as a slave, his struggles for an education after freedom, and his successful efforts at building Tuskegee Institute, a school for African Americans and the largest educational institution of any kind in the South. They portrayed his life as a symbol of the best that the United States had to offer: boundless opportunity. Where else, other than here, could a former slave become a highly acclaimed citizen in the country of his enslavers?

Since few of the authors knew Washington personally, many necessarily based their obituaries on secondhand information. Although they could have secured their knowledge from reading decades of news reports, most of the writers learned about Washington's life from published biographies and autobiographies. Washington determined that no better method existed for him to solicit moral, political, and financial support for Tuskegee Institute and his program of African American progress than to present the public with accounts of his life. The educator believed that his life served as a real representation of what most other blacks could and would achieve if provided the opportunity. Washington wanted very much for philanthropists, especially rich white ones, to deem the training provided at the Tuskegee Institute a necessary prerequisite for the masses of blacks seeking the realization of the nation's abundant opportunities. Thus, Washington wrote his several autobiographies primarily to inspire philanthropists to donate money to the institute.

Either Washington or his associates wrote several of the accounts written about his life before the 1901 publication of his most renowned autobiography, *Up from Slavery*. For example, the *New England Magazine* in October 1897 published "Booker Washington and the Tuskegee Institute," an article written by Thomas J. Calloway, a Tuskegee Institute employee. Max Bennett Thrasher, one of the few white workers at the institute, published an article and a book about the life of Washington. In May 1899, the *Appleton's Popular Science Monthly* published his "Tuskegee Institute and its President." The next year, Thrasher published *Tuskegee: Its Story and Its Work*. In the process of promoting the school, the book detailed Washington's life and his views. The previous June, *New York Teachers Magazine* had printed Washington's "My Life Work at Tuskegee, Alabama." Five months later, *Howard's American Magazine* published his short autobiography.[4]

Two of his autobiographies provided obituary authors with the bulk of their memories of Washington: *The Story of My Life and Work*, first printed in 1900, and *Up from Slavery*, initially published in 1901. The latter is actually the fourth edition of *The Story of My Life and Work*. After its publication, the book sold very well within and outside of the United States. These book-length self-portrayals, like the articles that he published, enabled the living Washington to help shape his postmortem memory. Since Washington tailored his autobiographies to inspire the philanthropic public, especially white northerners, to donate money to Tuskegee, he never intended for the books to stand as the complete, authentic account of his first forty or so years of life. He knew that the actual, enhanced, and mythical materials in the autobiographies had to generate social, political, and financial support for the Tuskegee Institute and his Movement. Thus, he embellished parts of his young life to more effectively pitch his plea. One of the more significant instances of falsification is that his autobiographies place the death of his mother as occurring after his first year of school at Hampton Institute. In fact, she died a year before he enrolled at the Hampton Institute. Portraying himself as a motherless schoolboy allowed him to emphasize to readers the tremendous obstacles he had to overcome to secure an education. Washington's autobiographies also symbolically suggested that the vast majority of African Americans needed help to overcome similar difficulties during their quest for the type of schooling that taught Yankee Protestant values. Washington's questionable accounts of his life reflected a long tradition of Americans who wrote self-portraits, especially those written as a part of the slave narrative genre.[5]

In a composition that possesses a style and a narrative similar to those in the autobiographies of Benjamin Franklin, Frederick Douglass, and many other slave narratives, Washington wrote a very successful solicitation. During the process of rewriting his autobiography the second time, Washington penned a letter to the publisher of *The Story of My Life and Work* that clearly revealed his primary reason for republishing the saga of his life as a serial in the *Outlook* magazine. He states that *Up from Slavery* would bring Tuskegee Institute "before a class of people who have money and to whom I must look for money for endowment and other purposes." This strategy worked, attracting wealthy donors like George Eastman, the founder of Eastman Kodak Company, and Colonel Wardwell G. Robinson, a former commander of black cavalrymen during the Civil War, both of whom donated $5,000. Eastman did so after completing his second reading of *Up from Slavery* after its publication in book form. Robinson bequeathed the money to Tuskegee

Institute in his will. Over a number of years, Elizabeth Julia Emery, an elderly white American who lived in England, likewise sent several thousand dollars to Washington after reading the book.[6]

Up from Slavery inspired Julius Rosenwald, the president of Sears and Roebuck, to become one of Washington's most charitable benefactors. Rosenwald's biographer, M. R. Werner, alleged that "no book could have been calculated to interest Rosenwald more than" *Up from Slavery*. Having read the book, Rosenwald provided the Tuskegee Institute and the Tuskegee movement well over $200,000. His donations included $25,000 to help fund Washington's annual salary, $25,000 as a fiftieth-year birthday gift to the black educator, over $30,000 to construct schools for rural blacks living in Alabama, and $100,000 to the Tuskegean's postmortem commemoration fund. Although other factors also influenced Rosenwald, *Up from Slavery* contributed to opening both his heart and his pocketbook, and Washington and the Tuskegee movement reaped the rewards.[7]

There are no means for determining how many additional contributors read *Up from Slavery* or some other report concerning the late educator's life before giving money to the school. Washington, in his ongoing efforts to promote Yankee Protestant ethics, wrote *My Larger Education*, a sequel to *Up from Slavery*, as well as several other books, to raise funds for his school and the Tuskegee movement. None of books sold as well or attracted as much money as *Up from Slavery*, which clearly contributed to Washington's image as a master fund-raiser. The image inspired the *Natchez (MS) Weekly Herald* to anoint him "the most successful solicitor of funds the country has ever known." While raising money, his ostensible autobiographies helped to shape the public's perception of Washington during his lifetime. They contributed, as well, to people's posthumous memories of him.[8]

Washington's published writings, especially the autobiographies, project the man as what James MacGregor Burns has called a "transforming" leader. Such human beings "shape and alter and elevate the motives and values and goals of followers through . . . vital teaching." Washington considered himself first and foremost as a teacher. After developing a comprehensive goal that could appeal to a broad-based constituency, Washington, like all "transforming" leaders, attempted to teach his followers to embrace the cause, principles, and objectives he deemed most important. Washington's curriculum included lessons for both his black and white supporters. He sought to teach African Americans to recognize and take advantage of available opportunities. Washington placed the Yankee Protestant ethic at the core of his formal and informal curriculum. At the same time, he struggled to teach northern and southern whites his concept of the most productive means to assist African Americans with their efforts at improving their material well-being and national prestige.[9]

Most of the Tuskegean's obituary writers portrayed Washington as a leader. His writings, together with the many speeches that he delivered, seemed to have helped them acknowledge his leadership. Although a few articulators penned disparaging remarks about it, in their respective obituaries, the vast majority of the writers praised Washington's guidance without reservation. After his death, northerners as well as southerners celebrated Washington as a significant leader. Regardless of their location, identity, or style of presentation, these authors frequently hailed the Tuskegean's leadership as extraordinary.

Most of the writers published their laudatory articles in newspapers that targeted predominately white readerships. The *Rochester (NY) Herald*, for example, announced that Washington "was rightly esteemed as the leader of his race." Other mainstream papers printed similar or more favorable assessments of his leadership. The *Duluth (MN) Tribune* opined that the late Alabama educator "was as much the father of his people as was the white Washington father of this country." The *Pensacola (FL) Journal* alleged that Washington had "no equals" among black Americans. He achieved this position, argued the *Ansonia (CT) Sentinel*, "through sheer native ability and force." Washington's wise leadership, asserted the *Daily Oklahoman* (Oklahoma City), "enable[d] him to accomplish more for and among the negroes [sic] of the United States than any negro [sic] of his time." However, other obituaries observed that the Tuskegean's leadership transcended race. In the view of the *Rochester Chronicle*, Washington "found the right way for any oppressed race to advance, he was a leader, not only of negroes [sic], but of humanity." No publication proclaimed Washington's leadership in higher regard than did the *Harrisburg (PA) Daily Telegraph*, which held him "among the greatest leaders of men that history has known."[10]

Likewise, most of the published acknowledgments by blacks about the death of Washington recognized and praised his leadership. Those articulate African Americans, however, who refused to applaud Washington included Charles S. Williams, the minister of Cincinnati's Allen Temple Church, who asserted that the "race was too big to have one man lead it." Periodicals like the *Voice of the People* lauded both Washington's leadership and professionalism. It alleged that "no leader of the negroes [sic]" would ever match Washington's success at promoting industrial education for blacks. Proclaiming that he served an imperative role in the United States for blacks, the *New York Call* pronounced Washington "one of the most vital leaders of a great race."

That African American newspaper observed that Washington "came in a time when leaders like him were needed." Never again would blacks have another leader like the Tuskegean, speculated T. Thomas Fortune, Washington's longtime close friend, in an obituary printed in the *New York Sun*. Demonstrating a keen understanding of history, Fortune asserted that, without the conditions created by slavery, persons with Washington's characteristics could not emerge as leaders. Nor would African Americans ever again need someone to teach them the rudimentary knowledge of work and thrift, or the need to buy land, and ways to cultivate the good graces of southern whites. While not stating why, Robert L. Vann, a black man, wrote in a letter published in the *Pittsburgh (PA) Press* that his "entire race owes a debt of gratitude to our lamented leader," Booker T. Washington. The *Indianapolis Recorder* stressed the reasons that Vann and other articulators considered blacks debtors to Washington. It remembered the deceased educator as the "Negro's [*sic*] greatest leader, its Moses and its guiding star." Claiming that his influence transcended national borders, the *East Tennessee News* described Washington as "one of the world's greatest leaders," predicting that "every race of modern civilization will be affected" by his death.[11]

Several African Americans, including Timothy Thomas Fortune, however, took exception in print to the generally uncritical appraisal of Washington as a leader. Responding that George W. Forbes—a librarian, editor, and lawyer—wrote and published in the January 1916 issue of *AME Review*, Fortune asserted that the late educator "had feet of clay" and was "sensitive to the last degree" to his "own position and equally intolerant and scornful of that of others." After detailing the nature of their personal and professional relationships, which included his editing Washington's speeches, articles, and books, Fortune charged that the Tuskegean's relationship with President Theodore Roosevelt undermined his own partnership with the late educator. They eventually parted ways, according to Fortune, after the editor's health declined, and he lost control of the *New York Age* newspaper. Fortune proclaimed that "We did not fall out and quarrel; we were on speaking terms to the last, but he had no further use for me in his business because I had lost my health and newspaper, and because with my assistance he had been able to reach the point of leadership where he did not want friends to advise him, but persons to do what he wanted done."[12]

After charging that white men had named Washington as the leader of Africa America and provided him with "plenty of money to carry out the purposes of his leadership," Fortune stated that he did not regret helping the late educator to acquire and maintain his position. He professed that black people needed to increase their educational achievement while expanding and enhancing their businesses. He asserted that Africa America required "some intelligence and money to back up its much-talked about justice and equality." Claiming that he "helped rather than hindered" Washington with the necessary work, Fortune, despite his clay-feet assessment, decreed the late educator a "very great man" who "did a very great work."[13]

Although W. E. B. Du Bois recognized Washington's eminence, he published one of the most stringent negative assessments of the late educator's leadership. In an obituary published in the *Crisis*, which he edited, the official magazine of the National Association for the Advancement of Colored People (NAACP), he in turn recognized, praised, and criticized the Tuskegean's leadership. Du Bois, Washington's most vocal black detractor, called Washington the "greatest leader since Frederick Douglass, and the most distinguished man, white or black, who has come out of the South since the Civil War." Du Bois followed this acknowledgment with a short recounting of Washington's accomplishments for black people and an assessment of his shortcomings. "He never" asserted Du Bois, "adequately grasped the growing bond of politics and industry." Nor did Washington, alleged Du Bois, "understand the deeper foundations of human training." The *Crisis* editor faulted the Tuskegean for basing his concept of good race relations on a social caste system. Du Bois ended his obituary with the despairing statement that Washington had "a heavy responsibility for the consummation of Negro disfranchisement, the decline of the Negro college and public school, and the firmer establishment of color caste in this land."[14]

Articulators who questioned or opposed a significant portion of Washington's ideas and actions, like the commentator that wrote for the *Afro-American Ledger*, provided support for Du Bois's appraisal. The newspaper attempted to legitimize critical aspects of the obituary with the proclamation that Du Bois had completed a "profound study of the race question in its economic and sociological bearings." Displaying its knowledge of the content of the obituary before *Crisis* published it, the *Afro-American Ledger* labeled Du Bois a "severer" but "tolerant critic" of the Tuskegean. It alleged that, in a future issue of *Crisis* magazine, Du Bois would make a "thoughtful and generous estimate of Dr. Washington."[15]

Most black obituary writers responded unsympathetically to Du Bois's assessment of Washington's life. The reactions, ranging from dispassionate to confrontational, provided a partial insight into the two dominant contemporary schools of thought among articulate Americans, especially blacks, concerning Washington and his activities. Those periodicals edited by Tuskegee movement supporters, which included the *Georgia Baptist* and the *Atlanta Independent*, took offense to both the tone and content of the obituary that Du Bois wrote. Employing a sarcastic tone, the *Georgia Baptist* proclaimed that "it was left to Dr. DuBois to sound the only discordant note" about the professional work of Washington. The editor of the *Atlanta Independent* asserted that he ignored Du Bois's obituary, hoping that "other race journals" would also refuse to recognize its existence. Calling Du Bois's indictment of Washington "strange," the *Independent* stated that it countered "the great unanimity of opinions of Dr. Washington from all classes of men." After stating that it "is an awful thing to charge any man with interrupting the development of a people," the paper chastised Du Bois for living "in the cloister of theories instead of in the open of practice." It asserted, moreover, that the editor did not have the authority to act as a judge in "the court of the last resort as what is best for the race."[16]

One of the most adamant Tuskegee movement supporting newspapers, the *Chicago Defender*, also published a passionate reaction to the obituary by Du Bois. Known throughout its history as uncompromising in its stance against segregation and injustices toward African Americans, the *Defender* (from its founding in 1905) steadfastly supported Washington. Its founder, Robert S. Abbott, came to Chicago from St. Simon's Island, Georgia, by way of Hampton Institute. After graduating from Kent College of Law in Chicago and failing as a lawyer, Abbott established the *Defender*. His paper, long before the death of Washington, had a history of ridiculing Du Bois. After Abbot learned of Du Bois's obituary, he lambasted the editor of the *Crisis*. Alleging that not even the NAACP, and certainly not the Chicago branch, embraced his views, the *Defender* argued that Du Bois wrote "undoubtedly the most flagrant case of misrepresentation." Hyperbolically, Abbot indicated that only Du Bois wrote a "discordant" obituary that countered the "tributes to the memory of" Washington made by the "entire world." He further stated that "there is no excuse for this attempt to distort facts that are known to every American school boy. If Prof. DuBois would do his race a benefit he would lay aside petty animosity and strife-breeding and present a program of constructive work for the uplift of his people which this splendid opportunity affords him."[17]

*   *   *

Mindful that obituaries provide readers with character development guides, writers constructed a utilitarian posthumous memory of the late Tuskegean. Authors wanted their audiences to believe that Washington's adherence to Yankee Protestant values allowed him to overcome enormous obstacles on his way to prominence. They described one or more of the noteworthy impediments that Washington overcame over the course of his life. In doing so, the Tuskegean's obituaries taught their readers a desired set of ideas and behaviors that included setting worthy goals and persevering through adversity, as well as pursuing education, working smartly, laboring hard, and assisting mankind.

Even though the *Springfield (MA) Republican* quoted Washington's claim that he had no memory of slavery before the day his mother shouted "hallelujah" in response to learning of her freedom, many death notices briefly discussed the Tuskegean's life as a slave. In fact, periodicals with predominately white readerships often began their coverage of Washington's life with his birth as a slave. Newspapers like the *Boston Evening Transcript*, *Pensacola (FL) Journal*, *Indianapolis Star*, *New York City Press*, and *Salt Lake City (UT) News* proclaimed Washington's slave origin in the first sentence of their respective obituaries. African American–oriented publications also promoted the idea that innumerable opportunities existed in the United States, but the vast majority of them either downplayed the enslavement of Washington or ignored it. The *New York City Amsterdam News*, the *Chicago Defender*, and the *St. Louis (MO) Argus* subordinated the Tuskegean's slave legacy for a variety of reasons that might have included resentment and shame, as well as perceived irrelevance. Writers, regardless of their racial identity, seemed to have wanted their readers to conclude that Washington's overcoming his slave heritage validated the existence of immense opportunities available for all Americans, not just white ones.[18]

Obituaries that did discuss Washington's enslavement did not attempt to construct a memory of him that supported his often-stated adage that, during slavery, African Americans associated labor with bondage. Instead, obituaries focused on Washington's alleged experiences. Reporting on his diet as a child, the *Boston Evening Transcript* proclaimed that Washington received "two tablespoonful of molasses once a week." Regarding his early literacy education, the *Richmond (VA) Journal* purported that one of his master's daughters taught Washington the "A B C's." While the *New York Amsterdam News*, an African American–owned newspaper, reported that Washington's assigned duties included fanning "flies from his master's table," the *Harrisburg (PA) Advocate-Verdict* claimed that his slave labor included retrieving the mail from the post office. While his autobiographies do not claim that his master's daughter taught him the alphabet, or that he retrieved the mail as a slave, Washington did assert in *Up from Slavery* that he fanned flies.[19]

A surprising minority of those writers who mentioned Washington's bondage emphasized his low social status by claiming to report his monetary worth as a slave boy. After his original master, James Burroughs, died in 1861, the *Richmond (VA) Journal*, and several other newspapers, noted that

James's grandson, S. C. Burroughs, possessed an appraisal that assessed the five-year-old enslaved Washington at $400. During the only publicized visit that Washington made to the area of his birth, he encountered Burroughs and asked for a copy of the appraisal. Although few publications discussed the appraisal while Washington was alive, after his death, several obituary writers, in their promotion of the purported bountiful opportunities found in America, wrote about it. Even a former slave could become invaluable in America.[20]

Washington's obituaries generally indicated that fatherlessness and previous enslavement did not prohibit significant success in America. Most of the posthumous vignettes about Washington countered the notion that the social standing of a man's father predetermined his maximum potential success in the society. Omitting any mention of Washington's stepfather, Washington Ferguson, articles reported that the Tuskegean overcame, in his ascension to success and fame, the significant disadvantage of not having a father. In the retelling of Washington's life, his death notices signified to the large number of immigrant Americans and their children, that the United States, unlike European societies, offered opportunities for self-actualization to the most humble of its residents. In the process, Washington's obits contributed to undermining the southern ethic and all other aspects of hereditary predetermination.

Death notice authors eagerly retold Washington's dubious claim that he did not know his biological father. "Washington confessed," asserted the *Fort Plain (NY) Register*, "that he knew nothing of his antecedents, save that his mother was a slave." The *New York Sun* purported that the Tuskegean "had only the vaguest idea as to who was his father," while the *Allentown (PA) Morning Call* stated that Washington never knew his father. According to Marquis James, a two-time Pulitzer Prize–winning biographer, however, Washington indeed knew the identity of his biological father, James Burroughs. Moreover, Washington had a long-term relationship with at least one of the children Burroughs sired with a slave woman other than his mother. That child also grew up in the Malden, West Virginia, area. After he relocated to Tuskegee, he occasionally visited her.[21]

Reflecting the intense race consciousness during 1915 and 1916, white-oriented publications credited Washington's white father for much of his accomplishments. U.S. racism seemed to have inspired several writers to announce that Washington inherited much, if not all, of his capabilities from his unknown sire. "His mind," asserted the *Boston Herald*, "was more Caucasian than Ethiopian." The editor of the *Progressive Farmer*, Clarence Poe, wrote that the Tuskegean's "ability came from his white father rather than his

Negro mother." The nation's prevailing racial protocol demanded that whenever whites and blacks interacted with each other, whiteness had to trump blackness. This code stipulated that only in a very few areas—for example, rhythm and dance—could black people's ability reign supreme over that of whites. Hence, ironically, the genes that Washington inherited that allegedly provided him with the wherewithal and desire to achieve could have come from any anonymous white man. Writers espousing this racist theory, in essence, told their readers that only whites or other people with noticeably Caucasian antecedents could realistically hope to enjoy Washington-like success and esteem.[22]

Other publishers and private citizens that championed a more open society challenged Poe and the other advocates of the idea that black people lacked an innate ability to succeed. These writers sought to promote America as a place where all people could realize their dreams of achievement, and they wanted the story of Washington's life to exemplify that premise. In this vein, the *New Haven (CT) Register* reminded its readers that "it has been common to seek, either consciously or unconsciously, to deprive the negro [*sic*] race of the credit for Booker Washington by constantly reminding us that he was partly white." Referring to the notion that a white man gave Washington his ability as both candid and funny, the *New York News* asserted that "it is the way of the white South to lay claim to all that is good in the black South. Never before have we heard from the South of black blood not tainting and corrupting white blood." In addition, the *News* asserted that southern scientists had claimed "the mulatto was worse than either of the parent stocks." These learned men, the author asserted, claim that the mother's characteristics dominated and the child would inherit none of the white father's "virtues," but rather that the offspring would acquire "all of the vices" belonging to black people.[23]

Whereas the racial designation of Washington's father produced controversy, the failure of death notices to establish a consensus concerning Washington's age did not. Repeating Washington's assertions in his autobiographies, the *Geneseo (NY) Republican* contended that Washington never knew the exact date of his birth. Displaying its uncertainty, the *Piqua (OH) Call* reported Washington's birth year as "1857 or 1858." The *Two Rivers (WI) Reporter*, however, claimed 1858 or 1859 as the year of the Tuskegean's birth, whereas the *New York Daily Graphic* gave 1856 as the year, as did the *Indianapolis Freeman*, the *Montgomery (AL) Advertiser*, and the *Tuskegee Student* (Tuskegee Institute). The latter two papers based their conclusion on evidence provided by Booker's older brother, John Washington.[24]

Writers of obituaries who published Washington's age responded to reader interest in the measurement of time, a tool that allows people to calculate the speed of movements. During the era of Washington's death, Americans had begun to embrace the concept of time more tightly than ever before. The preoccupation with productivity during the industrial era inspired many middle-class Americans to display an increasing fondness for efficiency—the act of perfecting any activity within the shortest possible time period—a core principle within the Yankee Protestant ethic. In addition to permitting readers to compare their longevity with that of the dead, stating ages in obituaries allows the living to gauge the efficiency of both the dead person's life and their own. Although he lived longer than many Americans of his era, Washington's death notices informed their readers that the Tuskegean accomplished much more than the vast majority of people regardless of their age at death. Obituary writers, most often inadvertently, used a consensus memory of Washington to instruct readers how to live a more efficient life.

Although there is no firm evidence of how Booker Taliaferro Washington received any of his three names, authors ascribed meaning to his first and middle names. They constructed explanations of how he secured those names in a manner that assisted the authors with their efforts at teaching preferred Yankee Protestant characteristics. Some posthumous recollections of Washington implied that his mother, who possessed high aspirations for her son, named him Taliaferro in honor of a prominent family who resided in their area of Virginia. Indeed, anthropologists Richard Price and Sally Price assert that a name is "a document epitomizing personal experiences, historical happenings, attitudes to life and cultural ideas and values." Many of the death notices intimated that a name helped to determine a person's ultimate eminence. Hence Washington's middle name reflected Jane's determination to raise her son in a manner that would indoctrinate him to highly valued achievement and prestige.[25]

Some authors further alleged that Washington's mother, Jane, gave the name "Booker" to her son as a nickname in recognition of his affection for books as a youth. The *Utica (NY) Globe*, for example, reported that his "mammy called him 'Booker' because he liked to look at books, and the rest of the pickaninnies didn't." The *Globe*, and the other periodicals that made similar claims, manifested U.S. opinion makers' high esteem for literacy, a key component in the effort to improve personal economic status as well as increase industrial proficiency in the nation. In reality, Jane's thoughts concerning her son's personal status probably went little beyond her desire for his freedom from slavery. Perhaps she simply continued a practice common in the Hausa-speaking area of West Africa of giving sons the nickname Bukar, in honor of Abu-Bakar, the successor of Mohammed and the first caliph of Islam. Historian Basil Mathews maintains that West Africans pronounced the first syllable of Bakar as "book." An uncounted number of enslaved Africans practiced Islam.[26] There is no written record that any member of Washington's family or any other slave living in close proximity of his birthplace practiced Islam. Someone, likely a slave carpenter, who had worked or lived on Burroughs's farm attached an Islamic icon, a circular wooden plate with "a crescent and star carved in the center" to the gable of Washington's master's "small front porch.

*　*　*

In the process of constructing a memory of Washington as a hard-working American who attained greatness after triumphing over immense adversity, writers attempted to ensure that readers clearly understood that the Tuskegean enjoyed few accomplishments without some sort of struggle. This is especially the case regarding Washington's pursuit of formal primary schooling. These reports continued the theme of overcoming adversity through resolve and hard work. Using information gathered partly from his several autobiographies, many obituaries reported that Washington did not receive formal schooling until after the family relocated to Malden, West Virginia. Several published obituaries alleged that Washington attended school there while he worked in either a salt or a coal mine. The *Tuskegee (AL) News*, however, asserted that Washington secured a job only after starting school in Malden. While the *Tuskegee (AL) News* contended that John, his brother, not Booker, worked in a salt mine on arriving at Malden, the *Birmingham (AL) Age-Herald* alleged that the younger Washington "worked in the coal mines during the summer and attended school in the winter."[27]

Regardless of when or where he worked, the death notices emphasized Washington's overcoming substantial hardships to acquire a formal education, a growing requisite during the early years of America's industrial era. Some obits, like the one published by the syndicated *Afro American Page*, an agency that distributed new items to numerous African American–oriented journals, contended that his stepfather did not allow Washington to go to day school. Instead, he "managed to attend night school for three of four months a year." Other death notices repeated the claim Washington made in his autobiographies that he worked a split shift, one that began early in the morning and ended late at night, so that he could attend day school. The *Springfield (MA) Republican*'s portrayal of Washington's struggle for schooling included a claim that he sometimes walked miles "to be taught only to discover that the teacher knew less than he did." Washington's efforts to attain an education, the *Tuskegee Student* suggested, did not become much easier after he began working for the Lewis Ruffner family in 1871 as their houseboy. This tabloid reported that he attended school during the day while working "mornings and evenings."[28]

Washington's training at Hampton Institute spawned as much, if not more, interest among his obituary writers than his efforts at taking a common (grammar) school education. His determination, as indicated by the hardships he overcame en route to the Hampton Institute in Virginia, and his subsequent admission to the school provided the writers with an exemplary object lesson on the rewards people in America can receive if only they persevere. Similar to the efforts of many adults to inspire young people, many of the articles attempted to motivate readers with embellishments of the difficulties Washington encountered on his way to Hampton. Many of the articles reported on his mode of transportation to Hampton and the difficulties Washington endured while traveling. *New Age* magazine reported that "part of the time he walked." Printing a quote from an interview with Washington that supported this allegation, the *Springfield (MA) Republican* asserted that he "walked a good share of the way, rode a part of the distance on the train, and begged some rides." The *Utica (NY) Globe*, however, stated that Washington "made his way afoot to Hampton." Putting his journey in a vague context of distance, the *Little Rock (AR) Gazette* professed that Washington "walked across two states." Giving more specificity to the length of the trip; the *Brooklyn (NY) Eagle* reported that he "walked 500 miles to reach the school."[29]

Washington's journey to Hampton provided authors with a case study of how determined persons, living in this nation, could find enough money to help initiate their quests for success. Persons only needed the will to work menial jobs and the wisdom to husband their pay properly, key Yankee Protestant values. The *Springfield (MA) Republican* made this point as clear as any periodical. It reported that Washington once stated that when he arrived at Richmond he "had no money left . . . slept under the sidewalk for a number of nights." During the day Washington worked "unloading vessels," and several other jobs, until he "earned enough money to pay" for his trip to "the Hampton Institute."[30]

Journalists repeatedly credited Hampton Institute, which Yankee Protestants founded and operated, with more responsibility than any other entity or experience for creating the public Booker T. Washington. The *Portland (ME) Express*, for example, decreed the Tuskegean "a product of Hampton." The school provided the opportunity for "the power of his mind" to come "into evidence," alleged the *Salt Lake City (UT) News*. While enrolled, the *Philadelphia Bulletin* asserted that Washington "caught the inspiration at Hampton." Obituaries recognized General Samuel C. Armstrong as the person who shaped "the beneficent career of the negro [*sic*] educator." A Brooklyn newspaper announced that "due credit must be given to the work of the Hampton Industrial Institute, and its head, Gen. Armstrong" for Washington's accomplishments.[31]

Obituaries aimed at a primarily white readership informed readers that white people and an institution that they controlled played fundamentally important roles in the training of Washington. Many of them proclaimed that a white Yankee Protestant woman employed Washington in West Virginia immediately preceding his relocation to Hampton Institute. Washington's "first real start in life" occurred in Malden, declared the *Philadelphia Inquirer*, when he worked as a houseboy for Viola Ruffner, a white teacher originally from Vermont. After leaving her employ, he enrolled at Hampton Institute, a school widely known as an academy operated by whites. Washington obtained his training, asserted a newspaper in Brooklyn, "as a student and teacher at Hampton." The *Hartford (CT) Courant* made it unmistakably clear that Washington's career preparation resulted largely from the goodwill of white people: "General Armstrong, who founded Hampton Institute, was a white man." Thus the *Courant*, among other papers oriented toward white readerships, used Washington's life to demonstrate the advisability for opportunity seekers to secure tutelage from upper middle-class white people.[32]

Armstrong received his initial assistance to establish the school from the federal government's Bureau of Refugees, Freedmen, and Abandoned Lands (Freedmen's Bureau) and the American Missionary Association (AMA). Both organizations concurred with Armstrong's concept of education for the former slaves. Armstrong and his institute, one of dozens of schools established by white Yankee Protestant missionaries to train former bondsmen, embraced a philosophy that originated in the thinking of early nineteenth-century U.S. Calvinists. Armstrong's parents, originally northeasterners, served as Christian missionaries to Hawaiians. His father, a Calvinist reared in Pennsylvania, once served as the Hawaiian commissioner of education. Perhaps his father exposed him to the Hilo Boy's Boarding School, which became the inspiration for the Hampton Institute's curriculum and pedagogical model. That model dictated that teachers implement a manual labor system to reinforce the teaching of the dignity of labor and other Yankee Protestant values. It also enabled Armstrong to exploit student labor. These missionaries embraced the assertion espoused in the biblical verse Luke 6:40, which states that a student "fully trained, will be like his teacher." Armstrong and his all-white, mostly Yankee Protestant missionary teaching staff wanted Washington and the other Hampton Institute students to internalize those collective values. After the indoctrination process, the missionaries intended for the former students to teach the same skills and values that they learned at Hampton to other African Americans living throughout the South.[33]

Most newspapers intended for a primarily white readership did not mention Washington's black teachers in West Virginia or the training he received at the predominately African American–populated Wayland Seminary. Only a few newspapers, including the white-owned *Tuskegee (AL) News*, mentioned the seminary in their obituaries of Washington. The location of that paper, with its majority black population, as well as the long association it experienced with Washington and his school, could have influenced the nature of the *News*'s obituary. It repeated much of what the institute's student paper wrote about the deceased, including information concerning his training at Wayland Seminary.[34]

Perhaps a desire to acknowledge Washington's embrace of religion and thus more closely identify the Tuskegee movement with Christianity dictated that Washington's black obituary writers mention his time at the seminary. Whatever the reason, the African American–owned *Savannah (GA) Tribune* reported that "Washington went to Wayland institute in Washington D.C." While attending school at the seminary, asserted the *Indianapolis Freeman*, Washington received his invitation to work at Hampton. The *Afro American Page* reported that the Tuskegean attended Wayland for a year, even providing the name of his primary teacher, Dr. G. M. P. King. Articles denoting the direct influence of a religious school in the shaping of the pre-Tuskegee Washington reinforced the righteousness of Washington and his movement.[35]

*   *   *

Tuskegee Institute, more so than the seminary or any other entity, provided Washington with the wherewithal to perform good works. He, as the obituaries written in the *Long Branch (DE) Record* and the *Piqua (OH) Call* asserted, "was most generally associated" with the Tuskegee Institute. A Brooklyn newspaper asserted that the names of the institute and Washington would "ever be inseparably conjoined." Washington's skillful promotion of the school and its various educational and social activities inspired Americans to think of the institute as an extension of the man. Visually manifesting the interconnection of the Tuskegean with the school, the *Indianapolis Freeman*, a newspaper published by an African American, displayed large photographs of the institute's campus under the headline "IN MEMORY OF BOOKER T.

WASHINGTON." The African American–owned *Atlanta Independent* called the institute the conception of Washington's "massive brain." Washington's activities, claimed the *Williamsport (PA) Grit*, at times seemed liked they "began and ended in the Tuskegee institute."[36]

The Washington and Tuskegee symbiosis motivated obituary writers to remember the development of the institute and the evolution of the educator as a person as being the same phenomenon. Their memories of Washington's post–Hampton Institute years most often centered on the growth and the experiences of the Tuskegee Institute community. Obituaries often traced the origin and evolution of the school. Death notices, like the one published in the *Los Angeles Examiner*, reported that when Washington arrived in Tuskegee, the state had not provided a site or grounds for the school. Other papers, such as the African American–owned *Washington (D.C.) Bee*, and the *Duluth (MN) Tribune*, noted that the institute "started in a rented shanty church." A periodical aimed at black Methodists, the *Christian Recorder*, asserted that Washington held the institute's initial classes in "an old henhouse." In addition to securing facilities and staff for the school, the *Minneapolis (MN) Tribune* pointed out that Washington had to overcome the initial reluctance of many black people. Revealing its support for Washington's concept of education, the papers went on to state that unenthusiastic African Americans failed to "grasp the sound philosophy" of Washington's teachings.[37]

The accomplishments of both Washington and Tuskegee provided writers with plentiful examples of positive consequences resulting from employing such Yankee Protestant values as hard work, coupled with perseverance and a grand vision of community service. They seemed to have delighted in reporting the school's meager start and the many stages it passed through before becoming the exemplary model for the education of black people. Several newspapers published in-depth accounts of the school's evolution during the thirty-four years of Washington's principalship. For example, the *Sioux City (IA) Tribune*, in a lengthy report on Washington and the institute, noted the difficulties the Tuskegean, his staff, and students experienced before they successfully manufactured bricks that they used to construct many of the school's buildings. Woods Hutchinson, a physician, in a series of articles widely published after the death of Washington, wrote the most comprehensive account of the growth of the institute, its educational methods, the activities of its students and staff, and the services offered by the school. Hutchinson provided his readership with an eyewitness account of the day-to-day life at the school during the latter years of Washington's life.[38]

Many other obituaries cited the recent enrollment figures, the size of the campus, the type and number of courses, the amount of the school's endowment, and its operational budget. The syndicated *Afro American Page*, the *New York Evening Mail*, the *Portland (ME) Express*, and the *Birmingham (AL) Age-Herald* are cases in point. Although often the alleged facts in the various articles contradicted one another, they all attempted to highlight Washington's success in the developing of Tuskegee Institute. The *Afro American Page* reported that the school consisted of more than forty buildings on a 2,500-acre campus, with 662 students enrolled in the normal school and 150 in the training school. It offered academic classes and thirty-eight trade courses, employed 167 persons, and operated with a $325,000 annual budget. Along with asserting that the campus included some of the "largest if not acutely the largest buildings in" Alabama, the *New York Evening Mail* claimed that the Tuskegee Institute possessed "the largest group of buildings in the state." Proclaiming that no white institution could match Tuskegee Institute's wealth, campus acreage or size of its student body, the *Age-Herald* stated that the school had a staff of more than 200 persons, "a student body of more than 2,000, and an income of more than a half million dollars." Proclaiming that the school lay "just beyond the corporate limits of the tiny town" of Tuskegee, the *Daily Oklahoman* (Oklahoma City) asserted that the school "is as large as the town." The *Montgomery (AL) Advertiser* printed that the school "is certainly, in size an enormous institution and we are not prepared to dispute the statement that more money is invested in it than in any other educational institution in the South."[39]

Tuskegee Institute clearly impressed the authors, who publicized the school as an amazing entity. Over the years, Washington, a very skilled promoter, created for the institute an enormous amount of goodwill among many of the nation's leading opinion makers. Even though he fought to dismantle the southern ethic, Washington's uncannily successful promotion, along with the school's good works, even inspired white-owned southern newspapers to praise the institute. Its activities and reputation motivated the *Ocilla (GA) Star* to proclaim that the institute "had done so much for the Negroes of the South." It had, remarked the *Tennessee News* (Chattanooga), "an enormous influence over that part of the black belt of the South." Washington's Tuskegee propaganda machine seemed to have convinced the editor of the *St. Louis (MO) Republic* that the school's clout extended to all African Americans when it declared that the institute exerted a "powerful influence for good upon . . . 10,000,000" African Americans. Outside of the South, the school's eminence persuaded the *Sentinel*, a paper published in New York state, to claim that the institute had become "a center of Negro inspiration," which "stood for Negro independence and determination." At Tuskegee, announced the *New York News*, blacks "convince white citizens that the colored man can succeed and has succeeded." Perhaps the editor of the *Lynn (MA) News* held a similar opinion when his newspaper declared, "not one but many Tuskegees are needed if the Negro in the South is to have his far share."[40]

A number of writers remembered Washington as the head of an institution of national significance. For many of them, the late educator fashioned and effectively taught a curriculum at Tuskegee Institute that embodied values that they believed most Americans should learn and embrace. The alleged success at teaching Yankee Protestant values to African American students helped the school to secure a significant prominence. Its esteem inspired newspaper commentators, including those at the *Fresno (CA) Republican* and the *Chicago Journal*, to assert that the institute influenced the contemporary education of black and white children alike. That is what the *Chicago Journal* contended when it declared that the institute "had become a model for white schools as well as black." Washington's school, asserted the *Natchez (MS) Weekly Herald*, affected profoundly the educational fashion of the country." In its promotion of the Tuskegee Institute's curriculum and pedagogy, the *Detroit (MI) Journal* called for a wholesale reproduction of both. It declared that "when we copy Washington's work at Tuskegee we will then have started on the way towards true education for the masses."[41]

The consensus concerning the merit of Washington's pedagogy and curriculum did not translate into a broad-based agreement regarding the intent of his teaching. The *Des Moines (IA) Leader* correctly proclaimed "there has always been dispute over the aims of Tuskegee." Various published memories of the school's activities highlighted those differences. Papers like the *Montgomery (AL) Advertiser* asserted that the school trained "some worthy leaders of the negro [*sic*] race." Other periodicals, such as the *Philadelphia Press* and *Chicago American*, alleged that the academy taught the students how to make "an adequate living." More than a few of the death notices promoted the contention forwarded by the *Buffalo (NY) Enquirer*, which reported that the institute taught its students how to work. A sizable number of other publications told their readers that in addition to good workers, the institute trained "students how to be most useful as farmers" and as mechanics.[42]

Although the February 10, 1881, Alabama law that charted the institute declared it a normal school "for the education of colored teachers," only a few periodicals, including the *Tacoma (WA) Ledger*, noted that Tuskegee Institute prepared teachers. Most of the articles, like the one published in *Little Rock (AR) Gazette*, focused on vocational training at the institute, which it described as "a practical, not a theoretical, industrial school." The *Port Jervis (NY) Gazette* asserted that the institute provided young blacks a "place where they might learn how to utilize such industrial opportunities as opened to them." In an editorial that ignored the Tuskegee Institute's industrial train-ing, the *Buffalo (NY) News* asserted that the school never produced a politi-cian, statesman, artist, or a poet; instead, it prepared its students "for a life of . . . commerce that Booker T. Washington always contended his race was intended for."[43]

While obituaries attributed most of the credit for the founding and devel-opment of Tuskegee Institute to Washington, several also acknowledged the pecuniary and other forms of support that whites contributed to the school. Such references most often occurred in articles written by whites. These obituaries clearly asserted that Washington could not have developed the school, nor could the institute have acquired its acclaim, without the advice, support, and promotion of white men. Articles, like that printed in the *Hartford (CT) Courant*, and the *Springfield (MA) Republican*, placed lead-ing opinion-making white men at its core of their discussion of Washington and the Tuskegee Institute. The *Courant* stated that Washington "could not have done this work alone. White men helped." Similarly, the *Republican* informed its readers that "Washington's extraordinary success with Tuske-gee" could not have occurred without the assistance he received from both white southerners and rich Americans of northern European descent. Such obituaries legitimized the educator and his accomplishments while assigning partial ownership of them to white America.[44]

The esteem that many prominent and influential white men, northerners as well as southerners, held Washington is no secret, and reports of Washington's death sometimes emphasized those connections. Millions of whites, asserted the *Waterville (ME) News*, "understood and appreciated his work." His stand-ing among whites, alleged the *National Baptist Union Review*, allowed him to "get a hearing whenever he desired" with them; and "whenever he could get before an audience," reported the *Boston Herald*, "he won the respect of his white audiences." Whether they lived in the North or South, pronounced the *Jacksonville (FL) Times Union Current*, whites held Washington "in the highest honor." Their high assessment of him inspired the *Richmond (VA) Planet* to speculate that "probably no negro [*sic*] ever lived [who] was more honored by white men than" Washington. No other black person, as the *Union Review* claimed, "held the good will, the confidence and respect of," whites as did Washington. Indeed, his "indorsement [*sic*]" asserted the *Phila-delphia Public Ledger*, "was sufficient to muster the support of white people of influence in work which he or his people undertook."[45]

Most of these and other renowned white men became acquainted with Washington only after his speech at the Cotton States and International Expo-sition on September 18, 1895. The event in Atlanta during the opening day of the exposition, greatly impressed the vast majority of those people who attended, including news reporters. Although latter-day scholars, following the lead of W. E. B. Du Bois, tend to criticize parts of the presentation and characterized it as the "Atlanta Compromise," the vast majority of the reporting periodicals praised the speech. It so impressed President Grover Cleveland, a Democrat, that he publicly and privately praised the presentation and the presenter. Cleveland once proclaimed that he thought that "the exposition would be fully justified if it had not done more than furnish the opportunity for" the delivery of Washington's speech. Soon after the event, as the *Danbury (CT) News* asserted, "men and women of means began to want to assist Dr. Washington." Washington's presentation helped to inspire the great steel industrialist and philanthropist Andrew Carnegie to donate $20,000 to construct one of his famous Carnegie libraries on the campus of the Tuskegee Institute. This and other donations that followed Washington's exposition performance meaningfully enhanced the financially struggling school's ability to operate. More importantly, as the *New York Sun*, noted, before the 1894 Atlanta exposition, Washington "had acquired more or less local fame as an orator." The exposition speech, it declared, made Washington a national character and "the successor of Frederick Douglass as the leader of the Negroes."[46]

Some reporters credited the speech for winning "the sympathy and support of leading southerners." Southern papers seemed to remember the aspect of the speech that recognized social separation: "It was this sentiment, frankly spoken," wrote the *Norfolk (VA) Journal and Guide*, "that won for" Washington "the confidence of the South, which until his death remained unshaken." As reported in the *New York News*, Clark Howell, editor of the *Atlanta (GA) Constitution*, alleged that the address initiated "a moral revolution in America." The *Augusta (ME) Journal* emphasized the impact that the talk had on white southerners.[47]

Articles largely omitted Washington's other significant speeches. For example, they regularly overlooked his October 16, 1898, speech at the National Peace Jubilee celebration in Chicago. In this presentation, before President William McKinley and sixteen thousand other people, Washington clearly called for southerners to end racial discrimination. Before his largest audience, Washington declared that Americans had

> succeeded in every conflict, except the effort to conquer ourselves in the blotting out of racial prejudices. We can celebrate the era of peace in no more effectual way than by a firm resolve on the part of the Northern men and Southern men, black men and white men, that the trench which we together dug around Santiago, shall be the eternal burial place of all that which separates us in our

business and civil relations. . . . Until we thus conquer ourselves, I make no
empty statement when I say that we shall have, especially in the Southern part
of our country, a cancer growing at the heart of the Republic, that shall one
day prove as dangerous as an attack from an army.[48]

Although opinion makers throughout the South subsequently fiercely criticized him, Washington never disassociated himself from these assertions.

Also conspicuously absent from the death notices is the disturbance at a
1903 presentation in Boston and the beating he suffered in New York in 1911.
In the former case, Washington attempted to make a presentation at Zion
AME Church when several black people attempted to stop him from speaking
and in the process caused a general panic among the audience. News media
throughout the nation carried stories for days afterward about the disturbance and the nature of African American opposition to Washington. Very
few papers mentioned Washington's encounter with Henry Ulrich, a New
York white man who severely beat the Tuskegean for allegedly accosting the
white man's wife with the words "Hello, sweetheart." The authorities arrested
Ulrich, but a New York City court subsequently acquitted him. Although
deliberately silenced in the obituaries, court hearings related to the thrashing
received immense newspaper coverage.[49]

Washington's renowned dinner with President Theodore Roosevelt at the
White House, on the other hand, received attention in the obituaries. The
October 16, 1901, dinner had become a hotly contested topic in the news.
In the weeks following the dinner, newspapers across the nation, especially
those published in the U.S. South, editorialized the incident. The vast majority of southern periodicals oriented toward a white readership vigorously
denounced the president for inviting Washington to eat with him at the
White House. Since Washington, just three years earlier, had twice dined with
President William McKinley in Chicago without arousing controversy, the
timing and location of the dinner and not the company must have unleashed
the widespread irrational response to the occurrence. For most Americans,
the White House, more than any other national building, symbolized the
highest and the best of the nation. Conversely, they traditionally viewed
black Americans, regardless of their accomplishments, as the lowest and the
worst characteristics of the nation. A black man dining with the president
at the White House in 1901 created a convergence of diametrically opposite
symbols. The dinner occurred during an era in which a wide majority of
southern white opinion makers had agreed on the appropriateness of legally
restricting the civil and social opportunities of African Americans. They
sought to accelerate the disfranchisement and segregation of blacks living
in southern states. To those white opinion makers, Washington's dining with

Roosevelt suggested black social equality with the nation's foremost political leader. The act countered and undermined the white supremacy justifications for limiting the ability of African Americans to achieve self-actualization.[50]

Washington's death in 1915 reignited the controversy. With disfranchisement and the segregation of blacks, accepted as a fact in the South, and in many areas of the North, part of the southerners' debate absurdly focused on which meal of the day Washington shared with the president rather than question its propriety. Taking an evening meal in the White House at the request of the president did not promote an image of all blacks as social inferiors. Some reports portrayed the meal as evidence that Washington acted "indiscreetly" by dining with Roosevelt. Many obituary writers attempted to reduce the significance of the meal by incorrectly reporting that Washington and Roosevelt had shared an informal *lunch*. Somehow, for these writers, taking a casual noontime meal with an African American constituted a less odious challenge to white supremacy than sharing a formal evening meal. Consequently, many papers throughout the nation printed incorrectly that Washington ate lunch and not dinner with the president.[51]

Accurate versions of Washington's White House dining, like those published in the *Boston Transcript*, *San Jose (CA) Herald*, and *Salt Lake City (UT) News*, as well as the inaccurate ones, taught their respective readers an object lesson: They, regardless of the racial orientation of the publications, framed the White House incident as a reward. A few statements concerning Washington's death, like the one appearing in the *Savannah (GA) Tribune*, claimed that the meal signified that African Americans had reached "the same plane of equality as other races." Generally, obituaries suggested to readers that America publicly recognized its most accomplished citizens, and that persons of the most humble origins, even former slaves, could realistically secure enough personal prestige to merit a meal at the White House with the president. That is what both the *Terre Haute (IN) Star* and the *Genesee (NY) Republican* denoted. Roosevelt "saw fit to invite a distinguished citizen with a black skin to sit at his table" is how the *Star* interpreted the president's motivation. The *Republican* overtly proclaimed that Roosevelt's invitation to Washington "was just a recognition of the position which the educator held in the advancement of a large part of the population on the nation."[52]

*   *   *

Washington's renowned optimism had helped him achieve his venerated social position, and it provided much of the inspiration for the construction of the collective memory offered in his obituaries. Historically, Americans have held optimism as a highly valued personal characteristic. The belief that they could forge a better life on the American Continent inspired European settlers to colonize what became the United States. For more than a century before Washington's death, faith and hope for a better life motivated settlers and their descendants to travel to the nation's various frontiers. The bountiful U.S. economy, at the time of the educator's demise, provided substantial credence to the value of optimism and encouraged opinion makers to intensely cherish the belief. They held optimism, along with determination and hard work, as the three personal characteristics necessary for success. With memories of Washington's extraordinary positive thinking, death notices reinforced readers' belief in optimism. Papers like the *Kansas City (MO) Times* asserted that Washington "refused to be discouraged." In a letter published in the *New York Age*, Mary White Ovington, a founding member of the NAACP, claimed that Washington "was at all times an optimist." Proclaiming a universal admiration for the educator faith, the *Boston Transcript* stated that "all the world so honored" him for his "hopes for the future."[53]

Along with optimism, the obituary writers praised Washington's determination. Throughout the history of European settlement, Americans have placed immense value on steadfastness. The nation's unprecedented prosperity during the two decades before and after 1900 gave additional credibility to the trait. The popular press portrayed the men who led Americans in their very successful quest for personal and national prosperity as very strong-willed people. "Popular magazines of the day—Century, McClures, and Cosmopolitan—and widely-read novels" depicted business leaders as achieving success by being strong-willed. The widespread publicity that these "self-made men" received escalated the significance Americans placed on persistence. Having a clear understanding that many of his charitable countrymen held perseverance in high esteem, Washington often highlighted his own resolve, frequently stating examples of his willfulness in his fund-raising appeals, both written and verbal. Over and over, Washington told stories of how his determination helped him overcome immense problems in the very successful development of Tuskegee Institute. These anecdotes, especially those printed in *Up from Slavery* and his other autobiographies, provided death notice writers much of the information that inspired them to applaud Washington's resolve. Such lore inspired the *Waukegan (IL) Gazette* to proclaim the educator a "marvelous example of will power."[54]

Just as the living Washington successfully packaged his displays of determination into fund-raising appeals, obituary writers used many of those same expressions to champion individual willpower as a desired trait. Such statements, as the one printed in the *New York Evening Post* that Washington's success resulted from his "dogged determination to let no obstacle daunt him," strongly suggested to readers that in order for them to reach their respective goals they too must embrace steadfastness. Obituary writers wanted to strongly convey the message that "quitters never win" in the competition for success. The *St. Louis (MO) Republic* expressed this concept when it asserted that Washington's poverty, race, surroundings, "and the materials with which he proposed to work were all profoundly discouraging, but there was no discouragement in him." The *Waterville (ME) News* similarly asserted that Washington "never faltered in his purpose. He was true to the faith that was in him during many periods of discouragement."[55]

*   *   *

Most obituaries associated Washington's public life with labor. Even more so than optimism or determination, writers closely associated him with work. To them, Washington's life exemplified productiveness, a very important integral part of the Yankee Protestant Ethic. Revealing its adherence to the ethos, the *Birmingham (AL) Ledger* wrote that Washington possessed an "enthusiasm for work," and the *Pensacola (FL) Journal* stated that the educator's "heart was always in his work." Many of the notices, like the one titled "A Boy Who Worked," clearly pointed out that Washington's hard labor ensured his achievements. Washington, it asserted "rose to fame and usefulness through the indispensable medium of hard work."[56]

Since Washington purportedly worked for the aggrandizement of others, specifically the African American poor, and not for his personal betterment, his obituaries vigorously upheld that his labors deserved meritorious recognition. These notices conveyed to readers that all work that is moral is dignified, but those labors that enhance other people's lives are even more esteemed. Acknowledging the extraordinary value of Washington's lifetime toil as a philanthropic, the *Boston Herald* noted that his "work for the education and betterment of his race . . . made his name known the world over." Some periodicals constructed a Christlike metaphoric memory of him: the *Wichita (KS) Beacon* claimed that "he gave his life to a big work for this beloved race," whereas the *Philadelphia Inquirer* alleged that Washington "wore himself out in his labor for others."[57]

Not only did Washington work hard, but he often preached to others about the dignity of labor. For much of his public life, Washington packaged himself as a champion of work. He captured the nation's attention and a substantial amount of its support by preaching the dignity of toil. After his death, obituaries alleged that Washington "made all labor dignified." Supporters of Washington's teachings, such as the *Minneapolis (MN) News*, believed that black people's labor would "overcome all handicaps." This newspaper, among many others, held that African Americans, for a number of reasons including a heritage of slavery, possessed an underdeveloped appreciation of manual labor. They believed that Washington's lessons concerning work greatly benefited blacks as well as the nation, particularly the southern region. Washington's industrial education curriculum, many opinion makers reasoned, would help provide the South with an efficient labor class while stabilizing its social order. Their hope for this reality led obituary writers, like the one for the *Cleveland (OH) Plain Dealer*, to laud Washington for promoting the honor of labor. The newspaper's obituary asserted that to Washington "it was clear that negro [sic] independence depended on the negro's willingness to work. . . . he taught at Tuskegee and through the lecture platform the unmistakable sound doctrine that work meant salvation." For his efforts at teaching blacks to labor diligently, Washington received accolades from writers who represented the nation's businesses, as well as those who championed the U.S. working class, such as the *Worker*, which enthusiastically claimed that Washington "made more Negroes work than all of the slave masters who ever trod the soil of the South.[58]

Washington's labor created opportunities, recalled many of the obituaries. These reminiscences depicted the educator as a meticulous worker for the creation of new prospects for African Americans to prosper. While acknowledging that African Americans suffered from a shortage of opportunities, the *Brooklyn (NY) Daily Eagle* asserted that Washington labored to provide blacks with education and skills, the attributes they most often needed to prosper. A newspaper abroad made a similar assertion. Presenting a paradoxical, if not a contradictory assessment of the educator's work to increase black people's prospects for prosperity, the *New York Sun* recalled that Washington demonstrated "the capacity of the black man in those callings that are now open to him" rather than seeking new opportunities in those fields where "every factor was opposed to him." Washington taught black people to exploit their existing prospects "instead of emphasizing wrongs," the *Lonaconing (MD) Advocate* avowed. "Dr. Washington," it asserted, "emphasized opportunities."[59]

For a large number of Washington's obituary writers, the black educator's life provided tangible support for the premise that America represented one of the world's greatest chances for self-actualization. They used his life to counter some of the more pessimistic criticisms of the nation's emerging economic and social realities. Corporate capitalism and the mass immigration that it attracted, in the minds of many opinion makers, severely challenged the historic values of the nation. Social critics asserted that the United States always possessed poor people, but the combined forces of unchecked capitalism and immigration restricted opportunities, which would lead to the creation of a heretofore unknown permanent lower class. A society in which few Americans could realistically hope to improve their social and economic standing would produce class conflict, which in turn would disturb the nation's internal tranquility. The prospect of a social order similar to that found in many European countries displeased most U.S. public opinion shapers. Hence, those opinion makers who continued to view the United States as a land of boundless opportunity took satisfaction in discovering and proclaiming examples of upward mobility within their beloved country.[60]

Washington's life provided them with an excellent illustration. Obituary writers, black and white, straightforwardly told their readers that the Tuskegean's accomplishments resulted largely from the liberal number of opportunities for self-actualization available in the United States. Death notices like the one published in the *Bristol (CT) Press*, a blatantly self-evident pronouncement designed to calm readers' anxieties about America's changing society, told readers that Washington's career "would have been impossible elsewhere" and that Americans should remember that fact "in these troubled days."[61]

Despite racial discrimination and segregation, African American–owned periodicals tended not to begrudge the nation for providing blacks with fewer chances for self-actualization than it provided whites. Instead, newspaper editors like the one at the *Washington (D.C.) Star* retold Washington's life in a manner that praised the nation for the opportunities it did extend to blacks. "In the life of no other man of American birth" asserted the *Star*, "has the truth that 'the republic is opportunity' been quite so signally illustrated as in that of Booker T. Washington." The *New York Age* proclaimed that "if the lives of all the great men of this country were written out to be passed upon by the civilized world, not one would be a more impressive example to foreign peoples of the possibilities of American democracy than the life of Booker T. Washington." Reaffirming its endorsement of the United States as a nation of opportunities, the paper printed a letter from Richard M. Bolden, a preacher, who claimed that "the history of America will show that Dr. Booker T. Washington was a concrete example of the possibilities of a typical American." Chicago's leading black-owned publication, the *Defender*, republished the comments of the *Oshkosh (WI) Northwester*'s editor: "If this poor despised little 'nigger-boy' could get an education . . . why cannot any intelligent American boy look forward to a successful career?"[62]

Periodicals with predominantly white circulations echoed these sentiments. Many of these publications used Washington's obituaries to soothe, teach, and inspire whites. These journals declared to their readers that Washington's successes provided undeniable proof that the United States remained the land of democratic opportunity. The *New York World* rhetorically asked,

"If the United States is not still the land of opportunity, how are we to account for the career of Booker T. Washington?" In a like manner, the *Los Angeles Examiner* stated that Washington's life "is the best possible reply to those chronic pessimists who affirm that there are no longer any opportunities for the poor boy." Washington's life, proclaimed the *Tacoma (WA) News* is a "lesson to the world" and a "complete denial" of the pessimistic theory about Americans not having "equal opportunities."[63]

Booker T. Washington's success did not prohibit a number of obituary writers from crafting a memory of him that placed his accomplishments and prominence within a racial context. Some of them begrudgingly recognized that Washington's successes occurred within a social milieu that grossly restricted blacks while granting white Americans superior economic and social status. Other writers attempted either to ignore or to downplay the racial oppression that existed during Washington's lifetime. Americans believed in the concept of race more fervently in the period around Washington's death than they had at any point since the end of slavery, a half-century earlier. Black and white opinion makers manifested their extensive concern with race in virtually every published notice about Washington. Writers conspicuously and repeatedly informed readers of Washington's assigned race. The white-owned *Allentown (PA) Morning Call* stated that "In the death of Booker T. Washington, the negro [*sic*] race has lost its foremost representative and the man who more than any other was instrumental in putting the negro race on a higher plain in the country, both in ability and in respect." Likewise, the *Kansas City (MO) Star* remembered Washington as "proud to be a negro [*sic*]."[64]

The prism of race also played an important role in dedicating the contour of African Americans' collective memory of Washington. Like their white counterparts, black opinion makers accepted the social construct of race as a truism. Hence they too placed their recollection of Washington within a racial framework. The racial consciousness of black obituary writers and their seemingly ceaseless efforts to improve the community's self-concept necessitated that they would eagerly claim Washington as a member of their race while enthusiastically embracing his life's work. They constantly used the accomplishments and accolades of African Americans, especially those closely identified with the aspirations of the race, in their attempts to project a positive image of their racial community. Since no other contemporary African American possessed as much power and prestige as Washington, African American writers, like the one writing for the *Atlanta (GA) Independent*, maintained that Washington's "one effort was to uplift his race." For its part, a black American–oriented newspaper in Michigan asserted that the "average level of the Afro-American people has been raised and that Washington should receive "a large degree of [the] credit." His accomplishments inspired the *National Baptist Union Review* to advise black youths to use Washington's life as a model. The author recalled Washington as a man who at all times attempted to "construct the fortunes of his race."[65]

Washington's eminence in the collective expressions of African American obituary writers did not deter white authors from also recognizing the late educator as a significant representative of the nation's core values. They pictured Washington as a person who manifested such Yankee Protestant values as optimism, confidence, thrift, charity, self-denial, and hard work, while highlighting his life as an outstanding U.S. success story. To them, Washington's lifework and his cherished values, which included assisting poor people, especially African Americans in the South, clearly demonstrated a devotion to his country and a dedication to its betterment. Since these principles transcended Americans' intense race consciousness, many obituaries of Washington seemed to have wanted to forge all Americans into unified political body. In their respective death notices, both the white-owned *San Francisco Chronicle* and the *Baltimore (MD) Commonwealth*, a paper published for African American readership, hailed Washington as an important symbol of the core values that opinion makers wanted Americans to embrace. These and other obituary writers, in their communal process of recalling Washington's life, constructed an image of the black man that embodied the characteristics that an ideal American should display. They constructed a memory of the late black man that promoted the principles and behaviors that they believed would preserve the nation and provide its citizens with the best chance at attaining self-actualization. The public memory of Washington's model life projected to the world that the United States remained a land of abundant opportunities. As such, that memory motivated periodicals like *The Commercial Appeal* (Memphis, TN) to declare Washington "a valuable asset to the nation."[66]

3. "Taps"

The Funeral in Tuskegee

Immediately after his death, Booker T. Washington's family began preparing for his burial, to take place three days later, on Wednesday, November 17, 1915. His home, the Oaks, essentially became the dressing room to prepare Washington's body for his mortuary ceremony. Standing on a hill overlooking the Tuskegee Institute campus, the spacious red brick Queen Anne–style Victorian dwelling had five bedrooms and twenty-three other steam-heated rooms fitted with electric lights. Students who learned their craft at the institute built the Oaks, which served as an inspiration for their community. Washington had designed the asymmetrical house not only to provide lodging for his family and their many visitors, but also to symbolize the institute and the values it promoted. With its bold-colored interior walls, the Oaks stood as a tangible example of the opportunities available in the United States for blacks and other Americans willing to embrace the Yankee Protestant ethic, especially those tenets that promoted cleanliness, education, materialism, optimism, thrift, and work. The house, moreover, provided the academy's many benefactors with pronounced visual evidence that their bequests tangibly assisted Washington and the Tuskegee movement in their multifront culture war. It displayed the movement's success with its quest of modernizing young African Americans' vocational skills while teaching them a set of desired values.[1]

Organizers—of the ceremony, which included Washington's immediate family, the lead administrators of the Tuskegee Institute, and key members of the board of trustees—designed a burial ritual that would continue to impress and motivate students, patrons, and other members of the movement. The disposal rites for the educator's body served multiple purposes.

Transcending time and place, funeral rites are universal. Comprising one or some combination of wakes, lying in state, religious or other services, and disposal, these events commemorate the dead while benefiting the living. Societies use these rituals to assist their members to accept death and adjust to its consequences. The events, which most often are public rather than invitational, usually welcome all mourners, including persons who had no personal relationship with the deceased. The gathering of mourners creates mutual groups of supporters while authoritatively recognizing that the dead are no longer among the living. Funeral services, thus, act as public rites of passages while helping to forge and reinforce various bonds among the survivors. In the process, they routinely inspire attendees to shape a memory of the dead that instructs and motivates them to embrace the particular community's preferred ethics.[2]

The decisions that Washington's funeral organizers made clearly indicated their understanding of the role of death rituals. They staged a pageant designed to reenergize the movement's efforts at winning its cultural war. Organizers framed and promoted a favored posthumous image of the educator, his ethos, the institute, and most importantly, the Tuskegee movement. Washington, who often spoke simultaneously to ordinary southern blacks and prosperous northern whites, possessed a masterful understanding of the power of exhibitions. He conducted and participated in countless numbers of them. Washington used these presentations to exhort and garner support for the movement and most importantly its headquarters, the institute. The success of these pageants became imperative object lessons for Washington's survivors. As a collective, they had embraced the effectiveness of a well-choreographed demonstration before he had died. Hence, in their joint, ongoing effort to win the culture war, organizers orchestrated a funeral ceremony designed to shape a preferred postmortem recollection of Washington.[3]

Organizers realized that a multitude of people would actually, or vicariously, participate in Washington's funeral pageant. They clearly understood that thousands of sympathizers and reporters intended to attend one or more of the events related to the rites. Organizers recognized that some of the attendees would only view the body while it lay in state, that other individuals would attend the funeral service and not view the body, and that a large number of people would participate in both of these rituals as well as witness the interment of the remains. The attendees' presence and the significant interest that a sizable segment of the U.S. public possessed in the life and activities of Washington ensured that newspapers around the nation and beyond would publish detailed accounts of this noteworthy national and international event.

Grover Cleveland Thompson, a white undertaker and the postmaster for the town of Tuskegee, played an indispensable role in the pageant. Organizers employed him even after Margaret Washington received a no-cost offer to make the "funeral arrangements" from the Reverend Preston Taylor, a wealthy black mortician from Nashville. J. C. Napier, a black Nashville banker and the future president of the National Negro Business League, conveyed Taylor's proposal to the widow. Without providing any details concerning the person retained to prepare Washington's body, Emmett J. Scott, the late educator's longtime aide and secretary, informed the Tennesseans that Margaret Washington appreciated "most sincerely Rev. Preston Taylor's very kind offer" but that arrangements regarding the "burial have been completed." Since both black and white undertakers often competed with one another for the preparation of African American bodies during this era, the choice of Thompson did not cause any overt public concern. Ironically, Washington had two years earlier written the undertaker a gentle letter of reprimand. In what the educator characterized as "an act of friendship," he informed the undertaker that black people in the area disliked the poor appearance of the hearse that transported their dead and that they wanted its driver to wear proper funeral attire. Regardless of his services' previous shortcomings, Thompson's employment reinforced the symbiotic bond between the Tuskegee Institute and the town's white business community. Since Thompson belonged to the family that owned the Bank of Tuskegee as well as other businesses, using his services extended mutually beneficial commercial relationships with local whites. Washington, and other spokespersons for the movement, had preached, over the years, that such symbiotic associations, more so than anything else, would substantially improve relationships between blacks and whites.[4]

The funeral symbolized this creed, as well as the other doctrines and programs of the movement. The organizers took care to ensure that Washington's vast constituency would not think or feel that their mutually embraced doctrines and programs died along with the educator. Although Washington could no longer claim a national stage for his fund-raising efforts, organizers wanted his beliefs and agendas to remain nationally significant. They vividly grasped that Washington's public perceived him as the living symbol of the institute and the movement. Indeed, in many instances, especially when he attempted to solicit money, Washington's persona had overshadowed the movement's agendas. Washington had a great aptitude for ingratiating himself to potential donors. His personality, much more than his ideas or the movement, inspired patrons to donate money. Efforts to win the culture war, needed organizers to preserve and continue promoting Washington's civic ideas, educational programs, and fund-raising success.[5]

Thompson executed his duties well and significantly assisted the organizers with their quest. Out of consideration for expected mourners, the preparation probably included embalming. Although undertakers often embalmed Union soldiers during the Civil War, the practice did not come into wide use until after the 1920s. Northerners embraced this procedure substantially earlier than did southerners. After the embalming, and dressing, Thompson placed the body in a six-sided casket, a relatively new style of burial container. Prior to the early 1900s, survivors did not place the dead in six-sided casket boxes. They most often put them in eight-sided coffins. The interior of Washington's casket, which included a white cloth lining, enhanced the undertaker's effort to project him as resting rather than as deceased.[6]

Thompson's preparation of Washington's body provided survivors with a desired image of the late educator. It looked markedly younger and less fatigued than had the living Washington. A *New York Tribune* reporter alleged that the undertaker had lifted ten years of aging from his face. Thompson's achievement helped to shape a final, and in many cases a long-lasting, image of Washington.[7]

After the preparation, the funeral rites began with a procession on Tuesday, November 16. A second one occurred the following day. For ages, humans around the world have utilized funeral parades in constructing and reinforcing preferred memories of the dead. The most elaborate processions commemorate prestigious members of a community, most conspicuously heads of states and major military figures. A substantial segment of the U.S. population believed that Washington, the commander of the movement, had long acted as black America's titular head. His efforts to improve the welfare and prestige of African Americans earned him this lofty status. Recognizing his eminence, the processions helped to frame and promote a desired collective memory of the late leader that perpetuated his prominence and helped to memorialize him as a regal black American who had commanded the movement.[8]

The first parade started sharply at noon on Tuesday, November 16, 1915. Two students drove the hearse transporting Washington's body from the Oaks to the institute chapel in the center of campus. Acting principal of the school Warren Logan, Emmett J. Scott, and forty-four student officers marched in front of the vehicle. Although the chapel stood less than three hundred yards directly downhill from the Oaks, the parade took a circuitous route to the building to allow a large number of students and other members of the Tuskegee Institute community to view the procession and to pay homage to the memory of their late principal. The gazing students "stood, bareheaded, at attention while the cortege proceeded."[9]

Members of the procession placed the principal's body in the chapel to lie in state. As the first building that members of the institute's community both designed and constructed, it, more than any other campus structure, represented Washington's concepts of industrial education. Robert Robinson Taylor, the school's architectural and mechanical drawing instructor, drew the building plans, while students, using crafts they learned at the institute, erected the approximately 23,000-square-foot oak edifice. They gathered many of the materials used in its construction from lands that the institute owned. Students who worked in the institute's brickyard made the 1,200,000 bricks used in the chapel's construction. Other pupils cut down trees on land owned by the institute and sawed them into lumber. In addition, groups of students milled molding, laid bricks, and attached roofing. They also installed both the steam heating and electrical lighting, and designed the cornices and the pews. The auditorium accommodated 2,400 more people than any other building on campus.[10]

*   *   *

In the chapel, where the principal's body would lie in state, organizers deftly used floral arrangements to shape desired memories of Washington. Draping the chapel's auditorium "with palms and black and purple cloths," organizers placed the casket in the center of the venue a few feet in front of the pulpit. Organizers surrounded the casket, railings, and walls behind the pulpit with a mass assortment of very large floral arrangements. According to a reporter from the *Chicago Defender*, flowers "occupied every available bit of space in the spacious rostrum and in the choir loft." Organizers even covered the bottom two-thirds of the casket, "which bore neither name nor date, just 'At rest,'" with a blanket of chrysanthemums.[11]

From the time of ancient Egypt, humans have adorned the dead with flowers. Early Egyptians placed flower crowns on mummies and scattered their petals over the bodies to mask the pungent smells of the deceased. The Romans, in expressions of fond feelings, presented their dead with an abundance of flowers. While early Christian leaders expressed no unified thoughts about the role of flora in mortuary rites, many of them used flowers in the ceremonies. During the Reformation, Puritans denounced the practice, prohibiting the inclusion of flowers in their funeral rituals. After the mid-1700s, however, flowers grew in popularity at European and American Christian funeral services. By 1915, floral arrangements had become an integral part of most death rites. In that era, Americans readily accepted conspicuous displays of esteem and wealth in all areas of their society, including funerals. Just as the status and number of persons attending funerals symbolized the eminence of the deceased and the prestige of the survivors, so too did flowers.[12]

Sympathizers who lived far and near—blacks, whites, northerners, and southerners—brought or sent flowers to Washington's survivors. James R. Europe, the noted African American jazz musician, requested that Scott purchase and send him the bill for flowers that cost "any amount." Indianapolis attorney F. B. Ransom requested that Scott meet him at the local train station so that he could take a "special floral design" sent by Madame C. J. Walker, allegedly the richest black woman in the United States, directly to the chapel. Along with Walker's flowers, the Alabama Mosaic Knight Templars, an African American fraternal organization, delivered to the chapel a flower arrangement that caught the attention of Scott. He asserted that the Templars' floral design "was certainly a splendid testimonial to the love and respect which the order entertained for the great leader." Numerous other predominately black civic, educational, and business associations sent flowers. Members of Tuskegee Institute's industrial classes for girls provided the blanket of chrysanthemums placed on Washington's casket, while other student groups supplied other arrangements. Many white people in and around Tuskegee presented flowers. Altogether, survivors and sympathizers provided the ceremony with thousands of dollars' worth of flowers that more than filled two railroad boxcars.[13]

Whereas the floral arrangements represented wealth and prestige, the male student sentinels that served as honor guards of Washington's body signified the organizers' most valued objectives. Students, dressed in their mandatory military-style school uniforms, positioned themselves at the head and foot of the casket while the body lay in state. One guard stood about four feet away from the head of the casket and another stood approximately the same distance behind the first sentinel. Two other sentries took similar positions at the foot of the casket. These four honor guards strongly suggested to spectators that they ought to remember Washington as commander in chief of a peaceful army fighting on the front lines in the war against black people's degradation and deprivation. The presence of the sentinels sent a widely disseminated message that proclaimed that the average black youth, if provided the appropriate assistance and training, would become a model of decorum. Thus, these neatly dressed black youths participated in the efforts of both the institute and the movement to change the stereotypical image of blacks while symbolizing the potential of ordinary African Americans.[14]

Some reports estimate that twenty thousand people viewed Washington's body. These included the curious, survivors, and sympathizers. Starting at a little after 12:00 P.M., people from far and near filled the chapel and the surrounding grounds waiting for their turn to view the remains. Current students led acquaintances, former students, and sympathizers, in an "endless procession" that passed through the chapel. The sympathizers included an elderly couple who had walked a long distance to the campus. After arriving and seeing the long line, they approached one of the institute teachers and inquired about permission to view Washington's body. The male "'with trembling lips and eyes that overflowed asked:' 'Do you reckon they will let us see Booker?' and he hurried to explain: 'We have come so fur jus' to see him de las' time. Do you reckon they will mind us looking at him?'" The teacher arranged for a special escort of the couple to the casket. The viewing continued until the organizers closed the chapel doors at nightfall. Later they reopened the chapel to accommodate a trainload of sympathizers who had arrived from New York City. This large biracial group included members of the Tuskegee Institute Board of Trustees and major financial supporters of both the school and the movement.[15]

Railroads helped to bring more visitors to the institute than it had ever hosted at one time in its history. Mourners, including "leading" black residents of Nashville, negotiated with railroad companies for discounted fares. Riding on the Montgomery and West Point Railroad, some of the mourners disembarked at Montgomery, Alabama, and secured other means to complete their journey to Tuskegee. The remaining passengers continued from Montgomery to Chehaw, a town five miles southeast of Tuskegee. At that station, they either hired a hack to transport them to the school or transferred to a train on the six-mile-long Tuskegee Railroad line, which took them to the Tuskegee town depot, or to the station on campus.[16]

As Scott informed S. G. Elbert, a black Wilmington, Delaware, physician, no special train carried passengers to Tuskegee. However, the unprecedented demand for transportation to Tuskegee inspired railroad companies to provide passengers traveling to the school with exclusive cars. The Montgomery Tuskegee Institute Alumni Association secured a dedicated railroad car, while several Alabama state officials, and other white dignitaries, rode in another.[17]

Railroad cars, the *Montgomery (AL) Advertiser* proclaimed, brought "representative citizens" to Tuskegee. The newspaper used this popular circa-1900 term to characterize Americans who personified upper-middle-class respectability. The *Chicago Defender* chose to describe the same persons as "men and women of high degree." These, and other periodicals, recognized the social standing, residence, and race of Washington's sympathizers. They listed such mourners as William H. Baldwin III, a white founder of the National Urban League and the son of the late William H. Baldwin Jr., a former prominent Tuskegee Institute Board of Trustees member and one of Washington's dearest friends. Periodicals noted the attendance of George C. Hall, a noted black Chicago surgeon and Washington's personal physician; Samuel M. Newman, the white president of Howard University; Pinkney Benton Stewart Pinchback, the former black lieutenant governor of Louisiana; Charles F. Meserve, president of Shaw University; Alexander E. Manning, editor of the *Indianapolis World*, and Mary McLeod Bethune, the black founder of the Daytona Normal and Industrial School for Negro Girls (later Bethune-Cookman College). The papers reported the names of many other businesspersons, editors, educators, politicians, lawyers, and judges.[18]

*   *   *

Arguably, no other prior event had attracted more black leaders and opinion makers. The number of people greatly exceeded those who attended Frederick Douglass's memorial services in 1895. His rites had attracted the greatest number of influential blacks than had any other African American's memorial ceremony. The locations of Douglass's services explain part of the disparity. Whereas his rituals occurred in Washington, D.C., and Rochester, New York, far from the population center of black America. On the other hand, Washington's funeral took place near the geographical center of the Black Belt, an area from South Carolina to East Texas known for its dark soil and large African American population.[19]

Many of the black attendees held leadership positions in one or more associations. As part of what Samuel P. Hays calls the nation's "organizational revolution," African Americans in 1915 had greatly increased both the relative and absolute number of their formal leaders. The many economic, social, and technological changes that occurred during the late 1800s and early 1900s inspired blacks, like other Americans, to establish countless associations. Washington, who strongly believed in the power of organizations, and of the movement, contributed directly and indirectly to the founding of scores of African American–led associations. Along with Tuskegee Institute students and staff, black supporters of Washington established a myriad of schools and businesses as well as commercial organizations, professional groups, and civic leagues. These associations did not constitute a majority or a large plurality of the formal groups that enhanced the size of the black leadership class. They did, however, make an important contribution.[20]

Ordinary people, white and black, far outnumbered luminaries in attendance. They came from "every section of the country." Most of the sympathizers, though, lived in the surrounding hinterlands' farms, plantations, towns, and cities. Those mourners, who did not arrive on the rails, journeyed to the school and the surrounding areas by automobiles, "buggies, surreys, mule carts, and two horse wagons." More than a few of them even walked or rode on the backs of mules and horses.[21]

Many undistinguished whites also attended the burial rites. They too arrived from small towns, like Opelika, as well as from farms and plantations in the region. White attendees included youths similar to the small poorly clothed boy who stood at the end of the stage during the service, older men like the one without a collar and wearing a "dingy blue shirt and a coat somewhat tattered," as well as younger adult males who resembled the "two stripping fellows" sitting in front of the chapel and spitting "tobacco juice on the platform steps and on the floor." One white man, R. O. Simpson, a former Confederate soldier who claimed with pride to have fought with Robert Lee "from Manassas to Appomattox," attended. He asserted that "Washington helped the negro [sic]; he did. But he did more than that; he helped us whites, he helped me. He was the greatest friend of the south [sic], its great asset, and that sir, is why the great heart of the south [sic] is sad." The attendance of Simpson and the other whites at the funeral supports the statement that Albon L. Holsey, the former personal secretary to Washington, made concerning the funeral. He declared that "no color line" existed in the sorrow that the death of Washington created.[22]

Common black folks from all over America swamped the town of Tuskegee and the institute. They began arriving soon after the public announcement of Washington's death. A few of the "simple country folk" who had arrived hours or days before the funeral rituals "pitched camp, so to speak, on the football field," an area located down the hill and southeast of the Oaks. On this field, they prepared food and ate meals, "tethered their horses and mules." Many of these black people had known Washington personally. Over the years, he had treated them with kindness and generosity. In turn, they embraced the man, his ideas, and his work, becoming loyal members of the movement and its culture. Hence, these people perceived Washington's death as a great personal loss, and their tears gave testimony to their grief.[23]

Many of Washington's close associates secured more comfortable quarters, however. With only a small number of rooms available for rent in the town, various white Tuskegeans lodged in their homes many of the visiting mourners. Sympathizers, both black and white, packed "every bit of room in Tuskegee."[24]

* * *

On the morning of Wednesday, November 17, thousands of mourners and spectators left their places of lodging to stand along the roads between the Oaks and the chapel. They sought to view the final procession, and display both their condolences to Washington's survivors and the high esteem that the vast majority of them held for the late educator. To insure an orderly and safe procession, organizers had earlier closed the route that started at the Oaks and meandered to the chapel. At 10 A.M. a bugle call signaled that the march would soon commence and that spectators should collect and await the parade on the sides of the several roads that encompassed the route of the procession.[25]

The horn also notified all procession participants to gather at prearranged points and make ready to march. The institute band, at the head of the parade, led several battalions of male students, who had amassed on the drill grounds adjacent to the starting point of the march. The female students followed after organizing themselves on the lawn of White Memorial Hall, a girls' dormitory located a few yards from the drill grounds. Washington's family members rode in horse-pulled carriages behind the female students. Sixty-four honorary pallbearers and the six actual pallbearers, all African Americans, followed the family and walked just ahead of the institute's board of trustees. In a display of affection for the late William H. Baldwin Jr., the organizers allowed William H. Baldwin III to march with the trustees. Special friends of the deceased followed. They led the school's executive council, which walked in front of the academy's teachers. Alumni association members brought up the rear.[26]

Funeral organizers had selected active pallbearers from among key constituencies of the Tuskegee Institute community. They understood the potential threat Washington's death posed to the school and its mission. His demise initiated the real possibility of a radical alteration within the academy, one that could greatly affect the lives of the community's members and the movement. Survivors employed a technique that helped to counter the forces of disruption. Organizers identified and selected casket carriers from among four essential symbiotic segments of the institute's community: administration, faculty, alumni, and students. J. H. Palmer, the registrar, represented the administration; C. W. Greene, a teacher, symbolized the faculty; M. D. Garner and W. A. Richardson signified the alumni; and Tobert Pace and James Carlin exemplified the student body. As an embodiment of the school community, these representatives reminded spectators of the united effort within the institute, the citadel of the movement. In the process, organizers used this aspect of the mortuary rites to shape a memory of the deceased that advocated continuity for the school and the movement.[27]

The student-led procession walked slowly to the beat of muffled drums while the Tuskegee Institute's band played Frederic Chopin's "Funeral March" over and over again. Unlike the numerous previous occasions when the institute community marched briskly and "sprightly" to the chapel, the students did so this time "with a hung-down and saddened countenance," projecting their collective apprehension. During the process of parading, they created a memory of Washington as a hegemonic benefactor whose death would produce radical changes for their lives.[28]

The procession assisted the organizers with the logistics of seating the official mourning party. It insured an orderly entrance into the chapel for the deceased's family, special friends, and the institute community. The thousands of unofficial visitors gathered around the chapel before the start of the rites necessitated a systematic entrée, without which the official funeral party could not have taken their assigned seats in a timely manner. Before the parade arrived outside the chapel, sympathizers had occupied virtually every available space within the auditorium. Arrangers, yielding to the protocol of segregation, reserved approximately half of the hall seating spaces for white attendees, seriously limiting the space available for blacks not part of the official party.[29]

Whites overfilled their allotted seats and contributed to the more than four thousand unofficial guests occupying the chapel before the official party arrived. Members of the procession took their assigned seats. Hundreds of visitors, black and white alike, either stood along walls or sat in windowsills. Other persons, including the several thousand who followed the march, stood outside the building. A lucky few members of this horde maneuvered themselves into positions that provided a view of the service from the surrounding grounds. They observed the funeral through the chapel's windows and doorways. The remaining sympathizers mingled on the campus until the indoor portion of the ritual ended.[30]

*   *   *

With the school choir singing "We Shall Walk through the Valley and the Shadow of Death," the funeral began at 10:30 A.M. Although all spirituals and folk songs have multiple versions, no major periodical reported the particular lyrics sung that day. John W. Work published a popular version in 1940:

> We shall walk through the valley and the shadow of death
> We shall walk through the valley in peace
> If Jesus himself shall be our leader
> We shall walk through the valley in peace
>
> We shall meet our brother there
> We shall meet our brother there
> There will be no weeping there
> Will be no weeping there.[31]

In a later published version, the second verse is different:

> We shall meet those Christians there
> Meet them there
> There will be no sorrow there
> If Jesus himself shall be our leader
> We shall walk through the valley in peace.[32]

Washington possessed a deep and profound understanding of the relationship between black Americans and the spirituals. He called the music "plantation melodies." Enslaved for the first nine years of his life, Washington witnessed and experienced the important connection between the music and the bonded African American community. After emancipation, for a number of reasons that included the association of spirituals with slavery, some black people's attachment to the music lessened. The vast majority of freed people, however, including Washington, continued to sing and greatly value spirituals. As he grew into adulthood, Washington's appreciation of music did not diminish. Indeed, even the puritanical Hampton Institute reinforced his admiration for spirituals, as promoted by Samuel Chapman Armstrong, Hampton's founder and first principal. He regularly instructed his students to sing several songs at commencements and other school functions. In 1873, the year after Washington enrolled, Armstrong even assembled a touring choir that primarily sang spirituals.[33]

White people's positive responses to the songs caught Washington's attention. He observed the cheering receptions white visitors at Hampton gave them. Washington also learned of the very successful fund-raising tours of the Fisk University Jubilee Singers. Within seven years, from 1871 to 1878, the Jubilee Singers collected $150,000 while the Hampton Singers raised enough money for the institute to build a new girls' dormitory, completed a year before Washington's graduation. The immense cross-racial appeal of the spirituals, and their usefulness as a fund-raising tool, inspired Washington later to praise Fisk University enthusiastically. He asserted that if the school "had done nothing else or more, its work in gathering and popularizing these folksongs of the race has entitled it to be remembered with gratitude by the negro [sic] people and the world." Fisk's and Hampton's fund-raising successes inspired Washington to mimic their efforts at Tuskegee. By 1884, he had assembled a group of touring singers that included students and staff.[34]

Tuskegee chorales traveled with and without Washington. A flyer for December 1893 events at the Providence (Rhode Island) Island Bell Street Chapel listed Washington as a lecturer in its series of monthly presentations and announced that a "Quartette of men-singers, young colored students in the School, who will give the songs of the slave and freedman," would accompany Washington. Independently, the singers performed before 1,400 male and 130 female inmates at the New York State prison. Afterward, they sang at two area churches.[35]

Throughout his career, Washington promoted the songs. On campus, members of the institute community performed the songs after their evening prayers, at their weekly Sunday chapel talks, at special school functions, and at meetings of visitors. Over time, the singing of spirituals became a fundamental aspect of many of Washington's public presentations. He often requested their singing before making a speech. At some of the mass gatherings that Washington addressed, he would request a member of his delegation to lead the audience in singing one or more spirituals. They inspired Washington and improved audience receptiveness of his message. "He learned by observation that a few of these songs in an hour could create more friendship than months of philosophic arguments."[36]

Spirituals meant far more to Washington than a public relations technique and a fund-raising tool. He appreciated the aesthetics and other cultural significance of these songs. They helped him to maintain an emotional and intellectual connection with ordinary African Americans. He held the songs in high esteem, and he feared that black people, as they secured greater formal education, would "abandon the 'Spirituals' because they" would remind them of enslavement and denigration. Believing that black people possessed unique characteristics that they "should never discard or be ashamed of," Washington sought to create "an appreciation of the beauty of this music that it might be easy to preserve this undoubted cultural asset to the Negro for all time."[37]

Spirituals, like other aspects of Washington's burial ceremony, helped the funeral organizers to create a desired collective memory. As an icon, Washington appealed to the mass of blacks and a significant segment of white America alike. The funeral arrangers scripted the ritual to reflect and promote this dual attraction. Organizers realized that if blacks stop believing in the symbolism of Washington and withdrew their approval of the school and the movement, many white backers would end their political—and financial—support. Without such aid, the school and the movement would have an extremely difficult existence. The inclusion of spirituals in Washington's funeral helped perpetuate both the academy and the movement. The singing of these songs prompted sympathizers to remember Washington as an African American while providing the black community with a conspicuous vital role in the principal's funeral. In the process, organizers helped to create a memory of Washington that reinforced African Americans' commitment to the movement.

For years, Washington and his supporters asserted that the school and the movement's teaching would, over time, markedly elevate blacks in ways that white philanthropists would recognize as evidence of higher "civilization." This in essence meant that black people would have internalized and manifested desirable aspects of the Yankee Protestant ethic. Funeral organizers used the ritual to provide evidence of the civilizing effect that Washington, the institute and the movement had on ordinary African Americans.[38]

Regardless, numerous whites during the early 1900s, especially those who thought of themselves as members of polite society, valued emotional control as an essential trait of a civilized person. The scripted memorial services in Tuskegee established an atmosphere that minimized ostentatious mourning, indicating the organizer's desire to impress this segment of white America. The choir stopped singing just before John W. Whittaker, the institute chaplain and one of the service's co–masters of ceremonies, began speaking "the simple words of the most simple burial service."[39]

A former Black Belt country preacher and graduate of Atlanta University and Livingstone College Divinity School, Whittaker had a long but sporadic professional career at the Tuskegee Institute. Having applied to Washington for a job in 1887, Whittaker first served from 1888 to 1891 as the school chaplain. He left the school after three years but returned to its staff as a "traveling fund raiser" ten years later. Whittaker, in 1906, accepted the interim deanship of the institute's Phelps Hall Bible Training School. At the time of Washington's death, Whittaker had worked seventeen years with the Tuskegean. No other preacher possessed a more intimate knowledge of the school and its principal.[40]

Following Whittaker's "simple words," the choir sang "How Firm a Foundation," a performance intended to lessen the emotional intensity. This well-known hymn did not easily fit into African Americans' cultural crucible. Blacks preferred songs in a pentatonic musical scale that utilized energetic and inventive voices keeping time to complex rhythms. "How Firm a Foundation" offered none of their desired musical traits. Black mourners would have perceived its diatonic scale, simplistic rhythm, and rigidly set vocal patterns as stoic and uninspiring. Unlike the spiritual that preceded it, it did not elicit the arousing responses familiar to African American mourners but alien to many northern whites.

The hymn, like the preceding spiritual, conveyed a message of reassurance. With seven verses, the song told listeners that since God will never abandon them, they should not lose faith in their ultimate well-being:

> How firm a foundation, ye saints of the Lord,
> Is laid for your faith in His excellent Word!
> What more can He say than to you He hath said,
> You, who unto Jesus for refuge have fled?

The soul that on Jesus has learned for repose,
I will not, I will not desert to its foes;
That soul, though all hell should endeavor to shake,
I'll never, no never, no never forsake.[41]

Following the singing, Whittaker read passages from the Bible.[42]

At the conclusion of Whittaker's presentation, George Lake Imes, the dean of Phelps Hall Bible Training School and the funeral's other co–master of ceremonies, read additional Scriptures. Born in Harrisburg, Pennsylvania, he worked as the pastor of the Union Congregational Church and studied for a Bachelor of Divinity Degree at Hartford Theology Seminary in Connecticut. After earning that degree in 1907, Imes relocated to Nashville, Tennessee, preached at the predominantly black Howard Congregational Church, married Queen Patti Meredith, and began his studies for a master's at Fisk University. On completing his advanced degree in 1910, he accepted a job teaching English at the Tuskegee Institute. The following year, Imes taught classes for the institute's Phelps Hall Bible Training School. He became the dean of the school in 1912. A northern African American who possessed little or no firsthand experience with the South until relocating to Nashville, Imes became enthralled with Washington and his movement. This highly educated and talented black man would remain at the institute until 1935. During the last eleven years of his employment, and after the institute had evolved into a college, Imes served either as special assistant to the president or as secretary to the institute.[43]

Imes recited scriptures that conveyed desired spiritual and worldly messages. He read the fifteenth chapter of Corinthians, a text that Paul the Apostle wrote. Passages from the chapter affirmed Christians' fundamental belief in the resurrection of Christ and the temporariness of death. The chapter included warnings against sin, urging believers to abound "in the work of the Lord." Listeners could easily conclude that Washington labored for God and that the Lord would embrace his spiritual body. More importantly, these texts strongly encouraged the attendees to hold fast to their belief that good will trump bad, and by logical extension, that the movement, even without the living Washington, would overcome all obstacles and succeed in its culture war.[44]

After the bible reading, the choir started singing "Lead, Kindly Light, amid the Encircling Gloom." John Henry Newman, who would become Cardinal Newman, wrote the hymn in 1833 before converting from Anglicanism to Roman Catholicism. Written as a personal request for guidance, the hymn gained widespread appeal among English and American Christians, becoming one of President William McKinley's favorite hymns. Organizers of the president's funeral included it in the ceremony. Commemorators who did not attend the rites performed it in his honor at the "Union and Madison Squares, New York City." Without mentioning God, the song sought his assistance with its request:

> Lead, kindly Light, amid th' encircling gloom
> Lead thou me on!
> Keep thou my feet; I do not ask to see
> The distant scene; one step enough for me.
>
> I was not ever thus, nor prayed that thou
> shouldst lead me on;
> I loved to choose and see my path; but now
> lead thou me on!
> I loved the garish day, and, spite of fears,
> Pride rule my will: remember not past years![45]

Newman's hymn, like the living Washington and the ongoing movement, promoted hope and optimism, core aspects of the Yankee Protestant creed.

> So long thy power hath blessed me, sure it still
> will lead me on.
> O'er moor and fen, o'er crag and torrent, till
> the night is gone,
> And with the morn those angel faces smile,
> which I have loved long since, and lost awhile!

This hymn, like the previous one, helped to place Washington's memory and his funeral service within a cultural context acceptable to most of white America.[46]

*   *   *

The Reverend Hollis B. Frissell, the principal of Hampton Institute, offered a prayer at the close of the hymn. A native New Yorker, he possessed personal and professional relationships with many of the nation's most prominent families. Frissell had met some of them during his studies at Phillips Academy in Andover, Massachusetts, and at Yale University. After graduating from college in 1874, he taught for a few years before attending Union Theological Seminary. Following his graduation in 1879, Frissell took a job at the Madison Avenue Presbyterian Church as an assistant minister. A year later, he accepted Samuel Armstrong's offer of a job at Hampton Institute. By 1886 Frissell had become the institute's vice principal, and after Armstrong's death in 1893, its principal. His relationship with Washington began with his employment at

Hampton Institute and continued throughout the Tuskegean's life. A former teacher of Washington, Frissell became one of his close confidants. The two had worked closely together on issues relating to the education of black southerners.[47]

Frissell's appreciation of Washington and the movement inspired him to praise both of them. The words of the prayer, coupled with the passion and skill of its delivery, belied Frissell's reputation as a powerless speaker. Acknowledging God for an undetermined victory, Washington's life and faith, the prayer commended the principal for sharing "ill treatment with the people of God rather than enjoy pleasures of sin." Frissell thanked God for not allowing Washington, regardless of his personal treatment, to hate anyone. The prayer asserted that a meek, humble Washington taught people to love one another. It thanked God for Washington's "loving friends, for his devoted coworkers and pupils," and for the school. Several sentences of the prayer paraphrase Luke 4:18 and Matthew 11:4–6. In those verses, Jesus gives sight to the blind, makes the lame walk, provides hearing to the deaf, heals those with leprosy, "preached to the poor," frees the prisoners, and raises the dead. Although Frissell did not claim that Washington also was able to resurrect the deceased, he did allege that the principal's "life of service; . . . made blind eyes to see; that he like his Master, made lame men to walk; that he, too, brought liberty to the captives." Frissell's prayer credited Washington for making it possible for thousands of people to acquire "better homes and farms . . . schools and churches," and for assisting with the creation of "the thousands of purer and better lives."[48]

Before he ended his prayer, Frissell emphasized the desirability of sustaining the movement. Shaping his plea to align with the salient message of the day, Frissell alleged that those persons in his presence had rededicated themselves to Washington's "holly [sic] calling." He prayed to God for assistance to continue the work that Washington "gave his life."[49]

At the close of Frissell's prayer, the choir performed another spiritual. Several of the newspapers covering Washington's funeral, including the *Chicago Defender*, titled the song "Tell All My Father's Children Not to Grieve for Me." Very popular at that time with blacks, the song actually had several names. The *Savannah (GA) Tribune* named it "My brother's taken his crown and gone home." In his history of the Fisk Jubilee Singers, J. B. T. Marsh refers to the song as "Angels waiting at the Door." John W. Work's *Folk Song of the American Negro* lists it as "Don't You Grieve for Me." As with the title, there are several versions of the lyrics, since improvising is an integral part of singing spirituals and folk songs. Although the Tuskegee Institute singers performed the song with "brother" as the subject, printed versions of this song instead refer to "sister":

> My sister's took her flight
> And gone home,
> And the angel's waiting at the door;
> My sister's took her flight,
> And gone home,
> And the angel's waiting at the door.
>
> Tell all-a-my Father children,
> Don't you grieve for me;
> Tell all-a-my Father children,
> Don't you grieve for me;
>
> She has taken up her crown,
> And gone home,
> And the angel's waiting at the door:
> She has taken up her crown,
> And gone home,
> And the angel's waiting at the door.[50]

The lyrics to the spiritual suggest that Washington's lifeworks, teaching, and command of the movement merited a princely reception in heaven, and that other persons who desired such greeting should pursue similar endeavors.[51]

Frissell's prayer, the spiritual that followed, or some combination of these prompted widespread crying among the mourners. Some of the participants shed tears of personal grief. Washington's immediate survivors mourned the loss of a relative or close friend, and the institute faculty, staff, and students bewailed the death of their leader and benefactor. Many of Washington's associates lamented the end of his philanthropy. White supporters of the movement greatly regretted the loss of their primary biracial ombudsman and prototypical black American. Sympathy for the survivors might have prompted other mourners to cry.[52]

While the audience wept, the choir sang the widely familiar "Swing Low, Sweet Chariot." John W. Work, who classified this mourning song as one of the "sorrow songs with a note of joy," alleges that an encounter in antebellum Tennessee between a distraught slave mother and an old "mammy" inspired some unknown person or persons to compose the song. After learning that her master had sold her, but not her daughter, south to Mississippi, the slave mother became so distressed that she took the baby and searched for a suitable site to commit infanticide and then suicide. En route, the mother met an older enslaved woman who convinced the mother not to kill either her baby or herself. The aged slave told the mother, "'Don't you do it, honey; wait, let de chariot of de Lord swing low.'" Although the story is likely apocryphal, Work cites it as eventually inspiration for the composing of the renowned spiritual "Swing Low."[53]

As an African American folk song composed by a community of enslaved people, "Swing Low" manifested both the sorrow felt by the bondsmen and their optimism of a brighter tomorrow. As such, it aptly assisted the funeral organizers by reinforcing their desired message of hope and optimism. The song's promise of a trip to heaven promotes belief in a better future:

> Swing low, sweet chariot,
> Coming for to carry me home.
> Swing low, sweet chariot,
> Coming for to carry me home.
>
> I looked over Jordan,
> And what did I see
> Coming for to carry me home?
> A Band of Angels coming after me,
> Coming for to carry me home.
>
> If you get there
> Before I do,
> Coming for to carry me home
> Tell all my friends
> I'm coming too
> Coming for to carry me home.[54]

Following the singing of "Swing Low," Emmett Scott, the institute's secretary and longtime Washington associate, addressed the attendees. Bearing witness to the Yankee Protestant doctrine of modesty, a key principle taught by Washington, the institute, and the movement, Scott informed the gathering that the simplicity of the service reflected the organizers' attempt to fulfill the "specific request" of the late educator. He asserted that "We here have felt that this day is a day too sacred to have even a eulogy imposed upon it." Scott indicated that the unelaborated program did not fail to recognize, nor did it understate, Washington's esteem. He instructed members of the audience seeking a monument to the memory of the Tuskegean to "look about you—at these buildings and grounds, at this out-pouring of love, this tribute of affection and respect."[55]

In an assertion that indicated that Americans living throughout the nation embraced Washington and his works, Scott went on to note that the Tuskegean's survivors had received hundreds of notes of solace. Scott reported that sympathizers sent these messages to "cheer the wife and the children and those of us who have labored here with" the late principal. The secretary asserted that these communications substantiated the loss that both his nation and race suffered. Organizers, however, had decided that Scott would read to the assembly only one such note: the telegram from Seth Low, the absent chairman of the school's board of trustees. William G. Willcox, also a member of the board, who had traveled to the funeral from New York City in the company of William Jay Scheffelin, another board member, carried Low's message to the funeral.[56]

Seth Low had dedicated much of his adult life to public service. Born in 1850 to a wealthy transplanted puritan New England family in Brooklyn, New York, he graduated from Columbia College. Subsequently, Low took a junior partner position with his family's firm, A. A. Low and Brothers. Within a few years, Low became a senior partner and remained with the business until it ceased operations in 1888. Parlaying his volunteer work with the Brooklyn Charities into a Republican Party nomination for mayor in 1881, he secured election to the office and served two two-year terms. A year later, Low became president of Columbia University, a position he held until becoming mayor of Greater New York City in 1901. After his defeat for a second term, Low forsook elective politics but continued his civic work. He joined, in 1904, the National Civic Federation, an organization of elites working to solve conflicts between employers and workers. He became the president of the federation in 1908, serving in that position until his death in 1916. He had also accepted the presidency of the New York State Chamber of Commerce beginning in 1914. Low had joined the Tuskegee Institute Board of Trustees in 1905.[57]

Seth Low strongly believed in Washington and the works of the movement. As a paternal patrician who subscribed to the Yankee Protestant ethic, Low had for years sought to improve the material and moral condition of the nation's poor. His desire to assist dispossessed people led him to work with various charitable organizations. After Low joined the Tuskegee Institute Board of Trustees, he became a leading member of the movement. His knowledge that blacks, especially those in the South, suffered at the bottom of the nation's socioeconomic ladder motivated him to join the movement. Washington invited him to serve as board president after Low had served three years on the board; he accepted only after Washington agreed to a number of conditions, which included the appointment of a vice principal, enhancing the school's academics, improving the financial condition of the institute's farm, and reducing the school's administrative expenses. Low further stipulated that he would not donate any money to the school as long as he chaired the board. An energetic chairman, Low at times seemed obsessed with the efficiency of black workers. He thought that African Americans' economic and social enhancement depended on their mastery of proficient labor. Low concluded that the movement, more than any other force, would inspire African Americans to embrace the work ethic he preferred.[58]

Low's short and pointed funeral message primarily addressed the Tuskegee Institute community. Although it did not offer condolences to Washington's family, his note did maintain that the nation lost "a great patriot and the Negro race an inspiring leader." Low evoked Washington's memory only as an instrument to promote his desire to maintain the movement. He therefore did not make praising Washington the primary objective of his note. Low wanted his communication to inspire the school's administration, faculty, staff, and students to remain faithful to the school and the movement. He sought to reinforce their individual and collective commitment to the culture war. Low asserted that "it is now the hour to show without his [Washington's] magnetic presence, by your loyalty to the school and to his high ideals how truly you have caught the inspiration of his spirit and of his devoted life of service." After assuring the institute's community that the board of trustees would continue to support the school, he asked for their continued "loyal co-operation in keeping Tuskegee a worthy memorial of the great man with whom you have worked so long and well."[59]

Willcox, the board of trustees' official representative, spoke after Scott finished reading Low's note. A scion of a wealthy Staten Island, New York, family, Willcox's father, a Congregational minster, also practiced law and owned an insurance brokerage. His bother held a professorship at Cornell University, and a sister held a professorship at Wellesley College. Despite Willcox's success as an attorney, and his background and privilege, he retained an immense interest in education, especially the schooling of working-class children. Less than two months after Washington's funeral, he became president of the New York City Board of Education. During his tenure he campaigned to initiate and maintain the short-lived and narrowly implemented Gray Plan, an educational curriculum with many features similar to those offered at the Tuskegee Institute. The prospect of training efficient young laborers contributed to his supporting and joining the National Urban League, an integral part of the movement. Willcox, along with Washington and several other Tuskegee Institute Board of Trustees members and close associates, played crucial roles in the league's founding and early development.[60]

Willcox's address clearly manifested the organizers' overriding desire to use the funeral events to ensure the perpetuation of the institute and the movement. He assured the attendees that members of the Tuskegee Institute

Board of Trustees would continue supporting the institute and the movement. He offered "encouragement and confidence and hope and faith to the
Officers, Teachers and Students of the Institute." After extending the "heartfelt
sympathy" of the trustees to the institute community, Willcox stated that he
wanted to express the board's "absolute confidence" in the "future growth
and usefulness" of the school. Declaring that this "is no time for a eulogy
of Dr. Washington's life and work," Willcox prophesied that people would
later "gratefully accord to him a high place among the truly great men of
our beloved country." He asserted that the grief that they all felt at the loss
of their "beloved leader," who "seemed indispensable," should not prevent
them from taking courage and looking "forward with absolute confidence
and faith."[61]

The New Yorker promised that a new leader of the movement would
emerge and carry on Washington's work. Willcox declared that the Tuskegee community should not worry about the institute or the movement. He
asserted that Washington's lifework "is now firmly established in the confidence of both races. It cannot go backward; it must and shall go forward."
Willcox reminded the audience that throughout history, when great leaders
have died, new ones come forward who then went on to also achieve major
victories. God, he alleged, must have determined that "Washington's great
work was finished," and that his death would inspire survivors to accomplish
more than would have occurred if the Tuskegean continued to live for many
additional years. Willcox called for the institute's community to "take heart
and press forward . . . with fresh courage and enthusiasm."[62]

Pleading for cooperation within the institute's community, Willcox warned
against infighting. He proclaimed that in the continual pursuit of Washington's primary objectives, the "cause is everything, the individual is nothing."
Willcox asserted that the greater cause left no room for "personal ambition,
jealousy, or fractional difference." He called for every member of the community to take pride in their respective "share in Dr. Washington's work and
in God's work for the progress of the colored race." The principal's death,
Willcox claimed, created a crisis that necessitated an unprecedented amount
of unselfishness, disinterest, and faithful collaboration. He announced that
the "trustees will not fail you, and they know you will not fail them." Willcox
promised that the board, along with the school's community, "shall carry
forward the great work for the Institute" and the movement. After observing that Washington's death created sympathy that both blacks and whites
shared, and that the two groups would become more tightly bound, Willcox
alleged that "friends of both races will" substantially enhance their support
of the movement.[63]

Washington, Willcox purported, wanted a living memorial and cared little for an inanimate monument to his memory. Reiterating his theme of the desirability of maintaining the movement, Willcox avowed that Washington's "simplicity of nature, modesty and humility" prohibited the Tuskegean from seeking a memorial other than an "increased devotion and locality to this great cause." Asserting that if the community displayed their "appreciation of his life and honor his memory" as Washington would have wished, his demise would then become an "occasion for renewed consecration to the high ideals of which his life was such an example, and in which his memory will be such an inspiration."[64]

Willcox ended his statement with a response to the growing number of people calling for one or more tangible memorials to honor Washington's memory. While some of the persons requesting a permanent commemoration, like those in Newark, New Jersey, had no tangible proposal, other admirers, such as the Calhoun Colored School, made concrete suggestions. Supporters of the school, a Tuskegee Institute spin-off, located at Calhoun, Alabama, established a $30 scholarship in the name of Washington. Blacks at a mass meeting in Savannah, Georgia, enacted a resolution that requested all African Americans to recognize the birthday of Washington as a national African American holiday. In Mobile, Alabama, a group of blacks discussed building a "memorial in honor of Booker T. Washington." African Americans at a mass meeting in New Orleans made a more substantial suggestion. They agreed to commission the casting of a bust of bronze in the image of Washington and to place it in the city's public library. While the *New Orleans Picayune*, a white-owned newspaper, declared the Tuskegee Institute "the greatest memorial that could be erected," M. C. Runwick, a black man living in Lawrenceville, Georgia, prophetically called for the nation's African American population to donate money for the building of a monument that would cost $25,000. In just over six years, his proposal would become a reality.[65]

*   *   *

Following Willcox's presentation, the choir sang "Still, Still with Thee," a song with lyrics that Harriet Beecher Stowe wrote in 1855. The daughter of a Congregational minister, wife of a theology professor, and mother of seven children, Stowe died in 1896 as one of the nation's most famous writers. She authored no fewer than seventeen books and forty-three articles and pamphlets, but the publication of *Uncle Tom's Cabin* in 1852 secured her fame. That book sold 300,000 copies within the first twelve months; eventually, worldwide sales of the novel exceeded two million. Traveling road shows in

the North portrayed the novel's story on stage in town after town. Opportu-
nistic merchants sold a variety of items with pictures of the novel's characters
painted on them. The reception of the book in the northern states afforded
Stowe the illustriousness of a modern mega rock star. Her book became the
most widely heard voice of the antislavery cause. Many northern businessmen with financial interests in the South, however, denounced both Stowe
and her book. Responding to the novel's opinion-making impact, officials
below the Mason and Dixon Line suppressed and confiscated the novel. But
neither the criticisms of businessmen nor the actions of southerners stopped
the book from becoming a ubiquitous icon of the abolition movement. The
novel's influence even inspired President Abraham Lincoln, upon meeting
Stowe, to allege that it initiated the Civil War.[66]

Written in 1855, Charles Ward, Stowe's brother, and his coeditor, John
Zundel, published "Still, Still with Thee" in their *Plymouth Collection of
Hymns and Tunes*. Henry Ward Beecher, another of Stowe's brothers, wrote
the introduction to this compilation of over thirteen hundred hymns and
tunes. While "Still, Still with Thee" never became widely popular, Stowe's
prestige and the beauty of the song's poetic verses contributed to it becoming a favorite hymn in the collection. The hymn projects a deep and sincere
spirituality:

> Still, still with Thee, when purple morning breaketh,
> When the bird waketh and the shadows flee;
> Fairer than morning, lovelier than daylight,
> Dawns the sweet consciousness, I am with Thee.
>
> Alone with Thee, amid the mystic shadows
> The solemn hush of nature newly born;
> Alone with Thee, in breathless adoration,
> In the claim dew and freshness of the morn.
>
> As in the dawning o'er the waveless ocean,
> The image of the morning-star doth rest,
> So in this stillness, thou beholdest only
> Thine image in the waters of my breast.[67]

Perhaps admiration for Stowe, inspired Wilbur F. Tillett and Charles S.
Nutter to include "Still, Still with Thee" in their 1911 collection of hymns for
the Methodist Episcopal Church.[68]

However, symbolism and not popularity seemed to have motivated the
organizers to instruct the Tuskegee Institute choir to sing "Still, Still with
Thee" at Washington's funeral in 1915. The song became a tool of recruitment.

The hymn resonated with persons possessing a favorable memory of the abolition movement, in particularly white Yankee philanthropists. Although a significant number of ordinary African Americans had heard of *Uncle Tom's Cabin* and its author and even read the book, unlike a large number of whites, probably few of them knew that Stowe wrote the lyrics to "Still, Still with Thee." Understanding this reality, several African American–oriented newspapers chose to identify Stowe as the lyricist. Inclusion of the hymn in the service suggests that organizers strove to rekindle in the minds of racially liberal northern whites positive memories of the crusade to liberate African American slaves. The singing of "Still, Still with Thee" declared that the fight, now a cultural war, continued.[69]

A benediction completed the portion of the service that occurred in the chapel. Afterward, the rites moved to the front yard of the chapel. Chaplain Whittaker and several other clergymen led the pallbearers, who pushed Washington's casket out of the front door on a push truck, through the massive crowd that had gathered along the short route to the vaulted grave a few yards from the northeast side of the chapel. As the procession approached the tomb, brick masons completed the "walling up the grave and making the arch above the ground." Their tardiness resulted from Margaret Washington having changed her mind earlier in the day about the location of Washington's final resting place. Organizers had originally intended to bury Washington in the school's cemetery, alongside the grave of his first wife, Fanny Norton Smith Washington. Expressing her prerogative as the widow, Margaret selected a much more prominent site on the gentle slope of a hill several yards away. The final location provided persons traveling through the center of campus an unimpeded view of Washington's grave.[70]

Paradoxically, burying the principal signified both finality and continuation. Placing Washington's body in the grave declared to his survivors and all other interested parties that the Tuskegean, as a living entity, no longer existed. This proclamation, however, could potentially undermine the continual success of the movement. Survivors, proponents, and opponents alike all tended to view Washington and the movement as the same. Survivors did not want the man's death to signal the demise of the movement. Either politics or emotions inspired them to deny symbolically Washington's death. On some level, survivors concluded that preserving the man's body would assist them in perpetuating the movement. The process of preparing and then entombing the corpse in a vault designed to slow decomposition also helped to preserve a desired image of a virile resting Washington while symbolizing the persistence of an energized movement.

At high noon, and after one or more unidentified persons briefly spoke "the last words of the burial service," the institute bandmaster played "Taps" as the pallbearers slowly lowered Washington's casket into the vaulted grave.

Union brigadier general Daniel Adams Butterfield had composed "Taps" during the early months of the Civil War. Then thirty-one years old, Butterfield, a Utica, New York, native and a son of an American Express Company founder, commanded the Third Brigade of the Fifth Army Corps, Army of the Potomac, when he penned the twenty-four-note tune in July 1862. He claimed to have grown tired of hearing "Extinguish Lights," then the army's official bugle call to signal troops to turn out their lights. Having written "Taps," Butterfield then ordered Private Oliver Wilcox Norton, a bugler in the Third Brigade, to replace "Extinguish Lights" with the new tune at dusk. Before the war ended, both Union and Confederate commanders had adopted "Taps" as a bugle call. Although the United States Army did not adopt it officially until years after the Civil War, "Taps" had become integral to military burial rites by the time Washington died. Rarely, however, did burial rites for nonmilitary persons include the playing of the tune.[71]

Along with the funeral procession and the honor guards, the playing of "Taps" helped Washington's survivors construct particular aspects of the common memory that they wanted to promote. As performed during the entombment, "Taps" created a remembrance that closely associated Washington with the colossal number of fallen gallant warriors of the Civil War. This memory would inspire both of Washington's primary audiences—poor southern blacks and prosperous northern whites—to continue supporting the movement. Washington's survivors used "Taps" to stimulate and remind these utmost champions of the Civil War of their vested interest in a *complete* victory, one that freed African Americans from slavery as well as from economic and social degradation. Organizers needed both primary groups to support the movement strongly in its quest to win its cultural war.

*   *   *

As the sound of "Taps" faded, sympathizers ended their visit to Tuskegee and began their respective journeys home. For two days, a crowd of over ten thousand people, black and white, old and young, southerners and northerners had interacted with one another on the institute's 3,500-acre campus. Although Alexander E. Manning, a black editor of the *Indianapolis World* reported to Emmett Scott that a pickpocket victimized him, no journal published any accounts of crime or bad behavior during the several days of the mortuary ceremony. Mourners had visited the grandest institution for the education of African Americans in the nation while attending a masterfully organized funeral pageant. Together, the Tuskegee Institute and the memorial helped shape a desired memory of Washington that would reinforce commitments to the movement. More than anything else, arrangers wanted the burial ritual to counter successfully any possible defections from the force that had engaged in a multifront culture war under the leadership of Booker T. Washington.[72]

4. "A Debt of Gratitude"

Tributes across the Nation

On the day of his funeral, Wednesday, November 17, 1915, Tuskegee movement supporters across the nation held memorials for Booker T. Washington. From Louisiana to North Dakota, from Florida to Washington State, and from Rhode Island to California, they commemorated his life. While most Washington memorials took place later, movement supporters conducted countless of them on November 17. Perhaps for many attendees, these memorials, with the exception of the interment, served the same purposes as had the funeral itself. While generally not as elaborate as those held afterward, supporters employed several techniques three days after his death to memorialize publicly his life. Some mourners, like parishioners of predominately African American Christian congregations in Mobile, Alabama, rang church bells at 9:55 A.M., just before the funeral procession started in Tuskegee. Five minutes later, supporters of the movement in Austin, Texas, began ringing both church and school bells. Other supporters either lowered flags, closed schools, suspended commerce, conducted ceremonies, or adopted resolutions. A number of them embraced several of these activities in their efforts to venerate Washington's life and mourn his death.[1]

Organizers of these commemorations hoped to assist supporters with their grieving while inspiring them to internalize a constructed recollection of Washington. They understood that in addition to honoring the dead, commemoration activities are important tools of instruction. Organizers attempted to provide a preferred fabricated memory to people with no personal recall of identified events or Washington. For those individuals with a personal recollection of him and his historical actions, opinion makers used commemorative events to promote a desired reshaping of their remembrances. Promoters sought to construct a desired common recollection that fostered their favored worldview and priorities.[2]

Supporters of the movement held a stake in staging commemorations of Booker T. Washington. Organizers wanted their public glorification of his memory to help perpetuate political and financial aid from key white philanthropists. Supporters needed backing from selected whites to continue the dissemination of desired Yankee Protestant values to the masses of blacks. At the same time, supporters sought to inspire the white masses, particularly southerners, to become more tolerant of striving African Americans. To achieve these dual objectives, these culture warriors designed and executed an array of memorials for Washington.

Flying the U.S. flag at half-staff, like bell tolling, demonstrated one of the more conspicuous efforts to recognize and honor the life of Washington publicly. In several areas, supporters convinced government entities, business establishments, and private citizens alike to fly the national flags at half-staff, a gesture originally signifying the death of someone aboard a naval vessel. Later, military ground forces took to flying flags at half-mast to denote that one or more of their soldiers had died. When Washington died, flying flags at half-mast during peace time occurred primarily after the death of a prominent soldier, government official or private citizen. Only once before his death did a large number of Americans lower their flags in honor of a black person. They half-masted flags in recognition of the memory of Frederick Douglass—a suffragist, former abolitionist, and U.S. diplomat. After the death of Booker T. Washington, Americans for the first time half-staffed flags to acknowledge the passing of an African American with no history of military or meaningful government service.[3]

Two school districts, and perhaps more, authorized it for the day preceding interment. More than twenty-four hours before the funeral, the "colored school" in Tucson, Arizona, where Tuskegee Institute graduate C. C. Simmons taught, began flying its flag at half-staff. Across the country, Roscoe C. Bruce, the assistant superintendent of the Washington, D.C., public schools, helped to engineer the flying of flags at half-staff atop all of that district's African American schools. The son of the former Mississippi U.S. senator Blanche Kelso Bruce, Roscoe had become an integral part of the movement. After graduating from Harvard College in 1902, the Phi Beta Kappa headed the Tuskegee Institute's Academic Department. He relocated to Washington, D.C., in 1906, where he took a job as a principal. The following year, with a strong endorsement from Washington, he became an assistant superintendent. His job included supervising the African American schools in Washington, D.C.[4]

Bruce and other movement supporters persuaded officials on Wednesday, the day of the burial to lower flags adjacent to schools and other public buildings. The "Colored" schools in Washington, D.C., which had flown lowered flags the day before the funeral, also flew them at half-staff on Wednesday, the day of the funeral. On the West Coast, Judge Walter Bordwell, president of the Los Angeles Board of Education, directed *all* public schools—not just those for African Americans—to fly their flags at half-mast. Following suit, Los Angeles mayor C. E. Sebastian and the city council ordered the lowering of flags on all municipal buildings. The municipal governments of Boston and Cambridge, Massachusetts, lowered flags on all city-owned properties. The lowering of flags even occurred in several cities, like Highland Park, Illinois, which did not have a sizable black population. In response to a request from movement supporter, A. W. Fletcher, a wealthy businessman, and a group of other prominent white residents, Mayor Samuel M. Hastings ordered to half-staff the flag at city hall.[5]

Whereas a few private white citizens, like the managers of banks in Los Angeles, flew their institutions' U.S. flags at half-staff in honor of the memory of Washington, many more black civilians lowered theirs. For several days, African American movement supporters living in New York City kept their flags to half-staff. In New Jersey, the Colored Educational Conference requested that black people fly their flags at half-mast during the hours of Washington's funeral. George E. Cannon, a physician and a friend of Washington, chaired the statewide predominately black Educational Conference. He sent requests to supporters in Newark, Patterson, and other New Jersey cities to lower national flags in honor of Washington.[6]

*   *   *

In New Jersey and elsewhere, flag lowering did not fulfill the desires of many black businesspersons, some of the most fervent movement members, to honor Washington. African American proprietors in various locations across the nation ceased business transactions on November 17, the day of the funeral. The organization that Washington founded and headed until his death, the National Negro Business League (NNBL), led the movement to close black-owned businesses. On learning of Washington's death on Sunday, November 14, 1915, NNBL vice president Charles Banks telegrammed local NNBL chapters that same day to request that members and all other African American business owners suspend their commercial operations between 10 and 11 A.M. on the day of the funeral. He also asked that African American laborers, "with their employers [*sic*] consent, refrain from working from 10 until 10:10 a. m."[7]

Although white-owned daily newspapers helped Banks and the NNBL disseminate this request, most African American–owned journals did not. Generally, these papers published once a week only. Publishers of African American–oriented papers needed more time than the two days between Washington's death and his funeral to spread the call. As weeklies, the majority of papers targeting an African American readership did not publish between Sunday and Wednesday. African American–owned weeklies publishing on either Monday or Tuesday largely supported temporarily shutting down the commercial activities of black people in honor of Washington. A large plurality, if not a majority, of the publishers and their editors belonged to the National Negro Press Association (NNPA), an affiliate of the NNBL. Fredrick R. Moore, publisher of the *New York Age*, a leading African American–oriented journal, previously worked as the national organizer of the NNBL. He and other black publishers and editors who held membership in the NNPA had a stake in a widespread popular commemoration.[8]

White-owned dailies nationwide reported on Banks's telegrams to local NNBL chapters. The *Pittsburgh (PA) Telegraph* published a letter from a black man named Robert L. Varin, who enthusiastically endorsed the call and reinforced the paper's implied support of the appeal: "I am a negro [*sic*], and as such feel that my entire race owes a debt of gratitude to our lamented leader, and while we can never hope to make full payment, I feel that we can at least make a special effort in an honest endeavor to do him proper homage. Therefore, I suggest that as a fitting expression of respect, every negro [*sic*] enterprise throughout our country temporarily suspend all business for a least 20 minutes on Wednesday morning from 9:45 to 10:15, covering the hour of his funeral."[9]

Some black businessmen did not embrace the appeal, however. The president of the New Haven, Connecticut, Colored Business and Professional Men's Association, for example, expressed an unenthusiastic response to the idea. The city had no NNBL chapter, and the president of the association, attorney George W. Crawford, asserted that since he had received "no official communication asking such an observance . . . he did not think any such mark of honor would be inaugurated among members of his race" in New Haven. Although Crawford graduated from Tuskegee Institute in 1900, he did not support Washington or the movement. A member of the first board of directors of the NAACP and its Committee of 100, Crawford had signed "An Open Letter to the People of Great Britain and Europe by William Edward Burghardt Du Bois and Others," which took issue with the assessment of black America that Washington publicly espoused while visiting Europe. Along with Crawford and Du Bois, twenty-three highly educated

African American men signed the letter; including J. Max Barber, a founder of the Niagara movement; Archibald H. Grimke, a founder of the NAACP and former consul to Santo Domingo (now the Dominican Republic); and William Monroe Trotter, the editor of the *Boston Guardian* newspaper and a long-time Washington foe.[10]

Crawford did not represent the view of all black members of the New Haven Colored Business and Professional Men's Association. C. F. Baker, an owner of a New Haven funeral home and secretary of the association, supported the call for African American business owners to suspend commercial activities during the time of Washington's burial rites. Baker "thought the suggestion an admirable one." The association's secretary declared that he would ask black entrepreneurs in the Dixwell Avenue district of New Haven to cease operation, "if their business interests would permit," during the time of the funeral. In declaring his intentions, Baker made it clear that the association did not endorse his efforts.[11]

Baker's organizational endeavors mirrored those of many other African Americans. The night before Washington's funeral, the Augusta (Georgia) Colored Men's Business League met and resolved to ask black businessmen to close their establishments during the burial rites the next day. In Texas, the secretary of the National Negro Retail Merchants Association and movement supporter E. W. D. Welsh of Dallas sent a request "to all negro [*sic*] retail merchants throughout the United States to close their places of business" during Washington's funeral. An Indianapolis memorial committee asked the city's black entrepreneurs to cease business operations during the ceremony. Chicago's Robert Sengstacke Abbott, a graduate of Hampton Institute and the founding editor and publisher of the *Chicago Defender*, made a personal appeal to "all colored business men in Chicago to close their places between 10 and 11 o'clock Wednesday, the hour of the funeral of Washington."[12]

African American entrepreneurs who heeded these requests clearly reflected the movement's appeal while helping to boost nationwide commemoration of the life of Washington. While some of the businessmen closed their doors for only a few minutes, others kept them shut throughout the scheduled time of Washington's funeral. In Savannah, Georgia, "colored business houses were closed for a period during the funeral services" of Washington. African Americans in Fort Smith, Arkansas, suspended business activities between 10:00 and 10:30 A.M., and blacks in Pittsburgh, Pennsylvania, stopped between 9:45 and 10:15 A.M. In the cities of Boston, Massachusetts, Jackson, Mississippi and Lawrence, Kansas, "hundreds of Negro business and professional men closed their offices between the hour of 10 and 11 a. m." Closures occurred in New York City, Indianapolis, Chicago, and Mobile, Alabama. San Antonio's African American businesspersons shut their doors from 12:00 P.M. to the end of memorial services. On the West Coast, the *California Eagle* newspaper staff successfully convinced all but one "Race establishment in Greater Los Angeles" to cease operation during the hour between 11 A.M. and noon.[13]

After the *New York News* published an interview with one of its employees, Guilford M. Crawford, white-owned businesses in the Harlem area joined their black counterparts and suspended commercial operations. Despite reports of sympathy among some white owners for the movement to close businesses, the vast majority of them did not follow suit. In Chicago, Abbott claimed that many of that city's white businessmen told him they did not know of the agreed-upon time to honor Washington's life, insisting that "they would have been anxious to close their stores to express their feeling of respect" for him. The *Defender's* editor alleged that someone had failed to inform white Chicago business owners of the designated time to suspend commerce.[14]

No one made such an error in Tuskegee, Alabama. *All* businesses, black as well as white-owned ones, remained closed for most of Wednesday. Ernest W. Thompson, Tuskegee's mayor and editor of the *Tuskegee (AL) News*, requested in a personally circulated petition that white-owned enterprises in the town close for the duration of Washington's burial rites. All of Tuskegee's commercial proprietors signed Thompson's appeal. As a body, the town's business community also attended the funeral. Operating adjacent to the Tuskegee Institute, these white entrepreneurs made significant profits from the school and the movement's various outreach activities. Closing their businesses and attending the funeral publicly displayed their appreciation of both Washington and the movement.[15]

* * *

Like the businesses in Tuskegee and other places, a great number of public schools honored the life of Washington. With some noted exceptions, these academies primarily taught black children. At the most basic level, canceling classes and making other simple commemorations suggested to the students that their elders held Washington in high esteem and that they should do likewise. The formal lessons and pageants that many of the schools either sponsored or promoted helped to create and shape individual and collective memories of Washington. His vision and works inspired many public school officials to use his life as an object lesson. They wanted to convey to their respective student bodies a set of values and behaviors that they believed Washington and his public image typified.

Few academies suspended all classes for the day. Those that did conveyed clearly to students, especially African Americans, that Washington enjoyed high esteem as the race's premier leader. In the process of commemorating him, these closings produced an historical milestone. November 17, 1915, became the first day that any U.S. public school closed its doors to honor the life of a black man. Until that day, the protocol of white supremacy prohibited any such official recognition, especially in the former Confederacy. The closing of the public schools occurred in the "Old South," the region that the vast majority of African Americans lived.

Schools that did not open for instruction included those with predominately black student bodies: Austin, Texas; Vicksburg, Mississippi; Memphis, Tennessee; and Alexandria, Virginia. Lee Lewis Campbell, a black minister and publisher of the *Baptist Herald* in Austin, asserted that schools close in that city "out of respect" for Washington. Paying "suitable tribute to" the value of Washington's leadership, schools teaching black students shut their doors in Vicksburg, Mississippi, and throughout Warren County. Officials in Memphis, Tennessee, declared a holiday for black students to commemorate Washington's life. Public school administrators did the same in Alexandria, Virginia. Displaying similar motivations, as did their Memphis counterparts, they too wanted their black students to attend a ceremony that honored both the man and the movement.[16]

Throughout the South, as well as in a few locations in the North, public schools deferred regular course work rather than dismiss classes for the day. Some of the academies stopped their usual instruction for only a few minutes. Administrators of the African American public schools in Washington, D.C., who had authorized flying flags at half-mast, set aside a mere ten minutes to honor Washington. Roscoe C. Bruce, the black assistant superintendent "in charge of colored schools," directed teachers to suspend classes between the hours of 10 A.M. and noon. During that limited period, he wanted them to explain "why the personality and work of this great man should be respected by all Americans, particularly Americans of African descent." In Indianapolis, the teaching staffs of the various public schools with black student bodies conducted "brief and impressive memorial" services to honor Washington during the morning "exercise period."[17]

School districts that set aside more time to extol the life of Washington and the values that they associated with him, presented a variety of ceremonies. Teachers and administrators wanted their students to emulate specific aspects of Washington's character. The pursuit of this objective inspired the staffs at the "local colored schools" in Evansville, Indiana, to stop instruction at 10 A.M. in order to pay "respect to the memory of Booker T. Washington." Teachers at both the "city and county negro [sic] schools" in the Knoxville, Tennessee, area suspended classes during the same hour of the day. They told students about Washington's successes and asserted that pupils who mimic him would also become successful. Similar instructional recognition occurred in numerous other black-populated schools, especially in the South, including Birmingham and Tuskegee, Alabama; Fort Smith, Arkansas; Houston and Tyler, Texas; Sparta, Georgia; and Wheeling, West Virginia.[18]

In at least one school district, the superintendent directed that predominantly white as well as African American schools under his charge memorialize Washington on the day of his funeral. H. B. Wilson, the Topeka, Kansas, superintendent of public schools, admired Washington and the movement. Wanting his teaching staff and their students to appreciate Washington, Wilson ordered that all students in the third grade and above learn about "the history of the great negro [sic] educator's achievements." He left it up to the principals as to how they would carry out his dictate. In some schools, the principal gathered pupils in one room and told them about Washington's life. Elsewhere, teachers performed that task in their classrooms. Regardless of who spoke to the students, commemorations generally lasted approximately an hour. The superintendent's national recognition, along with the high regard that both local and state leaders held Washington, helped to provide Wilson with the clout necessary to overcome potential opposition to his order for a district-wide commemoration.[19]

* * *

Memorializing Washington in only one of Ohio's numerous school districts would not satisfy Frank W. Miller. This Dartmouth College graduate, son of German immigrants, issued an official statewide call for all public schools in Ohio to reserve part of their instructional day "to memorialize the great leader of the negro [sic] race and his work." A supporter of the movement, Miller proclaimed Washington a great man. He stated that, under leadership of Washington, blacks had "advanced" toward their goals and he had "elevated" their prestige. "As a consequence of this fundamental work," moreover "all mankind has been substantially benefited and the world is better for his having been." Miller went on to assert that presenting students with desired selected aspects of Washington's life would teach them "that he who persevere [sic] may win; . . . inspire them to live lives of sacrifice and usefulness . . . appreciate the fact that he who elevates mankind is humanity's greatest benefactor."[20]

Local African American supporters of the movement, and not educational leaders, led the efforts to mandate memorial services for Washington in the New Orleans public schools. No school official in the Crescent City had called publicly for any type of memorial before advocates of the movement approached them. The city did not possess powerful education administrators, like Miller or Wilson, who publicly expressed an interest in commemorating Washington. It did have African American residents who strongly supported the movement. Local supporters organized a committee to visit the school board with a request that African American students commemorate Washington on the day of his funeral. The board agreed to the appeal, directing the staff at "every colored school in the city" to hold memorial services during the hour of Washington's burial ceremony. The superintendent, on behalf of the board, ordered all teachers at predominantly African American schools to suspend ordinary instruction and "hold appropriate exercises in honor of Dr. Washington."[21]

Various schools dismissed classes early. In most areas of the nation, in 1915, African Americans could access only a few indoor facilities large enough to accommodate mass gatherings—most commonly church sanctuaries and public-school auditoriums. Education administrators whose schools hosted commemorations adjourned classes so their students and staffs could attend the programs, along with the public. That is what officials at the Booker T. Washington School in Houston, Texas, intended when they scheduled a memorial jointly with movement supporters. It would start at the same time that Washington's funeral commenced, as did a commemoration in the Beaufort, South Carolina, public school for African American students. A large audience that included the public-school student body, as well as pupils from the Beaufort Academy, a private, predominately black–populated school, and many of the local black residents, packed the institution's meeting hall. In Biloxi, Mississippi, authorities allowed a committee of movement supporters to hold a memorial in the chapel of the city's only public school for black students. The minister of the First Colored Baptist Church, the Reverend Dr. A. Bell, chaired the program, while the principal of the school, M. F. Nicholls, served as master of ceremonies. This relatively short service started at 11 A.M., with "a large gathering of the citizens and pupils" in attendance. It consisted of only one song, two ten-minute speeches, and three readings.[22]

Movement supporters planned to hold a similarly modest memorial for Washington at the Garrison Public School in Kansas City, Missouri. Open to the public, the memorial would include a few songs and speeches. Organizers included speeches from John M. Love, an educator, and the school's principal, R. T. Cones. Event planners promoted Howard Smith as a keynote speaker. A Baltimore, Maryland, native who graduated from Lincoln University in Pennsylvania and the University of Pennsylvania Medical School, Smith became active in the local Democratic Party when he relocated to the Kansas City area. His political connections assisted him in accruing several high-profile jobs, including physician for the Industrial Home for Negro

Orphans, and in 1915, superintendent of the Jackson County (MO) Home for Aged and Infirm Negroes. Smith's professional and political work, however, did not prevent him from becoming a civil rights activist. He served as the vice president of the Kansas Branch of the NAACP. Smith's medical career, political connections, and community activism enhanced the attractiveness of the intended commemoration.[23]

Some schools that held public commemorations staged elaborate ceremonies. Organizers of these events presented programs that for the most part mirrored the vast majority of countless Washington memorials held on the day of his burial. Organizers succeeded in attracting a wide variety of people to the ceremonies. Attendees came for different reasons. Many of them might have perceived the rituals as entertainment, coming just to enjoy the spectacle. Another segment of the audience might have sought to exploit the rituals' social, economic, or political networking potential. Any number probably simply wanted to express their appreciation of Washington and mourn his passing in a collective public setting.

Movement supporters held a memorial pageant at the predominately black–populated Lincoln High School in Wheeling, West Virginia. This commemoration, unlike the funeral at the Tuskegee Institute, did not include spirituals in the program. The music selected for the ceremony lessened the projection that blacks enjoyed a markedly different culture than did the whites who attended the memorial. Organizers authorized the singing and playing only of songs familiar to the majority of white Protestants, in particular Methodists. Lincoln students opened the service by singing the Methodist hymn "O Paradise," a popular early-1900s song of mourning that praised the afterlife for a weary Christian. Later in the service, a pianist played a solo version of "In the Sweet By-and-By," a Christian ballad that two white Americans, Sanford Filmore Bennett and Joseph Philbrick Webster, wrote in 1868. Before the conclusion of the commemoration, students sang "Abide with Me," a Methodist hymn that Henry F. Lyte wrote in 1847. A student octet closed the memorial with a rendition of Cardinal John Henry Newman's "Lead, Kindly Light."[24]

Organizers of the Lincoln High School commemoration interlaced the music selections with a prayer and four eulogies. After singing the opening hymn, the Reverend W. W. Hollinger, pastor of the Simpson Methodist Episcopal Church, led the congregation in a prayer. Like the songs, he used the call on God as a teaching tool. While helping to establish a desired ambience, the prayer, like the music, contributed to organizers' efforts to instruct attendees on how to feel and think. Subsequent to the prayer, J. H. Rainbow, the Lincoln principal, "paid a glowing tribute to Dr. Washington" in his efforts at educating African Americans. He and the other eulogists constructed addresses in a way that highlighted and reinforced the preferred values and behaviors that organizers wanted the attendees to internalize. They promoted significant aspects of the Yankee Protestant ethic. Whereas Rainbow used the story of Washington's lifework to teach the value of philanthropy and education, H. H. Jones, a teacher, and W. O. Davis, a prominent preacher, retold the widely known saga of the Tuskegean's perseverance, optimism, and work ethic. The fourth eulogist, D. W. Turpeau, a local resident, spoke on "Washington's One Ideal." Although reports about the memorial did not divulge the "Ideal," it is conceivable that Turpeau referred to the Tuskegean's frequent request for biracial cooperation.[25]

Promoting that concept is what supporters intended to accomplish during a commemoration that they planned to hold at the Muskogee, Oklahoma, Negro Manual Training High School. Organizers of this memorial wanted their program to attract schoolchildren as well as interested residents. Although they expected "Nearly all of the negro [sic] population of the city and some from the country" to attend, they also wanted white people there. Thus, the planned program placed all of the members of the city's predominantly white board of education on the dais while several local black and white luminaries presented speeches. Organizers included Robert Van Meigs as one of the scheduled speakers. A white native of Pineville, Missouri, and a Chicago School of Divinity graduate, Meigs served as pastor of the First Baptist Church of Muskogee. His appearance alongside the white members of the school board would prove substantial symbolic support for Washington's longtime call for biracial cooperation. Their presentations would become an extraordinary accomplishment in Oklahoma, a highly racially segregated state in 1915.[26]

Seeking white people's attendance and participation in the commemoration did not hinder organizers from celebrating Washington's African American culture. In a report to the local newspaper that advertised the scheduled program, they promised that a choir of African American students would sing "Swing Low, Sweet Chariot," allegedly Washington's favorite spiritual. Washington had frequently told Tuskegee Institute students, as well as members of the countless audiences who heard his speeches, of his affinity for spirituals. Organizers of the Muskogee commemoration included several of the hundred graduates of Tuskegee Institute residing in the area. They helped ensure that the other organizers appreciated Washington's professed partiality for plantation melodies and the songs' comprehensive representation of black people's culture.[27]

Predominate African American private primary and secondary schools, like their public counterparts, recognized the death of Washington on the day of his burial. Operating mostly in the South, these included the Greenville (AL) Baptist High School, the Asheville (NC) Allen Industrial Home School, and the Birmingham (AL) St. Mark's Industrial School. Each of these schools timed their respective rites to coincide with the scheduled start of Washington's funeral. Located approximately 85 miles southwest of Tuskegee, the Baptist High School conducted a ceremony that included the entire student body and faculty members as well as "many people of the town." Although few members of the public attended the Allen Industrial Home School commemoration, it seems to have strongly emphasized philanthropy, a Yankee Protestant ethic that Washington might have cherished more than any other. The presentations given during the service inspired the Allen students to donate money to a Winston-Salem, North Carolina, orphanage for black children. They also pledged to make annual contributions thereafter to the orphanage. While Reverend C. W. Brooks, the principal of the St. Mark's Industrial School, seems not to have stressed charity as much as the Allen Industrial Home School memorial presenters did, he accentuated two other aspects of the ethics Washington and his movement promoted. Brooks reminded his students of "the possibilities of life through industry and perseverance."[28]

Hampton Normal and Agricultural Institute (Hampton Institute), the industrial school that had taught those lessons to Washington, commemorated his life. Conducting services that commenced with Washington's funeral rites, the institute honored its most illustrious graduate. At this private industrial and normal school for African Americans, officials had often acknowledged Tuskegee Institute's worldwide prominence and Washington's immense fame during his lifetime. The memorial continued Hampton Institute's recognition of Washington and its longtime close relationship with the late educator. Hampton officials, as well as many other people, considered Tuskegee Institute a direct offspring of Washington's alma mater. A majority of Tuskegee's original teachers had attended the Hampton Institute, and they initially offered a curriculum similar to the one taught there. It, like the one taught at Hampton, emphasized the desirability of the fortunate providing charity to the needy. The Reverend Laurence Fenninger, Hampton Institute's associate chaplain, promoted benevolence in his commemorative address and served as the master of ceremonies. Calling Washington a prophet, Fenninger asserted that the late educator "had eyes that saw, ears that heard and a heart that understood . . . he strove to give sight to blind eyes, to unstop deaf ears, to bind up and fill with hope hearts that were broken. His were gifts that were increased by being shared."[29]

Approximately 60 miles northwest of Hampton, members of the predominately black Virginia Normal and Industrial Institute (now Virginia State University) community also recognized the memory of Washington. The tribute began at 10 A.M. in its Audience Hall. George Washington Owens made the first of four presentations. The first African American graduate of the Kansas State Agricultural College (now Kansas State University), Owens began teaching at the Tuskegee Institute the autumn after receiving his degree in June 1899. Nine years later, he relocated to the Virginia Normal and Industrial Institute and established its Department of Agriculture. In his address, Owens recalled working at Tuskegee Institute with Washington. He asserted that despite "difficulties and desolate surroundings," Washington's perseverance, labor, and ideas gave "to the world perhaps the most practical phase of education known to mankind." Following Owens, an unnamed Virginia Normal and Industrial Institute student presented an inspirational address to "the seven hundred boys and girls now attending this institution." Next, an unidentified former Tuskegee Institute pupil presented "appropriate remarks." The fourth and final speaker, President John M. Gandy, closed the services with comments. Known for his political astuteness, Gandy vigorously praised Washington as well as several other "prominent men of the race."[30]

Other predominantly black–populated, state-supported normal and industrial schools in the South memorialized Washington. The students and staff of Georgia Industrial College in Savannah started their services at 1 P.M., approximately the time of Washington's interment. Organizers of the ceremony placed movement supporter and the head of the school Richard R. Wright Sr. on the program. An Atlanta University graduate and a close friend of Washington, he spoke about the late principal's "life and work." Part of the "appropriate program" that the school's students planned included the reading of excerpts from Washington's writings.[31]

Like the Georgia Industrial College community, the Alabama State Normal School in Montgomery recognized the life and works of Washington. The Freedman's Bureau and the American Missionary Association had established the school at Marion, Alabama, in 1868 as the Lincoln Normal School. It relocated in 1890 to Montgomery after the state legislature renamed it the Alabama State Normal School. Washington initially opposed this relocation, but within a short time, he established a good working relationship with William Burns Paterson, the long-time president of Alabama State Normal School, and native of Scotland who had dropped out of school at the age of twelve. William Beverly became the first black president of the academy after the death of Paterson in November 1915. Intended to accommodate primarily the school's students and staff as well as other supporters of the movement in the Montgomery area who could not "for business reasons . . . go to Tuskegee," the commemoration started at 12 P.M. in the academy chapel.[32]

In northern states, staffs and students at normal and industrial schools like the Institute for Colored Youth (now Cheyney University of Pennsylvania) publicly and collectively expressed grief for the death of Washington. Washington had significantly influenced the evolution of their school. His involvement highlights the movement's influence in the early twentieth century. Richard Humphreys, a Philadelphia abolitionist Quaker who had emigrated from the West Indies, bequeathed $10,000 to establish a school to educate black children. From its inception to 1902, when movement supporters took control of the school, it offered a traditional curriculum. Afterward, its officials reorganized the curriculum, officials purchased a farm, and relocated the institution 20 miles west of Philadelphia.[33]

Washington influenced the school's leadership and curriculum changes. After Fannie Jackson Coppin, the longtime principal, retired, the institute's board of trustees asked Washington to suggest a suitable replacement. He recommended, and the board accepted, Hugh Mason Browne, the former head of the Hampton Institute Physics Department. Browne had taken a Howard University undergraduate degree and a master's as well as a doctorate of divinity from Princeton University. During his tenure, Browne implemented an industrial education curriculum and built an Andrew Carnegie–financed library in 1909. Carnegie, the school's most generous donor, contributed $10,000 for its construction. Four years later, Leslie Pinckney Hill replaced Browne as head of the school. Previously, Hill had taken two degrees from Harvard University before teaching several years at the Tuskegee Institute.[34]

As a leading member of the movement, Hill led the staff and students of the Institute for Colored Youth in commemorating Washington. After conducting "an impressive service," Hill, on behalf of his faculty, informed Margaret Washington that the school had held its own memorial. Although the Institute for Colored Youth lay far from Tuskegee, the faculty believed that the staff and students at the school "might give some expression, however inadequate, immediately to our own sense of bereavement." They seemed to have greatly appreciated Washington's exceptional influence and the movement he led.[35]

Perhaps the teaching staff at the Topeka (Kansas) Industrial and Educational Institute held similar feelings. With a significant number of former Tuskegee Institute teachers and students on its staff, and a curriculum similar to that of the Alabama school, many people referred to the Kansas indus-trial school as the Western Tuskegee. The Topeka institute did not begin as a Tuskegee offshoot. Within a few short years after its founding, however, it became all but an extension of its Alabama predecessor. Edward Stephens, a widely traveled colorful and glib educational entrepreneur, and Lizzie Red-dick, an elementary schoolteacher, cofounded the Topeka Industrial and Educational Institute in 1895. The academy began as a "kindergarten, sewing school, and reading room" for Topeka's small African American population. By 1898, the founders had secured enough donations to purchase a small building within the "black business district." In the following year, the state of Kansas gave the school $1,500. That same year, a group of prominent black citizens, including James Guy, an attorney, and George Shaffer, the minister of St. John African Methodist Episcopal (AME) Church, publicly and vig-orously complained about Stephens's lack of honesty and other moral fail-ings. Responding to the criticism, the state government stopped supporting the school financially, and in 1899 the school's board of trustees dismissed Stephens.[36]

Along with losing its founder and the state's financial contribution, the Topeka Industrial and Educational Institute suffered the death of its primary private benefactor: Eliza Chrisman, a local philanthropist who had made relatively large monetary gifts to the institute. These adversities prompted the trustees to resolve to reorganize and revitalize the school, and reach out to Washington. Agreeing to help, the Tuskegean recommended that the Topeka school hire William R. Carter as principal. A Tuskegee Institute graduate, Carter had taught and preached in several southeastern states.[37]

Under Carter's leadership, the school prospered. He implemented a cur-riculum and teaching technique modeled after that of the Tuskegee Insti-tute. He also hired several teachers who had either taught at or graduated from Washington's school. Carter's management style, the school's program of study, and the pedigree of its instructors seemed to have helped inspire the state of Kansas to resume and even increase its financial support to the institute. These funds allowed the institute to expand and to add additional courses. It subsequently purchased and relocated to a 105-acre plot east of the city and secured two gifts, totaling $15,000, from Andrew Carnegie. Washing-ton's considerable influence helped to improve the campus when he assisted the Topeka institute in its efforts to secure funds to construct a modern academic building, a two-story stone structure for the teaching of several trades, and a girls' dormitory, as well as an assortment of other structures.[38]

Organizers of the institute's memorial service utilized both visual and audio images. They hung pictures of the late principal along the walls of the auditorium and draped them in "the colors of Hampton, Tuskegee and Topeka Institutes." These images demonstrated the origin and continuation of the movement. They symbolically announced that with the training of Washington, Hampton Institute provided the movement with its foundation; the movement launched its cultural war at the Tuskegee Institute; and the Topeka institute would continue the campaign on behalf of the movement.[39]

This effort included lauding Washington's racial identity. The singing of only spirituals at the commemoration reinforced memories of him as a black man. The service began with the spirituals "Roll, Jordan, Roll" and "My Brother's Took His Flight and Gone." Later, the school choir sang "In Bright Mansions Above" and "We Will Walk through the Valley." Organizers closed the memorial with "Lord, I Want to Be a Christian."[40]

Organizers interspersed speeches between spirituals. After the completion of the singing of the first two spirituals, Richard Cunningham, an instructor and former Tuskegee Institute student, offered his eulogy, "Dr. Washington as Seen by the Tuskegee Student." His colleague, J. W. Fentress, followed with "The National Influence of Dr. Washington." Marie Brown Ferguson presented "Dr. Washington as Seen by His Teachers." A Topeka institute teacher and a Hampton Institute graduate, R. E. Malone delivered a lecture on the life and impact of Washington, "Washington as Seen by a Hampton Man." Since Principal William R. Carter had taken ill, M. W. Freeman, the assistant principal of the school, gave the keynote and final address, "Dr. Washington as I Knew Him." Similar to how many African American Protestants preachers augmented their sermons, Freeman sandwiched his eulogy between two popular spirituals.[41]

With less fanfare, predominately black–populated colleges held pageants in honor of Washington. Although twenty-three federal land-grant and state-supported institutions instructed African American students in 1915, only one, Florida Agricultural and Mechanical College, offered college-level courses. For the most part, African American students desiring college-level instruction had to attend one of the several dozen privately owned tertiary schools. The North had only two of these institutions, Lincoln University in Pennsylvania, and Wilberforce University in Ohio, while the South possessed the remaining privately owned colleges established for black students.[42]

Those institutions of higher learning honoring the memory of Washington on the day of his interment included Immanuel College. Located in Greensboro, North Carolina, it consisted of a secondary academy, junior college, and theology school. The Evangelical Lutheran Synodical Conference of the American Lutheran Church had established the college in 1903 at Concord, North Carolina. Two years later, it moved the school to Greensboro, close

to the states' predominately black–populated Agricultural and Technical
College. The conference wanted the school to train black theologians for
predominately African American Lutheran congregations. With Luther-
anism's limited exposure within Africa America, memorializing Washington provided the Lutheran missionaries operating Immanuel College with
a significant opportunity to teach desired values while further enhancing
their church's identification with blacks. The Reverend N. J. Bakke seized
the moment. At 10:00 A.M. in the school's chapel, Bakke, the field secretary
for the Evangelical Lutheran Synodical Conference, spoke to students and
staff about Washington's "life and works."[43]

On the far western side of the former Confederacy, Tillotson College and
Samuel Huston College, two predominately black–populated colleges in Austin, Texas, also had plans to honor Washington. The American Missionary
Association established Tillotson College. Although originally founded in
1846 to help end slavery, the association became the leading freedmen's aid
society in the nation after the Civil War. By 1900, it had established no fewer
than five colleges and forty-three normal schools that instructed African
Americans. The association named the college that it founded at Austin in
1881 after the Reverend George J. Tillotson. Named in honor of a northerner
and not Sam Houston the former governor of Texas, the Southern Education
Society of the Methodist Episcopal Church founded Samuel Huston College
in 1898. Both schools seemed to have conducted their rites only for members
of their respective college's communities.[44]

*   *   *

Supporters of the movement staged memorial rites for the public around
the country in a variety of population centers. Some locations, like Lawrence, Kansas, and Tacoma, Washington, had comparatively small African
American populations, while other urban centers such as New Orleans and
Memphis possessed greater numbers of black residents. Rituals occurred in
the South, Midwest, North, as well as the West. While organizers often conducted the ceremonies in religious edifices, they also staged them in meeting
halls, schools, auditoriums, and libraries. Whereas most often one or more
black persons initiated the call for the commemoration, white people helped
organize some of the rites.

A large majority of the commemorations took place in churches. The U.S.
race relations protocol, especially as whites practiced it in the South, dictated
the exclusion of black people from most public gathering places. Therefore,
African Americans in most areas of the nation did not have access to halls,
other than churches, large enough to accommodate a mass meeting. While

some of the memorials may have occurred in a relatively small number of churches with predominately white membership, the vast majority did not. Predominately black–populated churches hosted most of the rites. The denominational affiliation of congregations hosting the ceremonies included Baptists, Methodists, and Presbyterians. Reflecting black people's preferred affiliations, the commemorations most often occurred in Baptist and Methodist churches.

Both prominent and inconspicuous churches honored Washington. Boston's legendary Peoples Baptist Church and its African Methodist Episcopal Zion (AMEZ) Church held separate memorials. Movement supporters conducted rites at Smith Street Church in Poughkeepsie, New York. They held them at Bethel AME Church in Harrisburg, Pennsylvania, and in the sanctuary of the Central Baptist Church of Pittsburgh. They staged rites at the Zion Baptist Church in Norfolk, Virginia. Supporters residing in the southeastern state of Georgia honored Washington at St. Philip's Methodist Episcopal Church in Savannah and at Somerndike Presbyterian Church in LaFayette. In the mid-South, they memorialized him at the Mount Zion Baptist Church in Knoxville, Tennessee, and at the Ninth Street African Baptist Church in Fort Smith, Arkansas. Like Mount Zion AME Church in Pensacola, Florida, and the Big Zion AMEZ Church in Mobile, Alabama, many churches in the Gulf Coast states hosted commemorations. Movement supporters staged them at Mercy Street Baptist Church in Greenville, Mississippi; the Good Hope Baptist Church of Patterson, Louisiana; and New Orleans's First African Baptist Church.[45]

Supporters in small and large midwestern cities also memorialized Washington. "A number of colored churches throughout" Chicago performed commemorations. Movement supporters in Lawrence, Kansas, held a service at St. Luke's AME Church. In San Antonio, Texas, the Second Baptist Church also planned a tribute to the memory of Washington. Supporters in Los Angeles memorialized him at AMEZ Church. In the Pacific Northwest city of Tacoma, Washington, movement supporters used the local AME church's sanctuary to honor the late educator.[46]

Arrangers of many of these memorials enjoyed no direct connection to Washington. They, however, held Washington in high esteem and strongly supported the movement. Although the Reverend William M. Jones had no tangible ties to Washington, he presided over a commemoration at his Fort Smith (AR) Ninth Street African Baptist Church that the city's Colored Ministerial Conference sponsored. While Joseph B. Bass and his wife, Charlotte Spears Bass, initiated the movement to commemorate Washington in Los Angeles, neither had a direct tie to Washington. The pair owned and edited the *California Eagle*. A few years before marrying Joseph, Charlotte assumed ownership of the newspaper. Shortly thereafter, she hired Joseph to edit the *California Eagle*. He had previously published the *Helena (MT) Plaindealer* and had cofounded the *Topeka (KS) Plaindealer*. In a very short time, these two acquired a reputation of uncompromising pursuit of full citizenship rights for African Americans. Inspiring a community-wide remembrance of Washington helped their effort.[47]

Other arrangers of remembrances who had no personal affiliation with Washington included members of the National Association for the Advancement of Colored People (NAACP). As early as 1944 when Gunnar Myrdal suggested it in *An American Dilemma: The Negro Problem and Modern Democracy*, scholars have generally portrayed the NAACP as the archrival of both Washington and the movement. The organizers of commemorations in Tacoma, Washington, and Harrisburg, Pennsylvania, challenged this assumption. In Tacoma, the Reverend Henry Mansfield Collins, a member of the NAACP, helped organize a memorial held at the Allen Chapel AME Church. Collins had begun preaching at Allen Chapel Church after graduating from Fisk University and Wilberforce University. A Kansas City native, Collins had no institutional, professional, or personal links with Washington. Collins liked what Washington symbolized and chose to identify with him and the movement. Not just one member, but the entire Harrisburg, Pennsylvania, chapter membership manifested a strong endorsement of Washington and his movement. This NAACP chapter arranged the ritual for the late educator at Bethel AME Church in Harrisburg.[48]

While some of the organizers of commemorations taking place in predominately black–populated churches seemed to have possessed only an emotional or ideological affiliation with Washington, many other arrangers had conspicuous connections to him and to the movement. For almost thirty-five years, Washington and his supporters constructed a social, political, and financial network that spanned the United States. More than a few members of this network played leading roles in staging commemorations at churches across the nation. Aaron William Puller, the minister to Boston's Peoples Baptist congregation and a former Tuskegee Institute employee, participated in the planning and production of the memorial held at his church. The Pittsburgh Ministerial Union, which organized and held a memorial at the Central Baptist Church, included George B. Howard, a Hampton Institute schoolmate of Washington, who preached at the church. William M. Reid, a former roommate of Washington at Hampton, assisted with the ritual at Norfolk's Zion Baptist Church. Organizers of the commemoration at the AME Church in Savannah included Walter Sanford Scott, an 1895

Tuskegee Institute graduate and the vice president of a subsidiary of the NNBL, the National Negro Business League. The respective local NNBL chapters sponsored memorials for Washington in Greenville, Mississippi, and San Antonio, Texas. Business league members in Greenville held their commemoration at the Mercy Street Baptist Church, while those living in San Antonio staged one in the sanctuary of that city's Second Baptist Church.[49]

A desire to ensure that locals enshrined the memory of Washington and continued to support the movement motivated a group to organize a memorial at the First African Baptist Church in New Orleans rather than attend the late educator's funeral. Two days after Washington's burial, Robert E. Jones, a fervent black supporter of the movement from New Orleans, telegrammed Emmett Scott. In it, Jones explained why he, Walter L. Cohen, and Alfred Lawless Jr.—the latter two also local movement members—had not attended Washington's burial services because they felt that they "could do more in Mr. Washington's honor" if they remained in New Orleans in order to "conduct a big meeting at the time of his funeral."[50]

The trio, members of the NNBL as well as acquaintances of Booker T. Washington, had helped organize and manage Washington's highly publicized tour of Louisiana in the summer of 1913. Jones, a native of Greensboro, North Carolina, and an ordained Methodist Episcopal preacher who headed the New Orleans black YMCA and edited the influential *Southwestern Christian Advocate*, served on the NNBL's Executive Committee. An insurance broker, member of the local NNBL, and former federal employee, Cohen led the Louisiana Republican Party's black-and-tan faction. Lawless enjoyed an impressive professional life that included both preaching and teaching. At the time of Washington's death, he worked for the American Missionary Association (AMA), supervising the organization's "church work" in Mississippi and Louisiana while raising funds for Straight and Tugaloo Universities, which the AMA had established to educate African Americans.[51]

Local newspaper reports help organizers in New Orleans and elsewhere to attract people to various memorials. Far more white-owned daily papers printed accounts of forthcoming Washington commemorations than did the weekly published African American–oriented journals. In Savannah, Georgia, organizers relied on the support of the white-controlled *News* and *Press* newspapers to provide the public with information about their planned commemoration. The *New Orleans States*, the *Fort Smith (AR) Record*, the *Lawrence (KS) World*, the *San Antonio (TX) Express*, and the *Tacoma (WA) Ledger* are a few of the other white-owned daily newspapers that wrote reports about upcoming tributes. In doing so, they purposely—or, in some cases, inadvertently—enhanced organizers' efforts to immortalize Washington and to promote his movement.[52]

Newspapers provided other supporters with the time that the organizers intended for the services to start. Arrangers established several times to begin their respective commemorations. Like those persons who orchestrated the closing of businesses and staged rites at many of the schools, organizers of commemorations held at predominately black–populated churches often elected to start honoring Washington at either 10 A.M. or 11 A.M. Although railroad companies had standardized time zones in 1883, federal law would not mandate that the public follow suit until 1918. Without standardized time zones, arrangers of Washington's memorials could not know the local hour that corresponded with the start of his funeral. Reports of the wrong time may have confused organizers' commemorations. The uncertainty contributed to the decision of groups of organizers in various locations to initiate ceremonies at different times during the morning. The commemoration held in Norfolk, Virginia, began at 10 A.M. Organizers in Tennessee (Knoxville), Louisiana (Alexandria), and Kansas (Lawrence) selected the same hour, whereas arrangers in Arkansas (Fort Smith) and Washington (Tacoma) started their rituals at 11 A.M.[53]

Other African American movement supporters staging rituals at predominately black churches scheduled these later in the day. While a number of organizers selected times that would easily accommodate schoolchildren, other arrangers attempted to hold commemorations at hours that would maximize the number of adult attendees. With local pupils in mind, organizers in San Antonio scheduled the memorial in the Second Baptist Church to begin at 1 P.M. Members of the NNBL, the organizers of the proposed commemoration, publicly asserted that "the negro [sic] schools of the city" would cease classes at noon so students could attend. Displaying their interest in maximizing the attendance of working people as well as students, movement supporters in Greenville, Mississippi, and Savannah, Georgia, started their respective memorials after 8 P.M. Remembrances that occurred after the time of the funeral in Tuskegee clearly manifested their arrangers' desires to use their constructed memory of Washington to instruct and influence the behavior of the greatest number of blacks as possible.[54]

Movement supporters flocked to Booker T. Washington commemorations. Like those who attended his funeral, they came to memorials held at churches for a number of reasons. Sensing the potential for a large gathering, arrangers like those in San Antonio, Texas, predicted that "all negro [sic] citizens will turn out" to honor Washington. In Charleston, West Virginia, arrangers publicly asserted that "leading negro citizens from all parts of the State" would attend the memorial conducted in the sanctuary of the Second Baptist Church. Organizers of rites staged at the First African Baptist Church in New Orleans proclaimed that their event successfully attracted a "representative gathering" who participated in "a most impressive and solemn occasion." African American supporters of the movement who attended the memorial held at Norfolk's Zion Baptist Church overfilled the edifice's "main auditorium, lecture room and gallery." A remembrance at the Mount Zion Baptist Church in Knoxville, Tennessee, attracted "a large audience," as did one at the Somerndike Presbyterian Church in LaFayette, Georgia. At the Mount Zion AME Church in Pensacola, Florida, almost two thousand supporters commemorated Washington.[55]

✴   ✴   ٭

Persons who presided over these gatherings reflected organizers' attempts at constructing commemorations that maximized the effectiveness of the lessons presented. From the start of the program to its end, arrangers attempted to present prayers, songs, poems, speeches, and persons that seemingly represented desired values and ideas. In pursuit of this goal, organizers selected local prominent African American men to serve as masters of ceremonies. No woman played this role in any of the commemorations. The men selected enjoyed above average esteem and material success. Their prestige enhanced the efforts of organizers to concretize preferred aspects of the Yankee Protestant ethic for audiences.

Arrangers selected masters of ceremonies from diverse vocations. Organizers in both Mobile, Alabama, and Harrisburg, Pennsylvania, chose physicians to symbolize their objectives: H. Roger Williams in Mobile, and C. Lennon Carter in Harrisburg. The president of the Mobile Business League, an affiliate of the NNBL, Williams moved to Alabama after he graduated from Walden University and Meharry Medical School in Nashville, Tennessee. Before his college career, Williams had lived and secured training as a printer in New Haven, Connecticut. Carter graduated from Wayland Seminary in Washington, D.C., and the College of Physicians and Surgeons of Boston. After relocating to Harrisburg, he served as vice president of the Pennsylvania National Medical Association.[56]

Preachers most often served as masters of ceremonies. Although some groups of arrangers, like those who conducted a memorial at the Zion Baptist Church in Norfolk, Virginia, chose educators as masters of ceremonies, organizers commonly picked ministers who had attained an above-average formal education. Historical realities and racial protocol predetermined that most of these men received some, if not all, of their formal training from Protestant educators. White Yankees, or their black disciples, had taught the African American preachers who served as masters of ceremonies for Booker T. Washington memorials. Some of them, including T. D. Lee, who presided over the commemoration held at St. Luke's AME Church in Topeka, Kansas, attended industrial institutes. Lee graduated from Hampton Institute, a normal school. Other hosts had taken college degrees, as well. A. W. Puller, the master of ceremonies at the People's Baptist Church in Boston, graduated from Bucknell University; and the preacher who presided at Allen Chapel Church in Tacoma, Washington, Henry Mansfield Collins, graduated from Fisk University. Regardless of the type of school or its location, the white teachers and their black counterparts strongly promoted the Yankee Protestant ethic. With their above-average schooling, the pastors displayed a greater amount of leadership skills than less-educated blacks did. Such virtues, coupled with their alleged divine calling to represent the interests of God among both the nonbelievers and the faithful, provided many preachers with significant status. More so than any other factors, this perceived prestige seemed to have inspired organizers of commemorations to select ministers to direct many services that honored Booker T. Washington.[57]

Masters of ceremonies at all of the memorials held in churches helped to interlace music skillfully with other aspects of the remembrance program. At many of the memorials, music greeted attendees upon entering the auditorium. Organizers at the Big Zion AMEZ Church in Mobile, Alabama, for example, started their commemoration with a song. A choir at the service at the Good Hope Baptist Church in Patterson, Louisiana, sang the hymn "Nearer My God to Thee." The popularity of that hymn transcended race. Both black and white Protestants often performed it. A Briton, Sarah Flower Adams, had written the hymn for her pastor, William J. Fox, the renowned Unitarian minister and member of the British Parliament. It became even more popular after an account circulated about President William McKinley's last words: "nearer, my God, to Thee."[58]

Arrangers who did not begin their services with a song made strategic use of music during the memorials. The memorials that occurred at the Mount Zion Baptist Church in Knoxville, Tennessee, and at the First African Baptist Church in New Orleans, for example, presented programs "consisting of appropriate music." These services and other commemorations manifested recognition of the power of music on the human psyche; it often reinforced or changed its listeners' feelings about themselves and their surroundings. Acknowledging music's general appeal, advertisements for upcoming memorials, like the ones promoting memorials at St. Phillips AME Church in Savannah, Georgia, and at Allen Chapel AME Church in Tacoma, Washington, emphasized the musical segments of their proposed remembrances. Organists contributed to the musical performances at several commemorations. Some programs offered only one or two musical pieces; other services integrated instrumentals and songs throughout the tribute. While most programs presented a choir consisting of members of the host church or various groups of schoolchildren, a number of memorials included songs that individuals or small groups performed. Several tributes, including the one at the Good Hope Baptist Church in Patterson, Louisiana, featured congregational singing.[59]

Many musical selections represented both the U.S. Protestant traditions and the wide, transracial appeal of Washington and his movement. As had the organizers of his burial rites, arrangers of these memorials included the singing of Protestant hymns. While promoting mourning and conveying the Protestant concepts of a worry-free life and the heavenly rewards of peace and love for the righteous and faithful, the hymns helped attendees conceptualize the memory of Washington. Either consciously or not, organizers selected hymns that meaningfully contributed to the projection of the living Washington as an honored member of society. Soloists, trios, choirs, and congregations sang hymns promoting the Protestantism that Washington shared with the majority of African Americans and whites alike. They performed many hymns that white Protestants wrote, including "Asleep in Jesus," "Lead, Kindly Light," "Nearer, My God, to Thee," "Peace, Perfect Peace," and "What a Friend We Have in Jesus." Frequently preformed at funeral services, the communal words of these Protestant hymns conveyed messages of absolute sorrow while also promising eternal well-being for both white and black believers.[60]

Organizers did not exclude spirituals from the music program. While the Yankee Protestant tradition may have influenced the creation of many spirituals, their lyrical construction, dual messages, and polyrhythms emerged from the African American musical tradition. Serving the same purpose as hymns, spirituals provided listeners with a more emotional, if not, uplifting sensation. Like Washington, a countless number of black people embraced these folk songs. Spirituals such as "Swing Low, Sweet Chariot," which a trio sang during the commemoration held at the Somerndike Presbyterian Church in LaFayette, Georgia, and "Steal Away to Jesus," which choirs of schoolchildren performed at the Zion Baptist Church in Norfolk, Virginia, acknowledged Washington's African American heritage and the Christianity that most blacks embraced.[61]

Some memorials began with a prayer of invocation, and many of them ended the service with one. The organizers' piety, the nature of the rites, and the location of the memorials inspired arrangers to incorporate several aspects of worship services held at Protestant churches. Since public praying is an integral part of Christian rituals, organizers arranged for one or more preachers to offer prayers during the memorials. The Reverend M. Wooten presented the opening prayer at the St. Luke AME Church in Lawrence, Kansas; in the midst of the service at the Good Hope Baptist Church in Patterson, Louisiana, the Reverend J. C. Rochelle offered his; and the Reverend F. C. Campbell provided the benediction at the Norfolk (Virginia) Zion Baptist Church. Even though the Bible makes conflicting assertions about the appropriateness of praying in public (see, e.g., John 11:41 and Acts 20:36), the practice helps create a desired atmosphere while inspiring listeners to embrace preferred beliefs.[62]

Scripture reading enhanced that effort. As Protestant Christians, organizers strongly believed in the necessity of the faithful possessing firsthand knowledge of the words of God as written in the Bible. Christians, especially Protestants, often displayed a robust faith in the power of biblical text to influence beliefs and behaviors of persons who have read or heard the Word. In reading scripture during the memorials, organizers continued an old tradition among Christians and their Jewish predecessors. In both the Old and New Testaments, examples of public uttering of sacred texts are found. The first biblical report of someone publicly reading scripture occurs in the Old Testament book of 2 Kings 22:3. Several passages in the New Testament, especially John 8:32, vigorously encourage the wide dissemination of the Holy Word "If you make my word your home, you will be my disciples. You will know the truth and the truth will set you free." Since many attendees, as Christians, believed that "all scripture is God-breathed," these words resonated with former slaves and their descendants. The public utterance of scripture manifested both the organizers' dedication to religious tradition and personal freedom. The program at Bethel AME Church in Harrisburg, Pennsylvania; Big Zion AMEZ Church in Mobile, Alabama; and at the Good Hope Baptist Church in Patterson, Louisiana, included scriptural readings.[63]

Reading scripture, performing music, and uttering prayers combined to construct a desired context for eulogizing Booker T. Washington and promoting the movement. Using selected remembrances and interpretations of the man's life, arrangers used these memorials primarily to teach attendees a favored set of values and a desired pattern of behavior. However, eulogies taught these lessons more directly and arguably more effectively than any other aspect of the commemorations. Some of the speakers lectured. That is what John A. Brashear did at the memorial in the Central Baptist Church in Pittsburgh, Pennsylvania. Other orators, like the Reverend F. D. Williams, during the commemoration at the Good Hope Baptist Church in Patterson, Louisiana, delivered sermons that eulogized Washington. Focusing on his Christianity, his teaching, his publications, and his ability to inspire, A. B. Singfield delivered a eulogy at St. Philip's Methodist Episcopal Church in Savannah, Georgia, titled "The Agitator."[64]

*   *   *

Several secular auditoriums, too, hosted gatherings of Booker T. Washington commemorators. Although movement supporters in Muskogee, Oklahoma, conducted a memorial in the town's convention hall, a much more impressive one took place at Church's Auditorium in Memphis, Tennessee. Members of the local NNBL organized the Memphis tribute and timed the start of the ritual to coincide with the beginning of Washington's funeral. The service took place in the auditorium that Robert R. Church Sr., the son of a slave woman and a white riverboat captain, built in 1899. Before he died in 1912, Church had amassed more than a million dollars of assets. Widely regarded as the first African American millionaire, he invested most of his wealth in Memphis real estate. At a cost of $50,000, Church built his auditorium and an adjoining park. Designed to seat 2,500 persons, NNBL organizers attracted approximately five thousand black and white people to Church's Auditorium for the ceremony.[65]

Many factors contributed to the large assembly. Countless African Americans in the Memphis area held Washington in high esteem, and the presence of many of them at the services demonstrated a widespread desire to honor his endeavors and memory. Some of Memphis's most accomplished African American men and women held membership in the local NNBL. Their community standing helped to legitimize the ceremony and attract a cross-section of local blacks as well as several white officials. G. N. McCormick, a spokesman for the mayor and Dr. A. A. Kincannon, superintendent of public schools, attended. Kincannon had received permission from the Memphis Board of Education to declare "a holiday in all the colored schools so that the teachers and students" could attend the memorial. The *Memphis (TN) Appeal* and *Scimitar* newspapers, on the day before the event, published reports informing readers of the upcoming program, inspiring many of them to attend the service.[66]

Members of the audience experienced a focused ceremony. With Bert M. Roddy, a NNBL member and bookkeeper for the black-owned Solvent Savings Bank, as master of ceremonies, organizers initiated the service with music. A choral class from the Howe Institute, a private academy that offered the first high school curriculum for black students in Memphis, sang John Henry Newman's "Lead, Kindly Light," a hopeful and optimistic song. Afterward, the Reverend J. A. Lindsey, pastor of Avery AME Church, led the audience in prayer.[67]

Following Lindsey's heavenly plea, the orchestra of W. C. Handy, the "father of the blues," accompanied a mass singing of "Lift Every Voice and Sing." Brothers James Weldon Johnson and J. Rosamond Johnson wrote the song for the February 12, 1900, celebration of the birthday of Abraham Lincoln held in Jacksonville, Florida. Within a few years, "Lift Every Voice and Sing," had become known as the "Afro-American Hymn" (later as the "Black National Anthem"). Without identifying any specific group of people, the song proclaims past tribulations, faith in the present, and hopes for the future.

> Lift ev'ry voice and sing,
> 'Til earth and heaven ring,
> Ring with the harmonies of Liberty;
> Let our rejoicing rise
> High as the list'ning skies,
> Let it resound loud as the rolling sea.
> Sing a song full of the faith that the dark past has taught us,
> Sing a song full of the hope that the present has brought us;
> Facing the rising sun of our new day begun,
> Let us march on 'til victory is won.
>
> Stony the road we trod,
> Bitter the chastening rod,
> Felt in the days when hope unborn had died;
> Yet with a steady beat,
> Have not our weary feet
> Come to the place for which our fathers sighed?
> We have come over a way that with tears has been watered,
> We have come, treading our path through the blood of the slaughtered,
> Out from the gloomy past,
> 'Til now we stand at last
> Where the white glean of our bright star is cast.
>
> God of our weary years,
> God of our silent tears,
> Thou who has brought us thus far on the way;
> Thou who has by Thy might
> Led us into the light,
> Keep us forever in the path, we pray.
> Lest our feet stray from the place, our God, where we met Thee;

Shadowed beneath Thy hand,
May we forever stand.
True to our God,
True to our native land.

This song deftly expressed the core tenets of Washington and his movement's public teachings.[68]

Providing comfort to the mourners, the Howe Choral performed the hymn "In the Upper Garden" and a version of the spiritual "In the Sweet By-and-By." The singing of the latter both recognized the Tuskegean's affinity for plantation melodies and, as an indigenous African American folk song, reinforced black group consciousness. "In the Sweet By-and-By," like "Lift Every Voice and Sing," assisted ritual planners in making the ceremony in Church's Auditorium a communal experience for African Americans.[69]

Six black male speakers of diverse backgrounds made short presentations. The group included the Reverend I. S. Lee, an AME preacher; Edward Cliffinger, principal of the Lemoyne Institute; J. M. Jones, principal of a public school; T. H. Johnson, president of Woodstock Training School; the Reverend R. J. Petty, entrepreneur and minister of the Macedonia Baptist Church; and M. V. Lynk, president of the University of West Tennessee. All gave talks relevant to the occasion, but for the sake of brevity, each speech lasted no longer than three minutes.[70]

Four leading members of the NNBL presented longer addresses. A local teacher, D. W. Cary, discussed Washington's work as an educator. The pastor of Metropolitan Baptist Church in Memphis, L. J. Searcy focused on the Tuskegean as an entrepreneur. Wookstock Training School president and spokesperson for the local NNBL chapter, T. J. Johnson, presented "an excellent tribute to the deceased educator." Author and pastor of Tabernacle Baptist Church in Memphis, Sutton E. Griggs, made the closing address, which "drew many lessons from the life of Washington, and urged his hearers to emulate his virtues and support the principles for which he stood." Before Handy's orchestra played the recessional, organizers read several resolutions glorifying Washington.[71]

*   *   *

Nationwide, supporters lionized Washington in proclamations. Commencing the day of his death, sympathizers, like the Chicago Federation of Colored Organization adopted declarations. Any number of groups, both black and white, and not just persons attending commemorations, adopted and sent resolutions to the survivors of Washington. Some groups also sent copies to newspapers for publication. On the day before Washington's burial, black students at Iowa State University adopted a proclamation expressing grief, sympathy, and memories of Washington. Their resolutions, as well as others, reinforced both emotional and philosophical identification with the late Washington and the surviving leaders of the movement.[72]

A diverse collection of persons residing throughout the nation, some of them attending commemorations while others did not, sent declarations that acknowledged Washington's commanding position within black America. Attendees of a memorial that occurred at the St. Paul AME Church in Houston, Texas, adopted a resolution that teachers at the city's Booker T. Washington School wrote. It proclaimed Washington "one of our . . . most noted . . . leaders." Members of the Providence (Rhode Island) Westminster Lodge embraced him as a "friend and leader, whose fellowship was an honor to enjoy and whose leadership was a pleasure to follow." While members of the Negro Employees of Los Angeles called Washington the "greatest leader" of the race, a small group of blacks who had relocated from Alabama to St. Louis adopted a resolution calling for "other Leaders of the Negro Race" to emulate him.[73]

For the majority of mourners, supporting the resolutions concluded their participation in the first nationwide day of commemoration for an African American—a remarkable occurrence! Although NNBL leaders had promoted business closures on the day of Washington's funeral, no person or group called for or coordinated these local tributes. This lack of central coordination in the staging and execution of the various tributes testifies to the local spontaneity of the events. The loss of Washington—the African American most closely associated with the decades-long culture war to convince southerners, particularly blacks, to replace their ethic with Yankee Protestants values—inspired thousands of blacks and a much smaller number of racially liberal whites to participate in countless commemorations. Their involvement in the widespread remembrances of Washington helped to construct and reinforce locally desired memories of the man and his work. Attendees of a memorial service, like the one held at the First Baptist Church in Little Rock, Arkansas, affirmed their support for industrial education, Washington's primary instrument to teach Yankee Protestant doctrines. Their resolution asserted that the congregation would support and strengthen its "abiding faith in the end and wisdom relative to industrial training for the masses," which Booker T. Washington "most ably defended, the value of which is daily being seen."[74]

Figure 1. Sometime in August 1915, a now-unidentified newspaper published the last known photograph of Booker T. Washington, posing with a number of longtime key members of the National Negro Business League. Reproduced from the collection of the Library of Congress

Figure 2. Booker T. Washington's grave near Dorothy Hall. Photograph by Arthur P. Bedou, Xavier University of Louisiana Archives and Special Collections

Figure 3. Funeral procession for Booker T. Washington. Photograph by Arthur P. Bedou, Xavier University of Louisiana Archives and Special Collections

Figure 4. Booker T. Washington's tomb, adjacent to the original Tuskegee Institute chapel, circa winter 1915. Tuskegee University Archives, Tuskegee University

Figure 5. Tuskegee Institute student cadet honor guards flank Booker T. Washington's casket in the chapel. Tuskegee University Archives, Tuskegee University

Figure 6. Flower arrangements accompany Booker T. Washington's casket as his remains lie in state in the Tuskegee Institute chapel. Tuskegee University Archives, Tuskegee University

Figure 7. Teachers' cottages at Greenwood, Alabama (near Tuskegee). Undated. Reproduced from Booker T. Washington Papers, box 933, Library of Congress

Figure 8. Booker T. Washington, at a Macon County, Alabama, tenant's house. 1914. Reproduced from Booker T. Washington Papers, box 933, Tuskegee Records, Photographs, Macon County, Alabama, Library of Congress

Figure 9. Clinton J. Calloway, director of Tuskegee Institute extension service, interviews the head of family in front of a dogtrot, or breezeway, log cabin. 1912. Reproduced from Booker T. Washington Papers, box 933, Tuskegee Records, Photographs, Macon County, Alabama, Library of Congress

Figure 10. Booker T. Washington's house, the Oaks. Undated. Tuskegee University Archives, Tuskegee University

Figure 11. The original chapel at the Tuskegee Institute. Undated. Tuskegee University Archives, Tuskegee University

Figure 12. Booker T. Washington astride Dexter on the Tuskegee Institute campus. Undated. Reproduced from the collections of the Library of Congress

Figure 13. Booker T. Washington. Undated. Reproduced from the collections of the Library of Congress

5. "Sermon Tonight on Booker T. Washington"

Months of Commemorations and Eulogies

Commemorations for Washington did not stop after his burial. While the greatest number of the memorials occurred during the three months following his November 17, 1915, funeral, groups of Tuskegee movement supporters staged memorials for the better of a year. During the days between the interment and August 1916, blacks and whites throughout the nation organized commemorations in venues ranging from places of worship to secular halls. Like all of the memorials, with the exception of the funeral, arrangers selected persons to present tributes honoring the memory of Washington. These eulogists possessed diverse personal histories and economic standings. Ordinarily an official eulogy is given at a funeral. For reasons never fully explained, organizers chose not to eulogize Washington during his burial rites. Arrangers did state that in the process of following the wishes of Washington, they would keep his funeral simple. Whether or not organizers believed that a eulogy would betray this objective is unclear. A service without a eulogy, however, would reduce the possibility of spontaneous outbursts of grief. Funeral organizers had made it clear that they desired to conduct what one observer called an "Episcopal burial service": a stoic, emotionless funeral. Even so, one or two of the songs performed during the ritual did inspire widespread weeping.[1]

Tuskegee movement supporters who subsequently eulogized Washington did not attempt to control emotions. They primarily sought to extol Washington in a manner that would perpetuate his Tuskegee movement. For the most part, organizers of the tributes in the months after Washington's burial acted spontaneously and independently of any command center. While these tributes manifested a widespread sense of loss and hopefulness, they—more so than the countless letters of solace, published obituaries, printed comments, and funeral attendees—signified the desire among a substantial portion of the nation's leadership class to perpetuate, enhance, and promote the Tuskegee movement. Prominent local, regional, and national businessmen, politicians, educators, and theologians, black and white, publicly praised Washington and the movement he had led. They spoke to an undocumented number of people across the nation. Although the individual motives of each of the numerous eulogists is not known, their combined presentations helped to maintain the essence of the movement while championing it to thousands of eager listeners.

Eulogists William Henry Lewis, however, proclaimed his motive. He declared on a cold wintery January 30, 1916, night, at a memorial held at St. Bartholomew's Church in Cambridge, Massachusetts, that he idolized Washington and that the late educator had become his friend whom he loved and worshiped as no other man that he had "ever known, save only" his father. While not as well-known today as such luminaries as Julius N. Rosenwald, Theodore Roosevelt, William H. Taft, Madame C. J. Walker, and other celebrities who eulogized Washington, Lewis enjoyed some national prestige. Many Americans, especially blacks, knew him as a former All-American collegian football player and the first African American assistant U.S. attorney general. No other African American had ever attained such a powerful federal position. Lewis once belonged to a group of college-educated men and women known as the Boston Radicals, who fervently disagreed with Washington's civic, social, and political views. A onetime prominent member of the group, Lewis once told Washington to return to the South and leave "matters political" to him and other radicals. His admiration of Washington began to blossom several years after he made his infamous dismissive remarks. It seems as though the ideas that Washington represented had inspired Lewis to become a leading proponent of the Tuskegee movement.[2]

Lewis had experienced a Horatio Alger–like life. Born in 1868 to former enslaved parents who raised him in Portsmouth, Virginia, Lewis, after graduating from public schools in 1884, enrolled in the Virginia Normal and Collegiate Institute's preparatory school. Dismissed for protesting the firing of John Mercer Langston, the institute's president, Lewis subsequently earned admission to Amherst College in Massachusetts. There he thrived both academically and athletically. Having graduated from Amherst College, one of America's most prestigious liberal arts colleges, he entered Harvard Law School. While a law student, Lewis joined the Harvard football team, becoming the school's first black varsity athlete. After he stopped playing, Lewis helped coach the team.[3]

Lewis, who went on to practice law and win three elections to the Cambridge Common Council and one to the Massachusetts House of Representatives, desired better race relations in the United States. His yearning helped inspire Lewis to transform his views concerning Washington and his movement. A few years prior to Lewis's leaving elective politics after suffering a defeat at the polls, Theodore Roosevelt, a fellow Harvard College alumnus and football enthusiast, replied to a letter that the black lawyer had written to him. Roosevelt's reply hinted that Lewis should consult with Washington about ways to lessen the degradation of black people. Roosevelt asserted that, since the policies of Reconstruction failed, "I am at my wits' end to know what to advise." He subsequently asked Lewis if he knew Washington, "a man for whom I have the highest regard and in whose judgment I have much faith. I wish that I could meet him and talk the matter over." At the close of the letter, Roosevelt expressed a desire to meet with Lewis, Washington, and Paul Dunbar to "talk the matter over at length." The governor's aspirations and the encouragement Lewis received from his wife, Elizabeth, a former Wellesley College student, seemed to have inspired him to contact Washington.[4]

Coincidentally, W. E. B. Du Bois had encouraged Washington to contact Lewis. Their letters crossed in the mail. Washington wrote to the attorney in early October 1901 that he believed the two of them would one day occupy positions to "serve the race effectually, and while it is very probable that we shall always differ as to detail methods of lifting up the race, it seems to me that if we agree in each doing our best to lift it up the main point will have been gained." Lewis replied that it delighted him to learn that their minds worked "in the same direction, as you had intended writing me before receiving mine of recent date." He asserted that he could not communicate to Washington the pleasure that he felt upon learning of the educator's "continued interest and good will." Lewis agreed with Washington's speculation that they could "work for the common end effectually, and without friction."[5]

Their relationship matured from the mere exchange of letters to one of significant mutual benefit. Over the next fourteen years, Washington, who constantly looked for talented African Americans to recognize publicly and promote, championed Lewis and his career. In turn, Lewis worked for and with the Tuskegee movement. Washington commissioned Lewis to perform legal work during 1902. With Washington's endorsement, and after he suffered his last electoral defeat, President Roosevelt appointed Lewis assistant U.S. attorney for the Boston area. Eight years later, President William Taft, with strong encouragement from Washington, appointed Lewis as a U.S. assistant attorney general. While working for the federal government, Lewis became an active member of the National Negro Business League (NNBL). He toured southern states with Washington and wrote a published account of their 1910 travels through North Carolina. Three years after the tour, Washington published an article in the *American Magazine* that lauded Lewis's life. Washington supported Lewis, and the Harvard man provided the Tuskegee movement with his talents and energy.[6]

When Lewis delivered his heartfelt eulogy of Washington on that cold January night, he had already acquired a considerable reputation as a masterful speaker. Author William A. Farris, a contemporary of Lewis, called the lawyer a "second Daniel Webster" with a thunderous "Niagara voice." Lewis would, almost a decade later, employ his oratory skills to hold "spellbound" a crowded Massachusetts State Legislature gallery during a speech in recognition of Abraham Lincoln's birthday.[7]

*   *   *

Placing eulogists in churches and other respected places increased the significance of commemorations. The tribute that Lewis delivered, as well as many of the other ones, occurred in esteemed venues. Generally, attendees place greater value on events offered within or close proximity to prestigious edifices than they do to those that are not. Although several Washington memorials occurred in New York City, none of them enjoyed as much public interest as did the one that took place in the opulent Carnegie Hall. Although supporters secured access to some grand locations, the vast majority of the eulogies occurred in modest surroundings. Leading members of the movement, however, gave tributes to Washington in some of the most prestigious venues available. It seems as though these distinguished spaces reinforced the importance of the eulogy and the person being praised. The location of these public proclamations mattered.

With the exception of Church's Auditorium in Memphis, the City Hall auditorium in Dallas, and the Majestic Theater in Waco, Texas, only a few meeting halls in the South accommodated them. Providing few special dispensations, the ritual of segregation dictated that whites restricted black people's access to southern public and private spaces. While many whites living in the South respected Washington, and some of them even held him in high regard, a significant number did not. During the last decade of his life, a cadre of notable white southern articulators voiced very strong negative sentiments about Washington and his activities. These effectively persuasive opinion makers reinforced the intense racism that helped to ensure that few commemorators of Washington would deliver eulogies in white-owned southern venues.[8]

While the North had more large meeting halls, the protocol of race and not the scarcity of accommodations prohibited the holding of memorials in many buildings in the South with spacious gathering places. Although racial segregation existed in the North, segregation seemed not to restrict markedly the types of places available to movement supporters for the delivery of tributes: they used the Shrine Auditorium in Los Angeles; the Woman's Christian Temperance Union Hall in Stockton, California; the Courthouse Assembly Hall in Minneapolis, Minnesota; Memorial Hall in Dayton, Ohio; the Wanamaker University Hall in Philadelphia; Carnegie Hall in New York City; and Symphony Hall in Boston. The greater and more opulent the space, the more prestige the eulogists and their messages achieved.[9]

Supporters presented the vast majority of the Washington tributes in less auspicious spaces. These relatively modest structures included meeting halls on college campuses. While numerous institutions of higher education hosted eulogies, no predominately white one did. The esteem many leaders of these schools awarded Washington did not seem to inspire them to honor the educator posthumously. White men, though, headed the vast majority of predominately black–populated colleges, and several of them provided space on their campuses for eulogizing Washington. For example, memorials took place in Austin, Texas, at Tillotson College, an AMA–funded school; and at Samuel Huston College, a Methodist Episcopal Church institution. In Mississippi, the president at Rust College, a liberal arts institution affiliated with the Northern Methodist Church, hosted a commemoration. The president at Immanuel College in Concord, North Carolina, sponsored a tribute to Washington. At Howard University in Washington, D.C., the school's white president permitted eulogists to present tributes in the impressive Rankin Memorial Chapel. These men grasped the value that a sizable segment of the local African American community, particularly their students and staff, placed on the life and works of the Tuskegean.[10]

African American leaders of other tertiary schools did not fail to comprehend that reality. In efforts to accommodate the desires of members of their institution's community, they too provided space to Washington's eulogists. Hightower T. Kealing, a strong supporter of Washington, former editor of the *AME Church Review* and president of that denomination's Western University in Kansas City, Kansas, hosted eulogists. A Washington champion, Richard Wright Sr., the president of Savannah State College, accommodated persons honoring the Tuskegean on his campus. Martin A. Menafee, the president of Voorhees Industrial School, an offshoot of Tuskegee Institute in Denmark, South Carolina, allowed a tribute. The heads of Cheyney Training School for Teachers in Pennsylvania and the Topeka Industrial and Educational Institute in Kansas arranged for speeches honoring Washington to take place on their campuses. The principals of both Hampton and Tuskegee Institutes authorized the delivery of formal speeches that venerated the life of Washington. While Tuskegee Institute waited until December 11, 1915, to eulogize Washington, Hampton Institute presented a tribute the day of his burial.[11]

Movement supporters rendered eulogies in both secondary and elementary public schools' auditoriums, as well. For years after the publication of *Up from Slavery*, countless public school officials held Washington up to their students as an ideal American culture warrior. He and the Tuskegee movement promoted an educational model that these officials believed would assist in the production of a desired society. Like Washington and his movement, they too favored a curriculum that stressed the dignity of labor and other selected aspects of the Yankee Protestant ethic. These officials, however, seemed to have misunderstood one of the other core principles of Washington's curriculum. The movement taught African Americans to value and foster entrepreneurism. As early as April 1888, Booker T. Washington delivered a speech at Lincoln University in Pennsylvania in which he asserted that "even the most prejudiced and bitter white man likes to comment with local pride on the business success of a colored man in his locality." Twenty-one years later, in a speech made at Fisk University, Washington asserted, "By the side of the teacher and minister we must have in an increasing number, the independent farmer, the real estate dealer, the mechanic, manufacturer, the merchant, the banker, and other kinds of business men and women." These proclamations countered the objectives of many leading education policy makers in the nation. Education reformers like James E. Russell, the dean of Teacher's College in New York City, wanted to limit young Americans' ambitions to become self-employed and instead accept their plight as industrial workers. He asked members of the 1908 National Education Association Symposium, "How can a nation endure that deliberately seeks to rouse ambitions and aspirations in the oncoming generations which in the nature of events cannot possibly be fulfilled? If the chief object of government be to promote civil order and social stability, how can we justify our practice in schooling the masses in precisely the same manner as we do those who are to be our leaders?"[12]

It is conceivable that a significant number of movement supporters staging memorials in public schools agreed with Russell. Indeed, Washington's death occurred during an era in which public officials began to encourage the community at large to utilize unclaimed spaces in school buildings. Many groups of supporters sought and received permission to deliver eulogies in school assembly halls. While the majority of the homages occurred at predominately black–populated academies, an ample number transpired at institutions with prevailing white student bodies, including Schenectady (NY) High School; Hutchinson High School in Buffalo, New York; Trenton (NJ) High School, as well as Norwalk High School in South Norwalk, Connecticut. Several different types of predominately African American–populated secondary schools hosted tributes. Comprehensive high schools (secondary schools that taught college as well as workplace-bound students) such as Clark Street High School in Evansville, Indiana; Summer High School in Kansas City, Missouri; and Summer High School in St. Louis, Missouri, accommodated eulogists. They joined the Colored Normal and High School in Louisville, Kentucky, and the Industrial High School in Birmingham, Alabama.[13]

Elementary schools afforded supporters considerably more possible venues than high schools. Whereas the movement to build public high schools did not accelerate until after the Civil War, Americans had initiated the crusade for the massive establishment of state-owned common or elementary schools in northern states during the early 1820s. In southern states, however, public elementary schools did not become ubiquitous until the Reconstruction era. For the most part, the quality and size of southern school buildings in 1915 and 1916, especially the ones black students attended, did not match those in the North. Although southern common schools designated for white students did not host eulogists that honored Washington, many northern elementary institutions with a primarily white student body did. These academies included rural schools like those located in Allen County, Ohio, as well as large urban ones similar to Public School No. 11 in Jersey City, New Jersey. They joined the countless predominately black–populated common schools in the South in hosting supporters who eulogized Washington. All of the "colored public schools" in New Orleans provided both time and space to Washington eulogists. Other public schools designated for black students that allowed for the honoring of Washington included those in Biloxi, Mississippi; Knoxville, Tennessee; Mobile, Alabama; Paris, Texas; Sparta, Georgia; and Vicksburg, Mississippi.[14]

In a number of urban areas, Young Men's Christian Associations (YMCAs) provided space for tributes. The Malden, Massachusetts, association hosted a Washington eulogist, as did the YMCAs in Springfield, Massachusetts, and Topeka, Kansas. Even in Madras, India, a group of association members paid a public eulogy to Washington. Established in the United States in 1851, seven years after its founding in England, the YMCA had become a significant cultural force in the United States. Originally the association only sought to unite like-minded young white middle-class male evangelical Protestants. When Washington died in 1915, YMCAs had become far more comprehensive: the association had begun recruiting industrial workers, Native Americans, and African Americans. It even sent recruiters to India and other non-Western areas of the world. Engaging these groups reflected the YMCA's acute concern with social stability, especially in the English-speaking world.[15]

Washington had experienced a long association with the YMCA, which he had assisted with its "Negro Work." Washington believed that the association reinforced many of the Yankee Protestant ethics that he and his movement promoted. During a well-received speech that he delivered at the Washington, D.C., Colored YMCA a year before his renowned 1895 Atlanta Cotton States Exposition address, he asserted that the association taught African Americans "how it is possible to make religion touch practical life." Washington further asserted that blacks learned from YMCAs how "to associate religion with cleanliness, with health, and with pure living . . . to associate religion with the reading of books, with opportunities for study and advancement in his trade or profession." In a number of other presentations, on and off the Tuskegee Institute campus, and in several published articles, Washington made positive references to the YMCA. During one of his weekly Sunday evening talks in 1901, he told Tuskegee Institute male students, "Don't be ashamed to go to the . . . Young Men's Christian Association."[16]

Like their male counterpart, Young Women's Christian Associations (YWCAs), such as those in Rochester and Yonkers, New York, hosted persons who praised Washington. Focusing on women, the association, as did the YMCA, augmented the proselytizing of the Tuskegee movement. Its objectives inspired Washington to establish a branch of the YWCA on the Tuskegee Institute campus. The association's work, moreover, inspired Washington to assist with the raising of funds for a kindergarten sponsored by the New York City African American branch of the YWCA. Even so, Washington's interaction with the YWCA did not match his collaboration with various YMCAs. He did, however, develop relationships of various degrees with several black and white supporters of the association. Washington corresponded with Bettie G. Cox Francis, a founder and first president of the Washington, D.C., African American branch of the association. He and Grace H. Dodge, a white woman who led the movement to establish a national governing body of the YWCA, enjoyed a long acquaintance. The two of them served as judges at the 1895 Atlanta Cotton States Exposition's Department of Education. Throughout his public career, Washington had encountered various other prominent members and supporters of the association. He even exchanged letters with the husband of Mrs. Robert E. Speer, the president of the YWCA's national board. Washington had a much closer relationship with several of the YWCA's major donors. A number of these, including Cyrus McCormick,

George Foster Peabody, John D. Rockefeller Sr., John D. Rockefeller Jr., and Julius Rosenwald, financially supported facets of the Tuskegee movement.[17]

Washington's relationships with Rosenwald and other influential Jews inspired Jewish congregations to host eulogists. Many of them seemed to have liked Washington's ideas, programs, and biography. Rabbi Max Heller eulogized Washington at the predominately African American Central Congregational Church in New Orleans. Temple Beth Zion in Buffalo, New York; Temple Israel in the Harlem district of New York City; and the Free Synagogue in downtown New York City are among other Jewish congregations that hosted tributes. Both in and outside of Alabama, Washington initiated and nurtured beneficial relationships with a number of important Jews. Washington claimed a lifelong admiration for Jews and identified with their biblical and latter-day histories, especially their struggles to overcome bigotry. His personal interactions with both U.S. and European Jewry as an adult reinforced his veneration for them. During the early years of the Tuskegee Institute, Jacques Loeb, a Montgomery, Alabama, merchant and a French immigrant, extended credit to the school when other white local storeowners would not. Loeb's successful trade with the academy motivated other merchants to cease shunning the institute. Whereas Loeb provided credit, other Jews contributed money to the institute and other aspects of the movement. None of them, however, donated as much to the institute and the movement as did Julius Rosenwald, who had joined the institute board of trustees in 1911.[18]

Across the nation, Protestant congregations hosted more tributes to Washington than any other religious group. Few Roman Catholic Churches provided venues for his eulogists. While eulogists seemed to have preferred large, prestigious edifices, the vast majority of these speeches occurred in small church buildings. These small edifices included the University Place Church of Christ in Waterville, Maine; Mount Zion African Methodist Church in Bridgeton, New Jersey; the Mount Moriah Baptist Church in Richmond, Indiana; St. Peter African Methodist Episcopal Church in Minneapolis, Minnesota; Second Baptist Church in Davenport, Iowa; Second Baptist Church in Oswego, Kansas; Ninth Street Methodist Church in Fort Smith, Arkansas; Bethlehem Baptist Church in Pueblo, Colorado; and elsewhere around the nation.[19]

Cities possessed the larger venues that hosted memorials for Washington. Most often, urban centers with the large hosting edifice also possessed a sizable black community. Several of the cities with large African American populations generally possessed more than one sizable black-owned church building that accommodated a tribute. Hence, African Americans living in such cities as Boston, New Orleans, New York City, and Philadelphia had opportunities to attend tributes in more than relatively large venues. Edifices hosting eulogists included the First Congregational Church in Atlanta; People's Baptist Church in Boston; St. John's AME Church in Cleveland; Fifth Street Baptist Church in Louisville; Central Congregational Church in New Orleans; Bethel AME Church in Harlem; Miller Memorial Baptist Church in Philadelphia; and the Metropolitan AME Church in Washington, D.C. Very few predominately white–populated churches of any size in the South hosted tributes. White people's embrace of the more extreme elements of the protocol of racism prohibited any congregation in the South—Catholic, Protestant, or Jewish—from publicly hosting tributes to the life of any black man, even one with Washington's prestige. More than a few predominately white congregations elsewhere in the nation ignored this excessive aspect of racism and accommodated Washington's eulogists.[20]

*   *   *

Regardless of the venue, organizers of tributes began announcing forthcoming eulogies shortly after learning of Washington's death. On Monday, the day after his death, newspapers—including the *Kansas City (MO) Times*, and the *Minneapolis (MN) Trip*—had published notices of forthcoming eulogies. That next day, even more newspapers—including those in Newark, New Jersey, and Lima, Ohio—advertised impending tributes to Washington. Although the bulk of the announcements appeared in November and December 1915, organizers, especially those in areas with sizable black populations, continued to hold eulogies for Washington well into 1916, with several of them occurring around his birthday in April. For example, supporters placed typical advertisements in the *Providence (RI) Tribune* and the *Kansas City (MO) Journal*. The *Tribune* matter-of-factly declared that "Memorial services for the late Booker T. Washington will be held tomorrow." In a similar fashion, the *Journal* asserted that "Memorial services for the late Booker T. Washington will be held at the Second Negro Baptist Church." Occasionally, the African American–oriented *New York Age*, a periodical that Washington once partly owned, and its Chicago counterpart, the *Defender*, published similar notices for upcoming eulogies planned for areas outside their respective home areas. The *Age*, for example, announced on November 18, 1915, that Tuskegee movement supporters would deliver eulogies in Charleston, West Virginia. Nine days later, the *Defender* proclaimed that a "monster memorial meeting will be held" in Columbus, Ohio.[21]

Rightly believing that including famous people on memorial programs for Washington would increase audience size, organizers advertised the most noteworthy eulogists available. During the thirty-five-plus years of his professional life, Washington and his movement had attracted men and women, blacks and whites, alike. After his death, many of his constituents ardently wished for the Tuskegee movement to continue. Washington's numerous eulogists reflected his multiracial, coeducational following, and prominent adherents eagerly answered memorial organizers' calls to eulogize him. Gender mores of the day dictated that males constitute the vast majority of America's prominent public figures, a reality that ensured that women would make up a smaller number of the eulogists.

Organizers did select several prominent female supporters to publicly praise Washington, including Mary E. Josenburger, a wealthy Fort Smith, Arkansas, African American businesswoman, who eulogized him. Her selection manifested Fort Smith memorial organizers' desires to promote both renowned and well-connected female eulogists. A woman with wide-ranging business, civic, and social networks, Josenburger enjoyed substantial esteem in the Fort Smith community. Born and raised in Oswego, New York, along the shores of Lake Ontario, Josenburger graduated from Oswego's Free Academy. After taking a degree from Fisk University in 1888, she taught at the State Normal School in Holly Springs, Mississippi, during the 1888–89 school year. The following year, she moved to Fort Smith, where she taught at a grade school and a high school. After marrying William Ernest Josenburger, a postman and mortician, in 1903, she quit the classroom. Her husband's death in 1909 necessitated that she take over the family's undertaking business. Josenburger's business activities did not prohibit her from serving as the register of deeds for the Grand Court Order of Calanthe, a fraternal benefit society. Focusing on other business concerns, she eventually stopped managing the mortuary. Josenburger's dynamic entrepreneurism amassed an alleged net worth of approximately $30,000.[22]

While receiving rents from several commercial properties, including an auditorium that once hosted Booker T. Washington, and serving on the board of the Standard Life Insurance Company, Josenburger became active in several civic organizations. Fellow members of the Order of Calanthe elected her supreme conductress. She served as the president of the local Phyllis Wheatley Club, a Fort Smith affiliate of the National Association of Colored Women's Clubs, and became the vice president of the organization's Arkansas State Federation. Josenburger also belonged to the Eastern Star and the American Woodmen fraternal orders. Her businesses, clubs, and fraternal activities did not hinder her from joining the NBBL and the NAACP. She became a life member of the latter organization. Thus, her training, experience, contacts, prestige, and wealth endowed her with an alluring persona that would attract a sizable audience to hear Washington eulogized.[23]

Supporters advertised that Celia Parker Woolley, a renowned white female Unitarian minister, would eulogize Washington at one of the several scheduled Chicago tributes. Born Celia Parker Harris to abolitionists in Toledo, Ohio, and raised in Coldwater, Michigan, Woolley, a white racial egalitarian, graduated from seminary in 1866. Two years later she married J. H. Woolley, a dentist. They relocated to Chicago, where she became an editor for the *Unity*, a Unitarian periodical, as well as an acclaimed published essayist, novelist, and theologian. With her African American friends Samuel Laing Williams and Fannie Barrier Williams, she founded the Douglas Center, the first settlement house for a mixed-race, middle-class population in Chicago. She intended the house to "improve the relations between the black and white middle classes." A strong supporter of the Tuskegee movement, Woolley had expressed strong displeasure with Du Bois. After the first meeting of the Niagara movement, Williams, a confidant of Washington, reported that she "had become thoroughly sick of Du Bois." Woolley's local and national prominence, along with her reputation as an advocate for improving race relations between middle-class blacks and whites, substantially increased the attractiveness of Chicago's Lincoln Center tribute to Washington.[24]

Although organizers mostly advertised black men as presenters, a number of white men's names appeared in published notices. A group of New York City organizers who planned to pay tribute to Washington at the Bethel African Methodist Episcopal Church headlined Henry Clews as the intended eulogist. A wealthy Wall Street banker, Clews had emigrated as a teenager from Great Britain. Clews secured his first New York job with the dry goods importer Wilson G. Hunt and Company. Within a few years, Clews left the firm to help establish and work for Livermore, Clews, and Company, a Wall Street investment bank. The company's success and Clews's widely known strong support for the Union during the Civil War inspired President Abraham Lincoln's secretary of the treasury, Salmon B. Chase, to award his company a contract to sell U.S. government bonds. Neither profits from the sale of war bonds or prestige for being one of only two firms that kept the federal government solvent during the war kept Clews's company from undergoing bankruptcy in 1873. After Clews's firm reorganized, President Ulysses Grant awarded it a contract to represent the U.S. government in all international monetary transactions. While fulfilling his U.S. federal fiduciary obligations, Clews served as the Japanese government's financial adviser.[25]

Clews's wealth and success, along with his marriage to Lucy Madison Worthington, President James Madison's grandniece, allowed him to associate and socialize with many of America's most renowned citizens. His prominence provided him access to numerous civil, political, and social organizations. Clews claimed membership to the National Institute of Social Hygiene, the New York Historical Society, the Society for the Prevention of Cruelty to Animals, the Geographical Statistical Society, the American Academy of Political and Social Science, the Grand Army of the Republic, the Union League Club, and the New York Committee of Seventy (a powerful and successful civic reform association). Although Clews became an associate and strong supporter of Washington and his culture war, he never sat on the institute's board of trustees or any other organization closely associated with the Tuskegee movement.[26]

Several days later, organizers of another tribute in New York City publicized William Jay Schieffelin as the featured eulogist at St. Mark's Methodist Episcopal Church. A member of the nation's financial and social elite, Schieffelin engaged in various high-profile civic and political causes. As president of the importer and pharmaceutical manufacturer Schieffelin and Company, he possessed the time and wealth to effectively crusade. His marriage to a great-granddaughter of Cornelius Vanderbilt awarded Schieffelin a substantial amount of social capital, a necessary commodity for an effective culture reformer. Schieffelin's academic achievement and veteran status augmented his prestige. He fought in the Spanish American War several years after taking a doctor of philosophy degree in chemistry from the University of Munich, Germany. Since he belonged to America's cultural elite, many civic, educational, and political organizations eagerly attempted to recruit him. A founding member of the National Urban League, Schieffelin had joined the New York City Reform Club, the Citizens Union, Joint Board of Sanitary Control in the Needlework Industry, the National Civil Service Reform Association, the Armstrong Association for Hampton Institute, the Hampton Institute Board of Trustees, and the Tuskegee Institute Board of Trustees. Schieffelin's longtime, firsthand knowledge of Washington and his extraordinarily high profile made him a very attractive person to publicly praise Washington.[27]

Apart from the organizers of a Chicago memorial service showcasing Julius Rosenwald, no other memorial attracted eulogists as wealthy and well-known locally as Clews and Schieffelin. Organizers, whether in or outside of major cities like Chicago and New York, recruited white politicians with substantial prestige within their respective communities. Promoters in Kansas City, Missouri, for example, advertised former mayor Henry M. Beardsley as a speaker at one of that city's several memorials for Washington. A lawyer and longtime president of the local YMCA, Beardsley possessed a reputation as a progressive social reformer. Supporters in Rochester, New York, successfully

solicited Hiram H. Edgerton, the city's very popular mayor and businessman. Organizers of an all-city memorial in Los Angeles offered the mayor
of that city, Charles Sebastian, as Washington's eulogist. A controversial man
from and of the people, Sebastian had moved to the city sometime around
1900 and worked as a common laborer, law enforcer, and police chief before
winning the mayor's office. Some of these men had never met Washington,
and none of them possessed a close personal relationship with him. For one
or more reasons, including public recognition and an honest desire to support the Tuskegee movement, they either sought or agreed to praise the late
educator.[28]

Like the movement supporters in Albany, New York, who advertised John
H. Finley, the state's educational commissioner, as a eulogist, several groups
of organizers announced previous holders of statewide offices as forthcoming
eulogists. The "Booker T. Washington Memorial Association of the Capital
district" in Albany highlighted Finley and several other notable persons. One
of a very small number of appointed state office holders chosen to eulogize
Washington, Finley, a native of Grand Ridge, Illinois, had known Washington for more than sixteen years. The relationship began in the 1890s during
Finley's tenure as president of Knox College in Galesburg, Illinois. Finley had
taken both his undergraduate and master's degrees from the college and had
earned a doctorate from Johns Hopkins University. Finley then took a job as
the secretary of the New York Charities Aid Association. Three years later,
he returned to Knox College as its president. Having served seven years in
that capacity, Finley then became the editor of *Harper's Weekly*. Soon thereafter he left the magazine to teach politics at Princeton University. College
teaching did not long hold Finley's attention. Within a year he left Princeton
to become the head of New York City College. He worked as that school's
president for ten years before becoming New York State Commissioner of
Education and president of the State University of New York. While living
in New York City, Finley became a fervent Tuskegee movement supporter.
At a 1910 fund-raising event that occurred at Carnegie Hall, for example, he,
James Hardy Dillard, the president of a major education philanthropic foundation, and Booker T. Washington introduced a movie concerning Tuskegee
Institute's educational activities.[29]

Supporters in Milwaukee, Wisconsin, pledged that former New Jersey
governor John F. Fort would deliver a tribute. Fort counted President Woodrow Wilson among his close comrades. President Wilson, a Democrat, once
called Fort, a Republican who had served as a New Jersey Supreme Court
Justice before becoming governor, a true friend. Wilson had appointed Fort
as special envoy to the Dominican Republic in 1914 and to Haiti in 1915.[30]

Several days later, newspapers advertised that former New York governor Charles Seymour Whitman would eulogize Washington in Albany, New York. Whitman and Washington had known each other for several years. As the district attorney for New York City when Albert Ulrich brutally beat Washington, Whitman indicted and unsuccessfully prosecuted the assailant. Regardless, the district attorney seemed to have gained Washington's admiration. He sent Whitman a note of congratulations for winning the election for governor of New York. Someone provided a copy of Washington's letter to the *New York Tribune*, which in turn published it. After reading the contents of the letter, many people concluded that Washington endorsed Whitman's aspirations to run for president of the United States.[31]

In the Columbus, Ohio, area, arrangers announced Ohio governor Frank B. Willis as Washington's eulogist at a public service in the city. A reputed "born campaigner," Willis became one of a small number of sitting governors to praise Washington at a public forum. He started life in Lewis Center, Ohio, a small town north of Columbus. Willis took bachelor's and master's degrees from Ohio Northern University, a teachers' college. Afterward, he taught economics and history at the university, won a state representative election, lost a congressional contest, passed the Ohio bar, and became a U.S. representative. Willis left Congress in 1915, five years after going to Washington, for the Ohio governor's office.[32]

Although he might have never personally communicated with Washington, Willis shared many of the same ideas on social and racial reform as did the Tuskegee movement. They both supported increasing the opportunities for ordinary people to improve their material well-being while assisting them with enhancing their moral principles. Willis and Washington, for example, strongly supported the prohibition of alcohol. The governor, moreover, projected himself as a racial liberal. Several weeks before Washington's death, the State of Ohio Board of Censors prohibited the showing of *The Birth of a Nation*. Willis had appointed two of the three members of the board and received public credit and criticism for the decision. It delighted the state's African American population. The majority of their voters would support Willis "for the remainder of his political career."[33]

A few memorial arrangers solicited noted northern Democrats to eulogize Washington. That small number included organizers in Minneapolis, who asked Minnesota's Democratic governor Winfield Scott Hammond. A reform-minded politician with a bachelor's degree from Dartmouth College, Hammond became principal of Mankato (MN) High School after his graduation. The following year, the local school board appointed him superintendent of schools. During the next six years, he read law and passed the state's bar examination. Afterward, he practiced law. Although in 1891 Hammond failed in his first attempt to win a congressional seat, he secured an appointment to the State Board of Directors of the Normal Schools of Minnesota. These institutions, like the Tuskegee Institute, primarily produced grammar-school teachers. After serving on the board for eight years, Hammond won an election to the U.S. House of Representatives in 1907. Minnesotans elected him governor three years later. As governor, Hammond would attract a large audience for his tribute to Washington. His experiences as a New England college student, as well as a teacher, principal, and a director for the state's normal schools gave him the insight, and, perhaps the enthusiasm, to deliver an eulogy that would present an above-average appreciation of Washington's life and professional career.[34]

Rarely did Democrat or Republican, current or former, politicians living in the political South (that area of the nation that allowed legalized slavery in 1860) agree to eulogize Washington. A noted exception, former Alabama governor, Emmet O'Neal, publicly praised Washington at a memorial service that the Alabama State Negro Teacher's Association sponsored. The association had not publicized widely or enthusiastically the upcoming eulogy. O'Neal had a better-than-cordial relationship with Washington. During his four-year term as governor, he proclaimed to Washington his commitment to provide blacks with "equal, exact and impartial justice and by every possible effort to aid" them in "becoming a more useful member of society." Governor O'Neal, who had publicly opposed lynching, supported the removal from office of a county sheriff who allowed a white mob to murder an African American in his charge. Washington had praised O'Neal for his antilynching stances and personally thanked him for commuting a death sentence of a black man. O'Neal supported Washington's fruitful attempt at securing money from the federal government to fund the institute's teaching of agriculture and its farmers' extension work. These as well as other deeds motivated Washington to request unequivocally that several of his major financial supporters recommend O'Neal to President Wilson for a position with the federal government.[35]

Whereas the protocol of racial supremacy impeded the recruitment of white southern politicians, it did not prevent the enlisting of former U.S. presidents. Organizers of a planned memorial in New York City announced that former president William H. Taft would eulogize Washington on December 2, 1915, at the St. Mark's Methodist Episcopal Church. Taft and Washington had maintained a friendly relationship since the former had served as secretary of war in President Theodore Roosevelt's cabinet. The late educator, however, did not support many of Taft's policies on southern politics and African Americans. As Secretary of War, Taft had very much disappointed Washington when he followed Roosevelt's direction to dismiss three companies of black troops stationed in Brownsville, Texas, after some of them exchanged gunshots with white residents of the town. After he became president, Taft further disenchanted Washington. Although Taft consulted with Washington and supported several issues important to black Americans, he often discounted his suggestions. Disregarding Washington's protest, Taft pursued a southern political strategy that included removing African Americans from federal offices and refusing to appoint any blacks to government jobs in the South if southern whites objected. Regardless of their differences concerning political and racial issues, Taft sent a handwritten letter of support to Washington during the Ulrich trial. Numerous newspapers, which had received copies from Washington, published the letter.[36]

No person other than the sitting president, Woodrow Wilson, could attract a larger audience to hear a eulogy of Washington than former president Theodore Roosevelt. In the process of planning a December 11, 1915, memorial that, unlike the funeral, would include eulogies, survivors and the leaders of the Tuskegee movement decided that Roosevelt should present one of the key eulogies. His status and commitment to the Tuskegee movement made him an obvious choice to deliver a eulogy. For more than fifteen years, Roosevelt had supported Washington and his movement. Even though the former president did not meet the educator until after he became the vice president of the United States, Roosevelt had expressed admiration for Washington. With the robust encouragement of the railroad man, W. H. Baldwin Jr., then the chairman of the Investment Committee of Tuskegee Institute Board of Trustees and Washington's dearest white male friend, Roosevelt and the Tuskegean quickly forged a bond. Within a few years the relationship evolved into one that substantially benefited both men. It further ingratiated Roosevelt with African American voters and with white racial liberals while providing Washington with significant prestige and influence. The dinner that the two shared at the White House in 1900 illustrated a relationship between a black man and a president of the United States unlike any other in the history of the nation. Roosevelt's 1905 speech during a visit to Tuskegee Institute reaffirmed the connection. After accepting Washington's invitation to join the institute's board of trustees in 1910, Roosevelt became one of its more active members and most prominent associates of the Tuskegee movement.[37]

Roosevelt and Washington's symbiotic association continued until the latter's death. While he could no longer provide Washington with the support of a sitting president once his term in office ended, Roosevelt continued to champion Washington and the Tuskegee movement after he left the White

House. Two years later, however, he managed to insult the black community once again. During the 1912 Progressive Party Convention, which nominated Roosevelt for president, he agreed to the disqualification of southern African American delegates. While Washington did not openly support the Progressive Party, nor did he favor the ousting of blacks from the convention, their relationship remained strong. Roosevelt continued to serve on the trustee board as one its most powerful and esteemed members. He, more so than other trustees, influenced the selection of Robert Moton to succeed Washington as the principal of the Tuskegee Institute.[38]

*   *   *

Only a very few tribute arrangers could realistically hope to get a former president, or any other person with substantial national or regional prestige, to deliver a eulogy at a tribute that they intended to organize. The vast majority of the white men asked to praise Washington publicly, however, enjoyed notable local stature and held positions of prestige in their respective communities.

George Edward Crothers, an attorney and state judge residing in San Francisco, joined a cadre of white lawyers who assented to applaud the life of Washington and the programs he sponsored. Organizers advertised that Crothers would deliver his tribute January 4, 1916, at the Bethel African Methodist Episcopal (AME) Church. Born in Wapello, Iowa, Crothers had moved to California with his brother Thomas in 1894. Along with future president Herbert Hoover, he belonged to Stanford University's first graduating class. After undergraduate school, Crothers took a law degree from the university and went into practice with his brother. Several years later, he became a Superior Court judge, a position he still held in 1916. As the first alumnus to sit on the Stanford board of trustees, Crothers worked tirelessly on behalf of the school. While he did not possess an overt relationship with any aspect of the Tuskegee movement, Crothers's appreciation for formal education may have inspired him to acknowledge Washington publicly.[39]

Like Crothers, Civil War veteran and a survivor of the horrendous Confederate Andersonville Prison, Judge Joseph W. O'Neall had no direct tie to Washington, either. He too, however, agreed to deliver a tribute to Washington. Organizers in Springfield, Ohio, scheduled the tribute for April 7, 1916, at Grace Church. In the fifty years after the Civil War, O'Neall had become a well-known and very much respected public figure. He returned to his home in Warren County, Ohio, after the war. For several years, O'Neall taught school, engaged in business, and passed the bar before being elected in 1879 as probate judge. In the meanwhile, he became a leading member of the Grand Army of the Republic (GAR), an organization of Union Civil War veterans. For several years O'Neall commanded the Ohio department of the GAR, and in 1915 his volunteer work with that organization led the governor to appoint him state commissioner of soldiers' claims. Although O'Neall had no history of openly working with Washington or his movement, perhaps his participation in a war to free African Americans, his imprisonment, and his concern for Union veterans compelled him to eulogize the most famous of all former slaves.[40]

Even more so than with lawyers, tribute organizers enjoyed significant success soliciting white male educators to eulogize Washington. They promoted Cyrus Northrop, president emeritus of the University of Minnesota, as well as many other renowned teachers and educational leaders as eulogists. From Ridgefield, Connecticut, Northrop became the president of the University of Minnesota after a twenty-one-year career of teaching rhetoric and English literature at Yale University, where he had earned both bachelor's and law degrees. Before his academic career, Northrop had edited a newspaper and worked two years for the Connecticut state legislature. These experiences, along with his forceful and eloquent speaking style, contributed to his success as a college administrator. During his twenty-seven-year presidency, the University of Minnesota markedly improved its academic standing while enrollment grew from 223 to 5,000. Similar to Washington, Northrop had successfully ensured the sustaining of a significant educational institution. The accolades that he received for this accomplishments made Northrop a very attractive eulogist at the Washington tribute on November 28, 2015, in Minneapolis.[41]

Los Angeles newspapers reported that John Willis Baer, president of Occidental College, would deliver a tribute to Washington the same day Northrop presented his eulogy. A native of rural southeastern Minnesota, Baer acquired the reputation as a "brilliant lay preacher" in the Presbyterian Church. He had served as the assistant secretary of the Board of Home Missions of the Presbyterian Church of the United States. In recognition of his contribution to the denomination, church officials selected him to moderate their general assembly, the first layman so honored. For over a decade, Baer worked as the general secretary of the Christian Endeavor Society before his appointment to the presidency of Occidental College, where he increased enrollment and relocated the campus. He held commonalities with Washington, whom he had known for years. Both had spent part of their youth living on a farm, and neither attended college. The two had traveled extensively. Baer, as a professional evangelical missionary, journeyed around the world, and Washington, in his efforts to promote the Tuskegee Institute and his movement, visited Europe twice and toured the United States widely.[42]

*   *   *

While organizers promoted the tributes of a number of other education stalwarts, including Frederick Burk, president of the San Francisco Normal School, and Charles F. Thwing, president of Western Reserve College, they also publicized forthcoming eulogies of white prominent ministers such as the Reverend Minot O. Simons. A Unitarian minister originally from Manchester, New Hampshire, Simons graduated from Harvard University with bachelor's and master's degrees. In 1910, officials of the Unitarian Church Conference elected him president of that body. Five years later, when the conference selected as president William Howard Taft, the chief justice of the U.S. Supreme Court, it also elected Simons as chair of the conference. In Cleveland, Simons served as the secretary of the executive committee of the Associated Charities, president of both the Sunbeam Association for Cripples and the Men's League for Equal Suffrage. His dedication to social justice inspired him in 1912 to call for a "New Abolition Movement" that would stop lynching and strengthen the civil rights of African Americans. Simons asserted, "until the American people decide to treat the Negro as a human being . . . we shall continue to have our civilization disgraced before the moral judgment of the twentieth century." His philanthropy and espousal of racial equity may have prompted organizers to request that he deliver a tribute to Washington. It would promote their struggle in the culture war.[43]

Arrangers in East Orange, New Jersey, proclaimed that the Reverend James M. Ludlow intended to deliver a tribute to Washington at the Ashland School. Ludlow, a renowned white Presbyterian minister, had a long relationship with Washington. As early as 1890, he had hosted a fund-raising meeting for Washington at the First Presbyterian Church in East Orange. Hailing from Elizabeth, New Jersey, Ludlow had taken both bachelor's and theology degrees from Princeton University. After graduation, the Presbyterian Church ordained him. He began his ministerial career in 1865 at the First Presbyterian Church in Albany, New York. He subsequently preached at the Collegiate Church in New York City and the Westminster Church in Brooklyn before becoming the pastor for the East Orange First Presbyterian Church. At the time of Washington's death, Ludlow served as the church's emeritus pastor.[44]

Reflecting Washington's esteem and the ubiquitous acceptance of the Tuskegee movement's tenets within the African American Christian community, advertisements of eulogies announced far more names of black preachers than white ones. No significant group of Americans supported Washington and his objectives stronger than black Christians. At the time of Washington's death, he enjoyed widespread support among all segments of his natural constituency—African Americans. For a variety of reasons, including his accomplishments, fame, humility, piety, prestige, and power, as well as his iconic racial status, thousands of blacks, Christians and non-Christians alike, identified with him and filled the ranks of the movement. Leadership positions, community esteem, and articulation abilities led African American tribute organizers to seek black preachers. Their appreciation of Washington inspired a large number of ministers to accept invitations to eulogize him. Blacks who pastored Protestant congregations of all sizes and in all sections of the nation praised Washington.

Among several speakers scheduled to praise Washington publicly at St. John's Congregational Church in Springfield, Massachusetts, the *Republic* highlighted the Reverend Dr. W. N. De Berry, the pastor of the church. For the two previous years, De Berry had served alongside Booker T. Washington on the Fisk University Board of Trustees. Born in Nashville, Tennessee, De Berry graduated from Fisk in 1896. Although he seriously contemplated attending medical school, De Berry instead followed his father's example and became a minister. He subsequently entered Oberlin College as a theology student. After he completed his studies, St. John's Congregational Church, with its congregation of no more than a hundred, called him to preach. Under his leadership, it grew to become the largest African American Congregational congregation in the nation. De Berry's church actualized a religious vision that in several ways augmented the Tuskegee movement. It adopted the precept, "its work in all its phases to the religious and social needs of the people whom it [served]." As did the Tuskegee Institute, the church established outreach programs. It created a night school that taught domestic science, a female "social center," a no-fee employment bureau, and a residence for employed single women. These programs amplified De Berry's Yankee Protestant theology, which embraced the key values of the Tuskegee movement.[45]

"Sermon Tonight on Booker T. Washington" is how the December 5, 1915, *Augusta (GA) Chronicle* announced that the Reverend Charles Thomas Walker would pay tribute to the late educator at Tabernacle Baptist Church in that city. Walker, a former slave and a graduate of Augusta Institute, now Morehouse College, had attained a reputation as a brilliant and charismatic theologian. One of his contemporaries called him the "greatest preacher the race had ever produced." His sermons, which he published along with religious articles and books, helped increase the congregation to two thousand.

They, and the many visitors to Walker's church, heard him in the largest and most attractive African American–owned edifice in the nation. Numerous churches around the nation had invited him to preach from their pulpits. He ministered to both predominately black as well as to white congregations. During a trip to the Middle East, he accepted an invitation to preach in London, England's Exeter Hall, the home of the Anti-Slavery Society, and at Charles Spurgeon's Tabernacle, the world's largest Protestant church. In the United States, such notable laymen as President William H. Taft and John D. Rockefeller, as well as prominent white ministers such as David Gregg and Amory H. Bradford, heard his sermons. In recognition of his theological gravitas, excellent hermeneutics, speaking skills, religious writings, and captivating personality, his contemporaries referred to him as the black Spurgeon. It made for an interesting comparison, since Victorian-age theologians had decreed Charles Spurgeon, a British Baptist preacher, "the last of the Puritans."[46]

Walker's life in many ways paralleled Washington's. He too began life as a slave, lived among rural blacks, never attended college, built a very large institution, associated with powerful people, achieved national fame, and championed the moral and material enhancement of African Americans. As Washington strongly believed that blacks needed more than the teaching of the abstract, Walker understood that they required more than an abstract theology. Throughout his career, Walker strove to help African Americans improve their quality of life. While simultaneously holding the position of pastor at four rural Georgia churches, Walker in 1880 accepted a call to pastor the First Baptist Church of La Grange, Georgia, where he established La Grange Academy for African Americans. Subsequently, he became pastor of the Tabernacle Church in Augusta, Georgia. There, Walker launched a school that taught African Americans, in addition to literacy, skills such as culinary, carpentry, and business. Between 1899 and 1904, Walker accepted a call to preach at Mount Olivet Baptist Church in New York City. With Washington's assistance, he led a movement to establish the celebrated New York City's 135th Street YMCA branch for African Americans.[47]

As early as 1901, Walker had become a confidant of Washington. He trusted Walker to champion the objectives of the Tuskegee movement. Three years later, at Washington's invitation, Walker participated in the January 1904 African American leadership conciliation conference at Carnegie Hall. He honored a request two years later from Washington to attend the Georgia Equal Rights Convention. The Tuskegean wanted Walker to minimize potential radicalism that might emerge from the meeting. After Washington learned of a scheduled international race conference in London, England, he again urged Walker to travel to Britain and represent the interests of the Tuskegee movement.[48]

Civil rights icon African Methodist Episcopal Zion (AMEZ) Bishop Alexander Walters lent his name to the roster of scheduled Washington eulogists. Organizers slated Walters to speak on December 2, 1915, at St. Mark's Methodist Episcopal in New York City. Born in Kentucky in 1858, Walters, like Washington, suffered the cruelties of enslavement. After receiving his basic education in his home state, the Kentucky Conference of the AMEZ licensed Walter to preach at the young age of eighteen. After preaching at several churches in Kentucky and serving as the associate editor and treasurers of the *Zion's Banner*, an AMEZ periodical, he moved to California in 1883. Walters's performance earned him the opportunity to pastor Mother Zion AMEZ Church in Harlem, one of the oldest African American churches in the nation. He took a doctor of divinity degree from Livingstone College, an AMEZ-sponsored school, at the age of thirty-three. The following year, 1892, he won an election to the AMEZ Board of Bishops.[49]

After becoming a bishop, Walters became a nationally known civil rights crusader and an important consultant to Washington. In recognition of his activism, members of the Afro-American Council, a national civil rights association, selected him as their first president in 1897. This organization manifested the continuing desire among leading articulate African Americans for a national organization that would fight for the citizenship rights of black people. A reincarnation of the earlier Afro-American League, the council sought to use public opinion, elective politics, and legal suits to obtain its objective. Walters's election as council president occurred after Washington's close friend Timothy Thomas Fortune refused to seek the leadership of the new organization. With the support of both Fortune and Washington, Walters served as council president for most of its existence. With a few notable exceptions, such as disagreeing with Washington's position on the Brownsville, Texas, affair, Walters strongly supported Washington and his movement.[50]

While Walters and other nationally known preachers appealed to a national audience, most of the ministers who supporters broadcast as forthcoming eulogists possessed, at best, a regional following. The Reverend L. R. Mitchell exemplified this group. On Sunday, November 16, 1915, the *Lima (OH) Gazette* noted that he would make an address concerning the life of Booker T. Washington at the Second Baptist Church. A former restaurant headwaiter, Mitchell trained for the ministry at Metropolitan Baptist Church in Indianapolis, his hometown. After ordination in 1903, he pastored at a few churches before answering a call to preach at the Second Baptist Church several months before the death of Washington. It is very possible that Mitchell met Washington as early as 1904, the year the NNBL held its annual convention in Indianapolis. Washington presided over that meeting, as he had during the three earlier ones.[51]

*   *   *

While not as frequently publicized as theologians, arrangers selected both regionally and nationally renowned educators as eulogists. They, more so than any other group of Americans, could identify with the tribulations Washington overcame to establish the Tuskegee Institute and to develop it into the most renowned predominately black–populated educational institution in the world. Black teachers often represented the most learned and sophisticated segment of their respective African American communities. Next to parents, they held the greatest and most consistent adult influence on the majority of black children. This reality, coupled with the respect that blacks held for teachers' education and occupation, as well as their above-average ability to communicate, ensured a high status within African American communities.

Elmer W. B. Curry of Springfield, Ohio, both preached and headed a school in Urbana, Ohio. His Curry Normal and Industrial Institute, modeled after the Tuskegee Institute, had operated for more than sixteen years when the *Springfield Morning Sun* announced that he would eulogize Washington on April 7, 1916. Curry began teaching young black children in a shed as a teenager while attending Ohio Wesleyan University in his hometown of Delaware. With a college degree in hand, he worked as an itinerate preacher and public schoolteacher for several years before establishing his school at Mechanicsburg, Ohio. After relocating the school to Urbana, Ohio, Curry began editing the newly published African American–oriented *Informer* newspaper. While preaching, editing, and teaching, Curry took a doctor of law degree from Wilberforce University and a doctor of divinity from Simmons College in Louisville, Kentucky. He did not allow his educational and religious work to hinder him from participating in politics and philanthropy. Curry actively campaigned for the Anti-Saloon League of America while holding leadership positions in the Independent Order of Good Samaritans, an African American temperance organization. A renowned persuasive public lecturer, anti-saloon advocators made him a much-sought-after speaker. Curry's puritanical and educational proclamations prompted commentators to refer to him sometimes as the Booker T. Washington of the North.[52]

In Kansas City, Missouri, John Robert E. Lee, the principal of Lincoln High School, eulogized Washington. He had worked closely with Washington. A native Texan, Lee graduated in 1899 from Bishop College in Marshall, Texas.

He taught math at the Tuskegee Institute for five years before taking a teaching job at Benedict College in Columbia, South Carolina. He returned to the Tuskegee Institute in 1906 as the director of the academic department. While in South Carolina, he served as the president for the National Association for Teachers in Colored Schools and worked as an organizer for the NNBL. He moved to Kansas City a few months before Washington died.[53]

Along with teachers and preachers, African Americans who belonged to a number of disparate occupations eulogized Washington. Communication skills and prominence contributed to them being asked to pay tribute to Washington. Attorneys, leaders of fraternal orders, civil rights activists, as well as other persons with public-speaking experience joined the list of educators and clerics in eulogizing Washington. Arrangers in Albany, New York, broadcast that attorneys Joseph N. Hawkins and W. Raymond Atwell would deliver tributes to Washington. Milwaukee, Wisconsin, organizers promoted attorney George A. Douglass's upcoming eulogy, while movement leaders in Chicago did the same for the one that lawyer Samuel Laing Williams would present. On the West Coast, arrangers in Pasadena, California, publicized that William Prince, officer of the local Independent Colored Brotherhood and Sisterhood, intended to eulogize Washington. A longtime civil rights campaigner, Prince had held offices in the local California Afro-American Congress and the Afro-America League. The announcement for the Pasadena tribute to Washington proclaimed that the president of the local Negro Voters and Taxpayers League, E. L. Gaines, would also eulogize Washington. While the promoters of eulogies scheduled in San Francisco did not advertise the participation of noted civil rights advocates, they did indicate that two unnamed former students of the Tuskegee Institute would discuss the life of Washington. Presumably, they would provide the attendees with a firsthand knowledge of how efficiently the school indoctrinated pupils with desired aspects of the Yankee Protestant ethic.[54]

Although not a Tuskegee Institute graduate, John R. Lynch, a black former Mississippi congressman, lived a life that exemplified several aspects of that philosophy, and organizers in Detroit, Michigan, clearly comprehended that his eulogy of Washington would attract extensive attention. Their advertisement proclaimed that Lynch would deliver his tribute on April 13, 1916. His address would become one of the many eulogies delivered during the month of Washington's birth. More than all but a small minority of eulogists and the audiences to whom they spoke, Lynch understood the period and domain that Washington had endured and witnessed. Lynch, as did Washington, had a white father. Lynch's father, though, owned him, and for years the two had a familial relationship. A native of Dublin, Ireland, his father failed to free his black family before dying. A Natchez, Mississippi, slaveholder and friend of the father inherited the family. Union troops had brought freedom to Lynch just as they had done with Washington. Although he learned to read and write as a slave, Lynch, as had Washington, attended a freedmen's school while holding a full-time job.[55]

Both Lynch and Washington, as young men, participated in local politics. After their initial political experiences, however, their lives took two different trajectories. While Washington departed the political arena to pursue instruction and become an educator, Lynch continued to embrace electoral politics. He started his political career as a volunteer with a Natchez Republican Party club. Lynch's work with the club impressed party officials, who convinced Mississippi Governor Adelbert Ames to appoint him to a justice of the peace office in Adams County. Within a year of his selection, Lynch won his first of two elections to the Mississippi State House of Representatives, where he also served as the Speaker. He left the Mississippi legislature after winning a seat to the U.S. House of Representatives in 1872. Lynch won reelection in 1874, 1876, and 1880. After losing the 1882 race, he returned to Adams County, Mississippi, to farm and study law while remaining active in the state Republican Party. Lynch took and passed the bar in Mississippi in 1896, and in the following year, he did the same in Washington, D.C. While living in the nation's capital, he worked was an auditor for the Department of the Navy from 1889 to 1893, secured an appointment as major in the United States Volunteer Army in 1898, and later became an officer in the regular U.S. Army. Retiring in 1911, he moved to Chicago, opened a real estate business, and returned to the practice of law.[56]

It is easy to imagine that Washington would have included Lynch in the group of blacks he described in his famed 1895 "Atlanta Exposition Address" as persons who began freedom "at the top instead of at the bottom." These people, Washington alleged, sought a "seat in Congress or the state legislature" rather than seeking "real estate or industrial skill," and believed that "the political convention of stump speaking had more attraction than starting a dairy farm or truck garden." Washington made these assertions seven years after Lynch delivered a speech at the 1888 Tuskegee Institute commencement. Even though he experienced a long personal acquaintance with Lynch and seemed to have considered the former congressman an acceptable African American Reconstruction politician, the two never established a close relationship. Lynch, however, had meaningful personal, political, and professional associations with several of Washington's intimate associates, including Robert Terrell, with whom Lynch had established a law partnership, and

Ralph Tyler, who at one time attempted to help him gain an audience with President Theodore Roosevelt. Even though Lynch and Washington did not often directly associate or communicate, they did admire each other.[57]

* * *

Although Lynch and other celebrated eulogists attracted attendees, publicizing the names of the groups organizing, sponsoring, and trumpeting the memorials helped to legitimize and further enhanced their attractiveness. For a number of reasons, including potential attendees, a desire to support cherished associations or their quest for vicarious prestige, knowledge of the sponsoring organizations increased and reinforced the appeal of tributes. Announcements of forthcoming tributes indicated that Protestant churches underwrote the vast majority of eulogies. While most of the promotions publicized that a single congregation would host a tribute, occasionally a consortium of churches sponsored one. Advertisements for eulogies that would take place at the St. Mark's Methodist Church of New York City clearly noted the Interdenominational Preachers Association as the sponsor. A much smaller number of promotions identified secular organizations as organizers. Some of them, like the Montgomery, Alabama Tuskegee Club, had a direct connection to Washington and his movement. Many of the other sponsoring groups, such as the Cleveland Association of Colored Men, supported the movement but possessed a more complex relationship with it. The association had evolved from the local NNBL affiliate, but eventually it merged with the NAACP. Several newspapers, moreover, announced that a few local NAACP branches, including the one in Detroit, Michigan, intended to sponsor tributes. Their patronage belies the persistent widespread, and often repeated, contemporary perception that members of the civil rights organization during Washington's lifetime adamantly opposed the man and his supporters.[58]

Many arrangers revealed that they anticipated a large audience to attend their respective tribute. Sponsors of the one planned for Huntington, West Virginia, proclaimed that they expected "a big memorial service." People preparing for the eulogizing of Washington in Vicksburg, Mississippi, predicted that "record breaking" crowds would attend the event. Tuskegee movement supporters in Los Angeles and Stockton, California, likewise planned for big crowds. Chicago organizers expected attendance at the one they had scheduled to "be the largest" ever to have taken place in the city. Arrangers in Columbus, Ohio, confidently declared that a monster tribute "will be held here." Several of the sponsoring groups, like those in Rochester, New York, and Indianapolis, Indiana, manifested the era's race consciousness when they attempted to convey Washington's immense esteem with the promises that their audiences would consist of both "colored" and whites.[59]

One of the thousands of black and white Americans who did not disappoint organizers included A. M. Barnett, an African American residing in Los Angeles. They probably would not have approved of how he transported himself to the tribute. After learning of plans for an elaborate memorial scheduled to take place in San Diego on May 9, 1916, from a porter who worked for J. W. Johnson, a Los Angeles business owner, Barnett told his informer that he would attend the tribute if he could find a car. Without permission, he took Johnson's car to San Diego. A few days later, law enforcement officers returned Barnett to Los Angeles.[60]

While few persons seemed to have felt as strongly as Barnett about attending tributes, people did fill venues. A number of variables interacted to determine the size of an audience at any given event, including the venue's location and size, the eulogist's popularity, regional demographics, the event's date and time, as well as the weather. Whereas in Malden, Massachusetts, stormy weather played a major role in limiting a tribute's attendees to sixty, more than five thousand persons in sunny Los Angeles attended one at the Shrine Auditorium. Since churches, especially African American ones, hosted the vast majority of the tributes, the size of the edifice dictated the maximum number of attendees. Most predominately black–populated congregations, even the most prosperous ones, owned buildings that seated no more than a few hundred people. Even with an audience that filled the venue completely, a condition that often occurred, eulogists usually spoke before no more than two hundred or three hundred people.[61]

Bigger venues tended to attract larger audiences. In Denver, hundreds of people occupied all the seats in Shorter AME's sanctuary. Over five hundred heard the eulogy at the Wanamaker University Hall in Philadelphia. Approximately the same number appeared at the city's predominately African American–populated Miller Memorial Baptist Church for a tribute. Twelve hundred persons heard Washington praised at the predominately white–populated Centenary Methodist Church in Portland, Oregon. More than twice that many crowded into St. John's African Methodist Episcopal Church in Cleveland, Ohio. A crowd of three thousand overfilled the Bethel AME Church in Indianapolis, and an even bigger one attended the tribute in the city's Tomlinson Hall. Just as they had during Washington's funeral the previous month, a reported overflow audience of four thousand occupied the Tuskegee Institute chapel to hear former president Roosevelt and others eulogize Washington. Two months later, "a tremendous outpouring of men and women of both races packed spacious Metropolitan AME" Church in Washington, D.C. Although thousands of people heard eulogies of Washington at Carnegie Hall in New York City, Memorial Hall in Columbus, Ohio, and the Shrine Auditorium in Los Angeles housed two of the largest audiences. Each venue accommodated no fewer than five thousand attendees.[62]

The number and size of the countless tributes testified to the public's esteem for Washington as a man and as an icon. Other than George Washington and Abraham Lincoln, the death of no other American had elicited similar acknowledgments. Movement supporters who arranged the tributes, and the countless people who attended them, reinforced the nation's perception of itself. Yes, Washington the man had achieved some incredible accomplishments. He had overcome abject poverty to lead the construction of the largest and most renowned educational institution for black people in the United States, and he had served as consultant to presidents and billionaires. Washington had organized one of the most successful and largest secular organizations of African Americans. He had possessed fame and power. These factors alone would have inspired recognition, but not the type, size, and number that occurred. Washington represented the nation's potential. His life story told the world that, in America, regardless of heritage or race, individuals could achieve their quest for self-actualization, if they adhered to the tenets of the Yankee Protestant ethic.

6. Gone but Not Forgotten

Eulogies and the Sanctification of Washington

More so than the funeral or the countless obituaries, William Henry Lewis and the other eulogists shaped, promoted, and perpetuated the Tuskegee movement's attack on the southern ethic. Leading members of the movement appreciated the power of their tributes. Along with honoring the dead and comforting the listeners, eulogies intrinsically instruct and motivate. Like all orators who honor deceased persons of high esteem, these speakers sought to sanctify the deceased, encourage audiences to accept the death, and provide support for the desired future. In the process of performing these tasks, speakers honoring Booker T. Washington conveyed particular aspects of his life, deeds, associations, and vision. Although eulogists discussed an array of topics related to the life and ideas of Washington, they stressed his characteristics that reflected and promoted tenets of the Yankee Protestant ethic. Eulogists hoped that the snippets of Washington's life that they conveyed would inspire audiences to embrace his creed, emulate designated facets of his behavior, and assist with the actualization of his long-term goal.[1]

Like all tributes to public figures, these eulogists presented portrayals that promoted their favorite values and personal attributes. Each of Washington's eulogists individually chose which ones to promote. Eulogists generally highlighted Washington's early childhood, education, personality, values, the Tuskegee Institute, as well as the tenets that he promoted and his role in U.S. race relations. Regardless of the selections, and without denying his blackness, eulogists portrayed him as a southern representative of the Yankee Protestant ethic. They wanted all African Americans to become culture warriors and to adhere to those tenets. While many of the eulogists eschewed subtleties and boldly requested that African Americans embrace the teachings of Washington, leading white members of the institute's board of trustees declared their continual support of the Tuskegee Institute and its movement's assault on the southern ethic.[2]

Movement supporters indicated that they understood how the ambiance of a site hosting a memorial affected the audience. They therefore transformed venues into somber ceremonial atmospheres that captured listeners' attention, intensified their receptiveness, and signified to them that they would hear, during the event, a message of grave significance. Some supporters utilized portraits to achieve the desired somber environment. Tribute organizers at the St. John African Methodist Episcopal (AME) church in Montgomery, Alabama, for example, augmented the sanctuary with a large photograph of Washington that they placed in center of the pulpit. This most visible and prominent location symbolically declared the event's purpose. Arrangers of eulogies that took place at the Lincoln House in Chicago strongly indicated that they wanted to portray the tribute as a patriotic event. These sponsors draped a U.S. flag over an oil painting of the late educator during the tributes. Arrangers in Rochester produced a similar effect. These supporters, while placing a photograph of Washington in a conspicuous location, draped the city's Convention Hall, the location of the tribute, with "American flags and black and white buntings."[3]

While some organizers chose not to display portraits, others supplemented, and complemented, pictures of Washington with a variety of items to enhance the desired effect of the commemoration program. They exhibited plants, typically flowers, along with drapes and pennants. In New York City, several leading florists pledged flowers and palms to exhibit during a forthcoming tribute. They intended for the plants to complement the drapes, buntings, and flags in the Bethel AME Church sanctuary. Arrangers of a eulogy at the Grand Opera House in West Chester, Pennsylvania, placed a "great wreath of flowers" over a "life-size portrait" of Washington and positioned the icon on the opera house stage. With the adornment of sanctuaries with "large flags" and red, white, and cloth, supporters at the Congregational Church in Redland, California, and the AMEZ Church in Newburgh, New York, conveyed both gravity and patriotism. On the pulpits they placed bouquets of chrysanthemums, flowers that many people associated with the solemnity of death.[4]

*   *   *

Just as supporters did at Washington's funeral, organizers surrounded the delivery of his eulogies with music. The day of the tribute did not influence the nature of the music. Sympathizers attending tributes on the day of the

burial, as well as those who participated in one or more of the later memorials, heard soloists, duets, choirs, and orchestras. Like the visual objects
that planners of eulogies displayed, music enhanced the program's overall
effect. Organizers seemed to have recognized clearly, as did theologians, the
particular influence musical selections had on audiences. They knew that
certain carefully chosen music, performed at a specific place in the program,
could increase listeners' receptiveness to rhetorical presentations. Although
organizers conducted tributes each day of the week, the majority of them
took place during regular worship services on Sunday. Hence, as a matter of
course, arrangers included musical selections as an organic integral part of
the tributes.[5]

At many tributes, attendees listened to either instrumentals or vocals as
they entered the venues. Organizers in Newark, New Jersey, intended for
the singing of "Nearer, My God, to Thee" to initiate their tribute. Supporters in Flushing, New York, scheduled the combined choirs from Ebenezer
and Macedonia Churches to sing "Lead Kindly Light" as an "opening cho-
rus." Arrangers of a tribute in Dayton, Ohio, asserted that "a 20-minute
concert of sacred music and old plantation melodies will be rendered by
the Peoples band just before the speaking." After members of the Tuskegee
Institute community conducted a "Booker T. Washington Memorial March,"
organizers initiated the December 12, 1915, memorial with the school's organ
and orchestra playing "Lead Kindly Light." A united choir at a tribute in
Indianapolis performed the Protestant anthem "All Hail the Power of Jesus'
Name." Performing these and similar tunes at the beginning of the tributes
reinforced the sacrosanctity of the eulogies.[6]

At most tributes, audiences heard renditions of spirituals as well as Protestant hymns. The singing of these so-called plantation melodies often
occurred after the presentation of one or more Protestant hymns and before
the presentation of a eulogy. At many memorials, singers performed more
than one spiritual. The most frequently sung plantation melodies included
"Every Time I Feel the Spirit," "Steal Away to Jesus," and "Swing Low, Sweet
Chariot." Including plantation melodies in the programs, which reinforced
the sacredness of the tributes, clearly indicated to the listeners that the forthcoming eulogies would honor a member of the nation's African American
community.

In addition to the sacred music, a relatively small number of memorials
included secular songs. At a tribute in the Glenwood Mission Inn in Redlands, California, an African American choir performed "Old Black Joe." A
song with racist verses, it conveys the enslaved Old Black Joe's anguish over

the death of friends and loved ones. While possibly evoking grief, the song's stanza that asks the question "Where are the hearts that once so happy and so free?" wrongly implies that former slaves like Washington once enjoyed a blissful existence in the old South. "My Old Kentucky Home," which the student body at the Rochester (NY) Washington Junior High School performed, creates similar portraits of past black lives in that slaveholding state. Lyrics of "My Old Kentucky Home" proclaim that "'tis summer, the darkies are gay." Harriet Beecher Stowe's *Uncle Tom's Cabin* inspired Stephen C. Foster to compose both "Old Black Joe" and My Old Kentucky Home." He performed these songs during the late 1900s in minstrel shows, a popular theatrical genre among working-class whites that frequently demeaned African Americans.[7]

Attendees at Washington Junior High School, furthermore, heard the students sing "Dixie," a very controversial song. A favorite of antebellum white musicians who performed as black-faced minstrels, "Dixie" had become very popular in all sections of the nation. During the first few months of the Civil War, both Union and rebel military bands frequently performed "Dixie." The Confederates eventually adopted it as their battle hymn. Federals, though, did not give up the struggle for the ownership of "Dixie." Several days after Robert E. Lee surrendered in April 1865, President Abraham Lincoln expressed Northerners' affection for the song when he asserted that the Confederates had "attempted to appropriate it" and that the attorney general proclaimed the song as the North's "lawful prize." Northerners won the war, but they lost the song. Dixie had become the anthem of the U.S. South, the region most closely associated with the oppression and exploitation of African Americans.[8]

Ironically, one or more black northerners composed the song. The Snowdens, a black family of talented musicians living in Knox County, Ohio, taught the song to Daniel Emmett, a white neighbor, who is most often given credit for composing it. Originally composed as a ditty that ridicules a naive white southern woman whose lover had broken her heart, the tune masterfully reflects African Americans' rich oral tradition of improvising and signifying.[9]

The singing of "Dixie" and other minstrels songs performed at Washington's tributes wrongly inferred that the eulogized black man who lived only a few years in the antebellum South cherished its worldview as well as its lifestyle. Minstrel songs commemorate a stereotypical mythical idyllic antebellum American southern place and ethic. In the process, they reinforced popular support for the prewar southern way of life. Hence, supporters who included music of this genre (minstrelsy) in their tributes seemed not to have fully understood the culture war that Washington fought. Accompanying eulogies with these songs countered the Tuskegee movement's efforts at promoting a memory of Washington that would inspire the continuance of the culture war against the southern ethic.

"The Battle Hymn of the Negro" made it clear to anyone reading or singing its lyrics that supporters of the Tuskegee movement intended to continue to fight. Several months after Booker T. Washington's death, a number of newspapers promoted the singing of "The Battle Hymn of the Negro" as a public display of honoring him. It is a dramatically different type of song than the minstrels, and from its performances emerges a significantly dissimilar effect on listeners. William H. Davis, the NNBL stenographer, wrote the words to the tune of "The Battle Hymn of the Republic," a onetime anthem for both the Union army and its abolitionists supporters. Although the composer of the tune is unknown, Julia Ward Howe, a New York Protestant, had written the words to "The Battle Hymn of the Republic." The tune may have emerged from an impromptu musical session at a Methodist Camp meeting. Since this Christian sect often welcomed African Americans at their religious gatherings, one or more of them could have participated in creating the tune. African Americans in Georgia during the Civil War called it "The Wedding Tune," whereas Methodist hymnals titled it "Brothers, Will You Meet Me?" Memorializing both John Brown the abolitionist and John Brown a Union soldier, the troops of the Twelfth Massachusetts Volunteers renamed it "John Brown's Body." After hearing the singing of that version, Julia Ward Howe wrote a new set of verses. She titled her militaristic marching song "The Battle Hymn of the Republic," which in turn provided part of the inspiration for the words that Davis composed to commemorate Washington.[10]

Even a perfunctory reading of the lyrics to "The Battle Hymn of the Negro" will quickly reveal that Davis, while not excluding any segment of America, primarily aimed them at Washington's supporters, especially African Americans.

THE BATTLE HYMN OF THE NEGRO

Our eyes have seen the glory of a Booker Washington.
He has fought a swordless battle for the cause of right and won.
He has made his race respected, though his life on earth is done
His truth is marching on!

Glory, glory, hallelujah!
Glory, glory, hallelujah!
Glory, glory, hallelujah!
Our Booker Washington!

We have seen him in the watchfires of our race's bitter woes
Beating down the flames of prejudice and making friends of foes.
We have heard his forceful pleadings, and our racial progress shows
This work of Washington.

We have heard his loving gospel urging "Brotherhood of Men,"
"Mutual Helpfulness" his doctrine, preached by action, tongue and pen.
Whites and blacks should live together—not as enemies, but friends,
For God is marching on.

He has sounded forth the trumpet that would never call retreat,
Prove yourselves useful Americans and never fear defeat.
Oh, be swift our souls to answer, make the victory complete
Of Booker Washington.

In the hills of "old Virginia" he was born in poverty,
With ambition in his bosom, even "up from slavery."
As he died to lift men higher, teach our children then to see
The truths of Washington![11]

In the fashion of an eulogy, "The Battle Hymn of the Negro" provides a partial biography, praises the deceased, lists desired virtues, and instructs the living; the lyrics of Davis's martial marching song recognize the cultural war that Washington had fought and that his supporters continued to wage. Davis intended for the song to rally Americans to remain supportive of the ideas that Washington taught and the programs he worked so steadfastly to implement. One of the song's verses proclaims that all Americans, not just blacks, needed to embrace the Yankee Protestant value of working on behalf of their neighbors. Other stanzas provide evidence that the collective black population maintained strong desires to pursue increased national status. They promoted a peaceful and respectful coexistence with whites, rather than an ongoing longing for a pre-freedom past.[12]

Although newspapers had publicized lyrics that Davis, a prominent member of the Tuskegee movement, wrote, it is not clear that any tribute performed the "Battle Hymn of the Negro." Attendees at several eulogies, however, did sing "America." Written and publicly sung for the first time in 1832, "America" had become a popular but unofficial national anthem. Samuel F. Smith, a Bostonian and Harvard College graduate, wrote the lyrics of "America" to the English melody "God Save the King" while studying for the ministry at Andover Theological Seminary. A German music book for schoolchildren, which printed the English melody with German patriotic lyrics, inspired Smith to write the words to "America." Written in 1744, this English nationalistic song had achieved international admiration. Songwriters residing in several states across Europe had appropriated and ascribed their nationalistic lyrics to the tune. Smith just followed their example.[13]

For more than 160 years before the death of Washington, Americans of all ages, sexes, and races had performed "God Save the King" and a variety of other songs, including America, to the melody. They greatly appreciated the relationship that music had with culture and politics. Hence they sang nationalistic tunes during every kind of public event. Americans performed them at celebrations and ceremonies, as well as at political and protest rallies. Opinion makers utilized patriotic songs to socialize and nationalize its citizens. Few songs, if any, performed this task as proficiently as "America."

AMERICA

"My country, 'tis of thee,
Sweet land of liberty,
Of thee I sing:
Land where my fathers died.
Land of the pilgrim's pride;
From every mountain-side,
Let freedom ring.

My native country! Thee,
Land of the noble free;
Thy name I love:
I love thy rocks and rills,
Thy woods and templed hills;
My heart with rapture thrills,
Like that above.

No more shall tyrants here
With haughty steps appear
And soldier-bands;
No more shall tyrants tread
Above the patriot dead;
No more our blood be shed
By alien hands.
Let music swell the breeze,
And ring from all the trees
Sweet freedom's song:
Let mortal tongues awake,
Let all that breathes partake,
Let rocks their silence break,
The sound prolong.

Our fathers' God! To thee,
Author of liberty!
To thee we sing:
Long may our land be bright
With freedom's holy light;
Protect us by thy might,
Great God, our King![14]

Like other nationalist Americans, attendees at Washington tributes embraced the song and its declaration of patriotism. Singing "America" at these ceremonies not only proclaimed their attachment to the nation, it rhetorically signified Washington's patriotism. Perhaps it even suggested that he embodied the essence of American values.[15]

*　*　*

A number of eulogists sought to inspire their respective audiences to embrace patriotism. Since newspapers and other periodicals published accounts of tributes to Washington, eulogists conveyed both orally and in print their assessment of his citizenship and patriotism. Advocates of the Yankee Protestant ethic, which by the turn of the twentieth century had become both a religious and a secular set of values, had folded the tenet of patriotism into their belief system. Black as well as white eulogists discussed it, and like all significant topics examined in the tributes, few noticeable differences between the two groups emerged in their respective presentations. Movement supporters, regardless of race, seemed genuinely concerned about a perceived threat to U.S. patriotism. During the two decades preceding Washington's death, tens of millions of new immigrants relocated to midwestern and northeastern urban centers from eastern and southern Europe. For the most part, Yankee Protestants and their allies distrusted the loyalty of these new arrivals, who they suspected held beliefs and displayed behaviors that challenged the core values of Washington's eulogists. For many Tuskegee movement supporters, only people who embraced their ethic could claim the status of patriot. Since the new immigrants' values and lifestyles concerned many of the persons who delivered tributes, their eulogies reflected their intention to teach patriotism.[16]

Eulogists thus envisioned and projected Washington as an American who loved his country. "Booker T. Washington was a good citizen," declared Daniel Carter Beard, a founder of Boys Scouts of America. Rabbi Stephen S. Wise and the Reverend William B. Suthern likewise testified to Washington's faithfulness to America. At a memorial held within the Free Synagogue within Carnegie

Hall, Wise, an NAACP cofounder and the congregation's leader, emphasized "the good which Dr. Washington did for the American people." Suthern, who preached at a Hartford (CT) African American AMEZ Church, announced at a tribute held at his church that Washington did not lack "Patriotism." Several weeks later, Stephen M. Newman, a former Congregational minster and the white president of the predominately African American–populated Howard University, attested to Washington's patriotism. During the delivery of his eulogy in the university chapel, Newman asserted that Washington "put patriotism above all racial or political considerations." In his December 12, 1915, tribute at Tuskegee Institute, Roosevelt provided the specifics to Newman's generality, alleging that Washington provided him with unselfish advice that "was for the best interests of the people of the entire country."[17]

Recognizing that certain values had desirable effects on many listeners and readers, eulogists professed Washington's religious beliefs along with his patriotism. Acknowledging his piety served several purposes. It most importantly placed his accolades in a sacred context. Thus, for many people, proclaiming Washington's faith further legitimized the eulogists' praises and increased listeners' and readers' receptiveness to the acclaims. With the exception of the Reverend Henry Y. Arnett, eulogists rarely identified Washington as Baptist. The Reverend B. Mack Hubbar of Baton Rouge, Louisiana, declared that, as a true "follower of Jesus Christ," Washington's theology did not allow "for any particular denominational creed." Hubbar and the other eulogists who discussed Washington's piety expounded on his love for the Christian God. Speaking in Jacksonville, Florida, Mrs. I. I. Keeniebrew alleged that "few give more attention to the daily reading of the Bible than [Washington]." At a tribute in Savannah, Georgia, Professor H. Pearson contended that Nathalie Lord, one of Washington's Hampton Institute teachers and longtime adviser, taught Washington "to love the bible [*sic*] as the Work of God." Former president Theodore Roosevelt and Howard University president Stephen M. Newman conveyed similar sentiments: Roosevelt avowed that Washington "walked humbly with his God," while Newman asserted that Washington possessed a natural "faith in God."[18]

His piety may have helped to project a humble appearance. Eulogists declared Washington a modest man, and neither his relationship with Roosevelt, nor any other powerful persons, generated a memory that contested this image. "Being of modest demeanor" is how Will H. Wethers characterized Washington at a tribute in Baton Rouge, Louisiana. William H. Lewis made the same claim in his eulogy. At a tribute in Tucson, Arizona, Colonel LeRoy Brown, a white military instructor at the University of Arizona, recalled that, as a young adult, Washington "was a quiet, unassuming man."

While stationed in Hampton, Virginia, he had met Washington, then an instructor at Hampton Institute. Industrialist, political boss, and former Tuskegee Institute trustee Hugh Hanna, at a tribute in Indianapolis, "placed Booker T. Washington second to no man in . . . humility." He claimed to have "never known a man who was more humble in spirit" than Washington. After pronouncing him "exonerated from egotism," Reverend William A. Harrod, the African American pastor of Shiloh Baptist Church in Hartford, Connecticut, described Washington "as modest and unassuming as the lily." Furthermore, eulogists alleged that Washington's demeanor projected an air of approachability. William Walcott, the assistant commandant of the military department at Tuskegee Institute, further testified to Washington's affability: "[he] was the busiest man" but "always accessible to everyone, great or small."[19]

Perhaps Washington's perceived quiet dignity fostered views of his humility. Eulogists described him as a distinguished man who did not talk much. W. B. Edwards told his audience that Washington "didn't converse much[,] only to ask questions." Washington's cultivated etiquette conceivably dictated that he, as Edwards alleged, "listened intently to what others had to say." At a tribute in New Jersey, former governor J. Franklin Fort's eulogy made a point of Washington's demureness. Fort declared that as Washington "lived, so he died, a quiet" man. His limited conversation might have helped to inspire the several eulogists who delivered tributes in New Orleans to emphasize Washington's "simplicity of style and manner." Imagining Washington as someone with a "charming reserve," with a "simple dignity," and "perfect poise" is how his friend and admirer William H. Lewis projected Washington at a tribute in New York. Washington's persona impressed Alice R. Hitchcock, a teacher in Newburgh, New York. "A man of fine presence, courteous, and refined," is how she recalled him in her eulogy. Eulogists thus testified that Washington had mastered one of the essential aspects of the Yankee Protestant ethic: "absolute restraint of oneself."[20]

Washington's finesse, purported eulogists, did not preclude his sense of humor. He often punctuated his speeches with stories, often at the expense of African Americans, to amuse his audiences. Washington frequently told jokes in Negro dialect that insulted many articulate black people. They certainly offended Mary Church Terrell, a black woman who advocated for African American and women rights. She criticized him in 1906 for telling jokes in public that mocked blacks. Eulogists did not, however, mention that his humor sometimes offended listeners. They only focused on the quality of his wit. A former Tuskegee Institute teacher, Mrs. I. I. Keeniebrew, recalled at a tribute in Jacksonville that Washington "had a keen sense of humor—no one appreciated a good joke more than he." It delighted Washington, she continued, to hear a new one. "He could illustrate a point," Keeniebrew purported "by his inimitable manner of telling a joke." William H. Lewis, who called Washington's humor a "characteristic of the race," claimed that the late educator could "convulse an audience with laughter."[21]

The Tuskegean's skills as an orator elicited high praise from his eulogists. Unlike some of the commentaries critics made following the Atlanta Exposition, tributes offered no mixed reviews. They declared his voice forceful while alleging that he delivered his talks fluently. During the years between Atlanta and his death, Washington presented hundreds of orations to thousands of people in a multiplicity of venues. He thus enjoyed ample opportunity to practice and to improve the quality and effectiveness of his presentations. Most people heard him after he had become an icon and had mastered the art of speech making. At a tribute in Peoria, Illinois, the Reverend S. B. Jones, pastor of the Ward Chapel AME Church, acknowledged Washington's proficiency. He purported that Washington's oratory "captivated thousands" of people. Other eulogists testified to the fluency of Washington's orations. At a memorial in Flushing, New York, Thomas H. Mackenzie, the pastor of the Dutch Reform Church, argued that Washington ranked with William Jennings Bryan and Bourke Cochran, a New York congressman, as one of the three "great orators of his day." William H. Lewis testified that Washington possessed the most eloquent voice of his day. After stating that Washington "was eloquent, powerful and effective, a speaker," as a Dr. Mevs of Baton Rouge, Louisiana, eulogized that "thousands of people, both white and black have been held spellbound by his matchless eloquence."[22]

Along with his voluminous publications, Washington's speeches conceivably inspired his eulogists to commend his instincts. They praised his wisdom. Frank P. Chisholm, financial secretary for the Tuskegee Institute, purported at a tribute in Hartford, Connecticut, at the AMEZ Church that Washington had both "good common sense" and "sound judgment." At the tribute in Carnegie Hall, William Lewis alleged that Washington owned "shrewd common sense." Hugh Hanna declared that no man owned more wisdom than Washington. Few persons possessed Washington's endowment of insight, intimated the Reverend Charles Franklin Thwing, president of Western Reserve University. While delivering a tribute at St. John's AME Church in Cleveland, Ohio, he stated that Washington "possessed the most uncommon gift of the day—abundant Common-sense." Thwing subsequently claimed that Washington's "soundness of judgment was one of the things" that attracted men to the late educator. At a tribute that took place at the predominately white–populated West Chester State Normal School in Pennsylvania, Principal George Morris Philips similarly declared that Washington's "good sense" impressed him.[23]

His intellect mesmerized African Americans eulogists. Although both northern and southern blacks applauded Washington's quality of thought, white extollers tended not to mention it. Perhaps they thought that his programs manifested nothing more than common sense, or that they merely mimicked those of the Hampton Institute. It is possible that white eulogists concluded that the conception of Washington's program emerged innately and not from rigorous systemic contemplation. An English teacher at the predominately black–populated Georgia State College in Savannah, H. Pearson did not convey any one of those opinions in his tribute. He declared that "Washington was logical" and a "practical thinker." In his eulogy, Tuskegee employee Frank P. Chisholm announced that Washington produced precise thoughts. His ideas convinced the Reverend Henry Y. Arnett that they possessed a dynamic "intellectual strength." Arnett made that assertion in a eulogy delivered at the Mount Olive AME Church in Philadelphia. "Comprehensible," logical, and "most convincing" is how Dr. Mevs described Washington's thoughts. During a tribute at Hampton Institute, William H. Lewis declared simply that Washington possessed "the spark of genius."[24]

His wit, demeanor, and intellect facilitated his skillful interpersonal exchanges with a wide spectrum of individuals. Rabbi Wise "styled" Washington as a "statesman" during a service at the Free Synagogue in Carnegie Hall. At Voorhees Industrial School in Denmark, South Carolina, R. F. Green, an African American shoemaking instructor, expressed appreciation for Washington's intervention on behalf of black people. He believed that for years Washington stood between black people and "the fierce hate and oppression of ignorance and fanaticism." Washington employed his extraordinary mediating talents to charm hostile whites. At the tribute in Varick Memorial AMEZ Church in New Haven, Connecticut, the Reverend D. S. Klugh extolled Washington's charisma, calling Washington a "man of great personal magnetism." Klugh, who had pastored and taught at the Tuskegee Institute, claimed that he had seen Washington "sway large prejudiced audiences as the great winds move the forest." Not only did Washington win over antagonistic whites, he asserted Charles Alexander, former publisher and Tuskegee Institute teacher, "found it possible to reach men who lived, virtually in steel cages, protected from the intrusion of the outside world." Alexander charged, in part, that "Washington's success was due to his fine diplomacy." Lewis attributed Washington's diplomatic acumen to his in-depth knowledge of human nature. During his Hampton Institute tribute, he alleged that Washington's "knowledge of human nature was instinctive, intuitive, and sometimes uncanny."[25]

While Washington's servile experiences surely inspired him to refine his skills at determining the aspirations, fears, and moods of the people, particularly whites, in his audiences, none of the eulogists made that connection in their tributes. They primarily discussed Washington's enslavement as inspirational. Lewis's Hampton Institute commencement address informed listeners that, as a newborn, Washington "laid upon a bundle of dirty rags upon the dirt floor of a log cabin, with hardly more thought given to his birth than that of a domestic animal." When the Civil War ended, contended William H. Lewis, Washington entered freedom as "an unlettered slave at the age of seven." William Lawrence, a bishop in the Episcopal Church, likewise emphasized Washington's disadvantages at birth in his tribute. He reported that Washington lived part of his youth without either a name or home. In Waterville, Maine, the white pastor of the University Place Church of Christ, Charles S. Melbury, indicated that Washington not only had no father to support him, he did not even know the man's name. Repeating one of Washington's often-fabricated claims, Melbury asserted that, as "a child of slavery," Washington did not "know his father or the date of his birth." References to the enslaved Washington intimated that if the late educator could rise up from slavery to achieve greatness, then Americans born in freedom had few or no excuses for not striving for excellence.[26]

As they did with the verbal sketches of Washington's enslavement experience, eulogists made object lessons out of the snippets of his early post-emancipation biography. They used these bits to teach their audiences the practicality of selected tenets of the Yankee Protestant ethic. While praising Washington for his accomplishments, the Reverend C. Waldo Cherry, pastor of the Central Presbyterian Church of Rochester, New York, promoted the dignity of labor and its rewards when he told an audience that before Washington headed the Tuskegee Institute and received an honorary degree from Harvard, he washed dishes in a hotel kitchen and worked in a coal mine. At a tribute in Indianapolis, D. P. Roberts, the pastor of Bethel AME Church, promoted perseverance. He reported that Washington arrived at Hampton Institute as a hungry, ragged boy "with only 5 cents in his pocket." In telling a similar story, William Walcott promoted both steadfastness as well as conscientiousness. He alleged that Washington's earnestness won him "the admiration of the woman at the head" of Hampton Institute, who in turn admitted him to the academy. Speaking at a New Year's Day tribute on the Howard University campus, eulogists Professor George W. Cook, Washington, D.C., school board member Thomas J. Jones, and Howard University president Stephen M. Newman promoted the tenet of thoroughness by repeating Washington's account of how he secured admission to Hampton Institute.[27]

Tributes overwhelmingly credited the school and its founder, Samuel Chapman Armstrong, for providing Washington with the knowledge that served him well as an adult. For the most part, they disregarded Washington's African American teachers and his education in predominately black–populated schools. Discussing Washington's education at a memorial in Redlands, California, Walcott ignored the Tuskegean's childhood black teachers. While briefly mentioning that "a white woman" provided Washington with his first schooling, he focused on the Hampton Institute. Across the continent at a commemoration in Hartford, Connecticut, the Reverend William A. Harrod neglected to report that black teachers taught Washington. He gave credit to Hampton Institute and the Wayland Seminary only. Rabbi Wise, in his remembrance, ignored Washington's pre-Hampton life. "A new conception of life" is what the teachers at Hampton provided Washington, contended the Reverend Samuel W. Beaven, assistant pastor at Lake Avenue Baptist Church in Rochester, New York.[28]

While discussing his post–Hampton Institute experiences, eulogists omitted mention of Washington's employment in Franklin County, Virginia, and of his postgraduate work at Hampton Institute. They did, of course, discuss the establishment of Tuskegee Institute and its early years. Some eulogies, such as the one that Miss Frances Fields presented at a Connecticut tribute, concentrated primarily on Washington's life at the institute. Other presenters delivered a more comprehensive biography. In his eulogy, Rabbi M. H. Harris of Temple Israel in Harlem provided a short account of how Washington became the principal of the Tuskegee Institute. "Do not imagine him summoned to take charge of a school that was established," insisted Harris. He told his audience that "Outside of appropriating $2,000 for its maintenance, the entire work of founding it from its very roots, organizing it, and calling it into being, was entirely left to [Washington]."[29]

While Sigmund S. Hecht, at the Los Angeles tribute held in the Shrine auditorium, claimed credit for assisting Washington during the school's "incipiency," a number of other eulogists recalled how Washington demonstrated the Yankee Protestant value of perseverance and relied on his work ethic to overcome adversity in developing the institute. Hecht, who worked from 1876 to 1888 as a rabbi in Montgomery, Alabama, helped Washington when the Tuskegee Institute experienced a growing student population and the administration possessed little money to construct new buildings to accommodate the increasing population. To expand housing opportunities, Washington directed a group of his students in the art of brick making that they used to construct desired buildings. The Reverends Beaven and Frissell communicated to their respective audiences that after the students failed several times in their efforts at baking the bricks, Washington pawned his watch to finance the eventual successful attempt. Over the years, determination and effort enabled Washington to manage the development of the largest predominately African American school in the nation. At the time of his death, contended A. E. Chester, a eulogist in Baton Rouge, Louisiana, Tuskegee Institute consisted of "103 buildings, large and small; 2345 acres of land; plant and equipment valued at $1,579,248; endowment Fund $1,901,129." These data, as well as the story about the bricks, served as object lessons for audiences: embracing the Yankee Protestant tenets of pragmatism, perseverance, and systematic work would ensure success.[30]

Dignifying labor, a most important facet of the Yankee Protestant creed, is a value that tributes closely associated with Washington. He had become one of the most renowned advocates of the tenet. Americans have never attached any black person closer to it than Washington. His contemporaries celebrated him for his support and affection for the concept. At a memorial held at St. John's AME Church in Cleveland, Ohio, the Reverend Charles Franklin Thwing reported that Washington once told him, on a trip the two once took together, that "it is a good thing for every man to have a hard job." Suggesting that Washington performed difficult labor, Governor J. Franklin Fort proclaimed him "industrious." Each of the three eulogists at Howard University agreed that Washington possessed a willingness to work. The Reverend Charles S. Melbury declared that labor helped to make Washington "a leader of his race," whereas A. E. Chester, eulogizing at Mount Zion Baptist Church in Baton Rouge, Louisiana, declared that "the most beautiful trait of the late Dr. Washington character was that he loved toil." Chester furthermore asserted that "no man ever worked harder and longer" than Washington. Trumpeting a similar judgment, the Reverend William A. Harrod announced that "No one standing at his grave can say 'Here lies a lazy man' but must say, 'Here lies a hero who wore out his life for the uplift, and honor of his people and his friends.'"[31]

Devotees of the ethic promoted conscientious work. Conveying a variety of labels and phrases, eulogists sought to communicate to audiences that Washington labored in earnest. Signifying that Washington took his labor seriously, the Reverend William B. Suthern stated that "Washington was assailed and many stumbling blocks were placed in his path, but he stood unflinchingly for the work that he had undertaken." Robert R. Cheeks, president of the Cleveland Association of Colored Men, indicated at the St. John's AME Church tribute in Cleveland that Washington did not allow anyone or anything to prohibit him from accomplishing his tasks. Cheeks proclaimed that Washington "realized what he had to do and did it." At the tribute in Baton Rouge, Louisiana, Dr. Mevs paraphrased a verse from Matthew 25:23 to express the seriousness and thoroughness of Washington's work: "well done thou good and faithful servant."[32]

* * *

Along with these and other tenets, eulogists discussed Washington's calling. While delivering a eulogy in Newburgh, New York, headmaster of the Newburgh Free Academy, the Reverend F. E. Stockwell proclaimed that God sent Washington to "perform a definite work." He thus authenticated Washington's calling, his lifetime labor. For Yankee Protestants, no precept held greater prestige. Faithfully fulfilling one's calling" had both religious and secular signification. To many practicing Protestants, it provided undisputable evidence that one belonged to God's chosen people. Seculars honored persons who pursued a calling out of appreciation for their ascetic, frugality, industriousness, conscientiousness, steadiness, pragmatism, neatness, and honesty. Americans associated these traits with reliable workers and successful businessmen. Although eulogists like the United Presbyterian pastor J. G. D. Findley alleged that "God inspired" Washington, secularists could embrace easily an nonreligious interpretation of the Yankee Protestant's concept of calling. Perhaps Bastian Smits, the minister at Detroit's First Congregational Church, conveyed the thoughts of secularists when he proclaimed Washington's "sole aim was to lift man."[33]

For Washington and other disciples of the creed, answering one's calling indeed emphasized serving humanity. Adherents worked not just for themselves but for the common good. Eulogists acknowledged the service that Washington provided to other people. The Reverend Richard R. Ball, in his eulogy in Hartford, Connecticut, made this point dramatically. Ball proclaimed that he did not agree with some of Washington's "views and acts." He further reported that no one, not even the most ardent Tuskegee movement supporter, had more "sincere admiration for" Washington's "eminent services to his race." The Reverend B. Mack Hubbard, speaking at the Mount Zion Baptist Church tribute in Baton Rouge, did not make Washington's service race-specific. He declared that Washington "was an apostle of the brother-hood of man," not just African Americans. Renowned newspaper man Milton B. Ochs voiced a similar sentiment. The youngest sibling of a Jewish family that controlled the *Chattanooga (TN) News*, the *New York Times*, and several other large newspapers, Ochs asserted at a Chattanooga tribute that Washington "taught and practiced . . . love of humanity." Emphasizing the importance he thought Washington placed on serving, Professor C. H. Condell, at a memorial service at the Baptist–sponsored predominately African American–populated State University (Simmons College) in Louisville, Kentucky, asserted that Washington "threw his whole being into the presentation of the needs of others." Presenting his tribute at the NNBL's annual meeting in Kansas City, Missouri, Emmett J. Scott, Washington's longtime private secretary, similarly noted that Washington "gave to his race and to his country all of the physical and mental vigor; he could give no more."[34]

Serving other people necessitated self-sacrifice, and devotees of the Yankee Protestant ethic embraced asceticism. Disciples believed that scientific or systematic work, along with self-denial, would help produce the wealth needed to enhance the common good, the noblest objective for both religious and secular supporters of the ethic. More often than other eulogists, current and former members of the Tuskegee Institute Board of Trustees, employees of the institute, and close friends of the principal—the core membership of the Tuskegee movement—discussed Washington's championing of personal sacrifice. In his eulogy, Hugh Hanna, a former trustee, referred to self-denial as "the greatest thing" that a man could give to his friend. At the Shiloh Baptist Church in Hartford, Connecticut, Frank P. Chisholm suggested that Washington forsook riches and personal pleasures in the "spirit of sacrifice." Knowledge of the Tuskegean's self-denial may have inspired John O. Thomas, the field secretary for the institute, to title his tribute at the Michigan Avenue Baptist Church in Buffalo, New York, "Dr. Washington as a Personal Friend and a Self-Sacrificing Worker for Humanity."[35]

John Wesley, a founder of the Methodist Church, asserted that "both industry and frugality . . . cannot but produce riches." He could have also proclaimed correctly that frugality, a key component of the ethic, augments labor and self-denial. It is harder, but not impossible, for persons to attain wealth without saving. With this understanding, Washington taught, spoke, and wrote about the value of thrift, and his eulogists acknowledged him for it. In his letter to attendees of the memorial held at Varick Memorial AMEZ Church in New Haven, former president William H. Taft included thrift as one of the several tenets Washington taught black people. Milton B. Ochs's eulogy stressed that Washington taught black people to save. His inspiration for teaching the wisdom of thrift, alleged William H. Lewis, derived from observing the black "tolling masses spending all they earned." Lewis contended that Washington told African Americans to "save; get a bank account!" He presented thrift, asserted Charles Alexander in the tribute at White Temple in San Diego, California, as one of the primary factors that would provide "the ultimate solutions of the perplexing problem of the negro [*sic*] life."[36]

Some tributes contended that a strong desire to assist African Americans with their efforts to increase significantly their material well-being and their civil status propelled Washington to answer his calling. Leading the battle to transform the poverty-stricken, overly race-conscious population of the U.S. South into a just, pluralistic, and prosperous citizenry became his lifework. Washington's aspiration, asserted the powerful black attorney and Republican politician, E. H. Wright, at a tribute in Chicago, resulted from "a dream in his early years and it was of service to his people, ideas of the masses, and his preparing of them for usefulness." This alleged vision inspired George Cleveland Hall, Washington's personal physician and one of the cofounders of the Association for the Study of Negro Life and History, to call the Tuskegean a prophet. Sharing the platform with Wright, Hall claimed that Washington "saw his great work ahead of him, and had lived to see" the Tuskegee Institute, "a great part of his dream," realized. Rabbi Harris indicated that the vision came to Washington after he accepted the job of starting the school. Washington, alleged Harris, "felt that he was called to help solve the problem of the freed negro [*sic*]." In his address at Carnegie Hall, Washington's successor as principal of Tuskegee Institute, Robert R. Moton, supported the argument that Washington used the institute to assist the masses of African Americans. He concluded that Washington struggled "so that men might have a chance through the great Tuskegee Normal and Industrial Institute."[37]

*   *   *

Yankee Protestants valued education highly. Formal learning, particularly the acquisition of literacy, enabled individuals to read God's word for themselves. It allowed each individual to obtain, without the mediation of a third party, an understanding of what God desired from his people. It assisted their efforts at establishing a personal relationship with their deity, which is a vital aspect of Protestantism. Education, moreover, maximized people's ability to realize fully their calling. As persons who facilitated learning, educators acquired prominence in their communities, and in the American South, they fought on the front lines of the culture war. Providing an education to southerners had become a significant struggle. For the most part, public education did not emerge there until after the Civil War. Poverty and a legacy of private instruction for a privileged few hampered its development. Yankee Protestants and their black southern allies struggled mightily to overcome those obstacles. Washington had become the foremost symbol and voice for the education of ordinary southerners, particularly African Americans.[38]

As a result, few educators in the nation's history had enjoyed as high status as had Booker T. Washington. Eulogists helped to insure that his prestige as an educator transcended his death. W. W. Wemple, the New York State commissioner of public safety, participated in that effort. Speaking in Schenectady, Wemple contended that Washington did much to uplift black people "along educational lines." Making a similar assessment, J. R. Thompson, the pastor of the Westminster Reformed Church in Newburgh, New York, asserted that Washington did well in securing educational opportunities for blacks. Moton's evaluations greatly exceeded the ones that both Thompson and Wemple pronounced. In an address delivered at a tribute that the Alabama State Negro Teachers' Association conducted, Moton announced that no black person had ever equaled Washington's pedagogical competence. He declared Washington the "greatest teacher . . . the negro [sic] race had produced."[39]

Other extollers did not use race as a qualifier in their praise of Washington for his achievements as an educator. A number of eulogists, including New York's Rabbi Wise, simply proclaimed Washington "a great educator." However, for the pastor of Bethel AME Church in Indianapolis, D. P. Roberts, Washington had become more than an excellent teacher. In his judgment, no one defended education as well as had Washington. Similarly, Michigan governor Woodbridge N. Ferris declared the Tuskegean the "prince of American educators." At an Alabama State Colored Teachers Association meeting in Montgomery, R. B. Hudson declared Washington a pedagogical revolutionary. A black businessman from Selma, Alabama, who had formerly taught school, Hudson proclaimed that Washington possessed a theory that "revolutionized the educational work of the entire country."[40]

Washington had won widespread support for his hybrid curriculum and pedagogy. Although he labeled his concept of education *industrial education*, it differed from traditional vocational training that many elites in the North promoted to the masses during much of the postbellum era. Washington commingled a limited vocational education with a heavy emphasis on traditional precollegiate academic courses while indoctrinating students with the Yankee Protestant ethic, especially the tenet that emphasized the dignity of labor. He sold his educational ideas as a way to enhance blacks' economic standing, and to develop racial interdependence to markedly improve relations between blacks and whites. Washington said, "It is along this line I think we have got to look for the final and safe settlement of many of the race difficulties." He did not argue for all blacks to secure an industrial education. Washington revealed that for some African Americans he believed "thoroughly in the value of the classical and [for] others the industrial and technical."[41]

He did support industrial education for most ordinary African Americans. Washington's eulogists, as they did while he lived, cheered him for his success at convincing civic leaders, politicians, and educators to implement his "revolutionary" concept of education. Some eulogists, however, took longer to appreciate Washington's educational philosophy than others. When he first graduated from a "negro [sic] college" in 1890, E. P. Roberts did not believe that most blacks should pursue an industrial education. Roberts, the pastor of St. Mark's Methodist Episcopal Church in New York City, claimed "that he soon learned, as most others who studied the question did also, that Dr. Washington was right in insisting that industrial and vocational training were the greatest necessities of the negroes [sic]." Washington's proficiency as a teacher moved Dr. Mevs in Baton Rouge, Louisiana, to proclaim the late educator to be "the great apostle of Industrial Education." The instruction might have inspired Henry H. Proctor, the minister of Atlanta's First Congregational Church, to avow that Washington would "go down in history as the leader of the race in industrial development." In Trenton, New Jersey, J. T. Young recognized that not all Americans agreed with such assessments, but he "defended Mr. Washington's insistence upon industrial education for his people." No need existed to champion it with Michigan governor Woodbridge N. Ferris, who eulogized that "the work done by Dr. Washington for the Negro race . . . in fitting it for industrial life is exactly what we are trying to do for the white man today."[42]

Tuskegee Institute officially added industrial training to its initial mission of teacher education in 1893, although only a small percentage of its students mastered a skilled vocation. Five years before Washington's death, Monroe Work, the institute's director of the Division of Records and Research, informed Washington and the executive council that teaching academics made up the bulk of the school's curriculum. All students, however, learned to endure, if not honor, menial labor: every student had to work at some task that contributed to the operation of the institute. A. E. Chester of Baton Rouge charged in his tribute that the "constantly expanding Tuskegee" reflected the emphases that the school's curriculum placed on the "dignity of labor." Commandant Walcott told his California audience that "wherever you find a

Tuskegee student you will find a thorough worker." Not only did Washington want his students to work diligently, avowed President Roosevelt in Tuskegee, he also sought to train them to "face life cheerfully and resolutely, bent to do the best they could physically, mentally, and morally."[43]

For many people, Tuskegee Institute had become synonymous with Washington. Eulogists reinforced this perception in their praises. William H. Lewis purported that "Washington grew as Tuskegee grew, in richness, prestige, power, and influence." This symbiosis had, over the years, inspired a number of eulogists to visit the institute and see its operation and physical plant. At a tribute held in Morristown, New Jersey, the local paper reported that a eulogist named Reed told of visiting the Tuskegee Institute, where his "eyes had never beheld such great work accomplished." Ella Flagg Young provided her audience with a more detail account of her 1912 visit to the institute, as well as her exceptions. "I went there, she admitted, with the same idea that I presume is in the mind of every one of my own race." Claiming that she had heard of the "great man Mr. Washington," Flagg reported that she had expected to see "work for a man of another race." To her amazement, it took her fewer than twenty-four hours to learn that the school possessed a "leader carrying out ideas which the people of my own race in this country had attained and which I had seen nowhere so exemplified in the work of the school as here." Proficient execution of its mission might have inspired the Reverend S. B. Jones, in his tribute at Ward Chapel AME Church in Peoria, Illinois, to declare Tuskegee Institute "the greatest school of its kind in the world."[44]

Twenty years earlier, the school's growing prestige and its principal's popularity in the lower South inspired the organizers of the 1895 Atlanta Cotton States and International Exposition to invite Washington to speak at the fair. He accepted the invitation and his speech became the hallmark address of his career. It literally made Washington an overnight national figure. While eulogists often referred to the speech, most of them did not dwell on it. Some eulogists, like the Reverend Henry Arnett, however, countered that trend. His tribute included an expanded discussion concerning the Atlanta speech. Eulogizing Washington at the Mount Olive AME Church in Philadelphia, Arnett asked his audience to recall how "the country was moved by that address." That Atlanta lecture, contended Arnett, provided Washington with an opportunity to display his intellect, purpose, and character. God, declared Arnett, seemed to have opened a door for Washington to tell black people to "drop your bucket where you are." To Arnett, this declaration instructed African Americans "to do well and with their might 'whatsoever their hands found to do.'" While Grace Vanamee, a leading white suffragist in New York, did not provide an interpretation of the address, she did highly praise it. At

the tribute held at the AMEZ Church in Newburgh, New York, Vanamee proclaimed that Washington's speech stood "out with only one equal in American
history, that of Lincoln's address at the Gettysburg cemetery dedication."[45]

After Washington's famed Atlanta speech, major philanthropists became
much more willing to provide Washington with funds for the institute. Since
the school continually needed financial donations, fund-raising became
Washington's first and most important duty. Although Jay Thomas, a teacher
at the institute, acknowledged in a eulogy at Temple Beth Zion in Buffalo,
New York, that Jews financially assisted Washington, Yankee Protestants
provided the bulk of the gifts. Washington traveled through much of the
Upper Midwest, Northeast, and the West seeking money for the institute
and for the Tuskegee movement in general. In his eulogy, the Reverend F.
E. Stockwell recalled that during his boyhood Washington visited his home
while soliciting funds. William H. Lewis remembered Washington "begging
almost from door to door" during his tribute of Washington at a Hampton
Institute commencement. Washington's speech at Atlanta and those that he
delivered over the next twenty years, testified Rabbi M. H. Harris, inspired
millionaires enthusiastically to "place their wealth at his disposal." According to the Reverend D. S. Klugh, they responded favorably to Washington's
preaching the "Gospel of moral regeneration and industrial salvation for the
negro [*sic*]."[46]

Major as well as small contributions enabled Washington both to expand
the institute and fund public outreach programs, or what he called "extension works." Washington believed that these activities helped "to elevate the
race and to improve conditions in the South." In his 1908 annual report to
the school's board of trustees, Washington wrote: "the number of students
reached directly in the class room does not, however, embrace all the work
done by the institution. It carries on constantly a wide range of what might
be designated as 'Extension Work.'" He claimed that "perhaps nearly half
the work done in [his] office has little direct connection with the matter of
operating the Tuskegee Institute." During the 1908–9 school year, extension works included publishing a weekly farm paper, conducting a Farmers'
Monthly Institute, offering a short course in agriculture, providing farmers
in Alabama (and, with support from the federal government), Mississippi,
and Texas with demonstrations to improve farming, agricultural schools
on wheels, blasting demonstrations, whitewashing houses fairs, county and
community fairs, farmers and workers conferences, night school, afternoon
cooking class, Tuskegee women's clubs, ministers' night school, county ministers' meetings, a children's training school, a circulating library, boy's clubs,
local and state teachers' conferences, visitations to a local jail, and a hospital.[47]

Other programs included and influenced a much greater number of African Americans. With local and state chapters, the NNBL encompassed thousands of blacks across the nation. After its 1900 founding in Boston, NNBL members elected to keep the league's national headquarters at the Tuskegee Institute until 1945. With a $500 grant from the Phelps Stokes Fund to promote the program, Washington convinced the league in 1914 to help sponsor a National Negro Health Week. He conceptualized the idea after learning that the Negro Organization Society of Virginia sponsored a successful Clean-Up Week in 1914. During that week, the society encouraged blacks in Virginia to clean up the grounds and buildings in their neighborhoods. In addition to the society's successful program, perhaps Washington's own deteriorating health played a part in his conceiving the National Negro Health Week program. Washington initially conceptualized a one-day event. He soon changed his mind and planned a weeklong program. From 1915 until 1921, the NNBL, the Tuskegee Institute, the Hampton Institute, Howard University, the Urban League, and other organizations financed the National Negro Health Week. The Julius Rosenwald Fund and the federal government started funding the program in 1921. Years of successful National Negro Health Weeks, and the desire to improve the health for all Americans, motivated the U.S. government, which took over the funding in 1934, to rename the program the National Public Health Week.[48]

Neither the National Negro Health Week nor the NNBL encompassed and enhanced as many African Americans' lives as did the schools that money from Washington helped to build. As early as 1906, Washington used contributions donated to him to help fund the construction of a rural school for southern African Americans. To encourage black communities to help themselves, Washington provided matching funds only. Local residents had to provide 50 percent or more of the money needed for construction. Until 1912, the year that Julius Rosenwald agreed to provide money to help build six schoolhouses, much of the construction funds came from donations that Washington received from Anna Thomas Jeanes, a Quaker shipping heir who had in 1905 encouraged Washington to build rural schools for southern blacks, and from Henry H. Rogers, a Standard Oil Company executive. Afterward, Julius Rosenwald became the foremost contributor. Until 1920 he headquartered the "Rosenwald school-building program at the Tuskegee Institute." When the program ended in 1932, Washington and Rosenwald's initiative had cumulated in the construction of 5,338 school buildings. Their efforts resulted in the building of 20 percent of all schools that southern blacks attended.[49]

Disregarding his school-building program, Washington alleged that in 1909 extension activities interacted at least once with 271,500 persons, and more than once with 58,000 people. Organizers of various local farmers' conferences throughout the lower South contacted over 25,000 people, and the conferences held at the Tuskegee Institute included almost 24,000 attendees. Washington, during his travels, claimed to have spoken to 130,000 persons that school year. With the institution of the National Negro Health Week in 1914, Washington extended the scope of the culture war. The programs, and the many published reports about them, endeared Washington not only to blacks of the Black Belt, but also to African Americans across the nation, whether they were landless or prosperous. As the essence of the Tuskegee movement, extension works impressed many northern white donors, and eulogists recognized him for it. He included it in his efforts, as Rabbi Harris's eulogy asserted, to teach African Americans "how to live." Robert Moton, in his New York tribute, mentioned weapons, including the Rosenwald Schools and the NNBL, that Washington used to teach life lessons. The effective employment of these tools seemed to have inspired Julius Rosenweld, in his Lincoln Center eulogy in Chicago, to proclaim that the prominence of the institute "is second by long odds to the great work that Washington did outside of Tuskegee."[50]

*   *   *

According to tributes, U.S. blacks very much needed Washington's assistance. Many eulogists seemed to have unquestionably accepted Washington's characterization of ordinary southern blacks during the early post-Reconstruction years. He had many times and in numerous places, publicized his contentions concerning their worldview and plight. Washington's eulogists repeated his allegations as self-evident truths. Referring to rural African Americans living in the Black Belt as "simple people, recently serfs of the soil," Harlem's Rabbi Harris claimed that they possessed no awareness "of the elementary conditions of life." In a New York City eulogy, William Lewis provided a rationale for the economic predicament of ordinary rural black people in 1881, the year Washington moved to Tuskegee. He alleged that "when Washington came upon the stage he beheld an emancipated race chained to the soil by the mortgage crop system and other devices." Washington's close companion and confidant, Moton, delivered a eulogy that rendered an even more pathetic picture of their lives. He claimed that the Tuskegean "found a mass of unorganized, unconnected people; untrained in self-direction, with little knowledge of self-support and citizenship." They experienced, he asserted, various degrees of ignorance and poverty. Moton further claimed that African Americans felt "more or less demoralized and discouraged; as suspicious and distrustful of their own race as of the white race; and in the main, following no especially constructive leadership."[51]

According to his eulogists, Washington used the Yankee Protestant ethic as his primary framework to provide African Americans with the necessary guidance. In a letter read aloud in Varick Memorial AMEZ Church in New Haven, President William H. Taft referred to "the homely virtues of industry, thrift and a persistent use of their opportunities." In a eulogy Moton delivered at the Alabama State Negro Teachers' Association meeting in Birmingham, he included industry and thrift as well as "morality, decent homes, clean bodies and minds, better methods of farming" in the list of lessons that Washington taught blacks. Former president Theodore Roosevelt likewise praised Washington for teaching African Americans honesty and cleanliness. More importantly to Roosevelt, Washington taught efficiency. He extolled Washington for his promotion of "the gospel of efficiency, the gospel of work." In his tribute, E. H. Wright praised Washington for pioneering "in the great demand of the present day for efficiency." Steadfastness is the Yankee Protestant value that the Reverend Henry Y. Arnett highlighted in his eulogy. He noted that Washington taught African Americans "that it was their place to stay on the job that was at their hand."[52]

If blacks would actualize Washington's messages, especially those stressing work and self-denial, eulogists claimed that they would enrich themselves and enhance their collective status. Yankee Protestants had long believed John Wesley's adage, and adherents loathed people who did not embrace it. Moton represented their feelings in his tribute at the Alabama State Negro Teacher's Association. He declared that blacks living in Alabama had "more to fear from the lazy, shiftless, ignorant, criminal negro [sic] than from any race prejudice in" the state. Moton proclaimed that blacks needed to follow Washington's teaching concerning the "necessity of decent living and the beauty and dignity of labor." Tributes like the one William George Bruce, the white secretary of the Wisconsin Manufacturers Association, presented at an AME church in Milwaukee manifested the widespread agreement with Moton. Bruce alleged that Washington "was wiser than other leaders of his race." He understood that African Americans could not "progress" without vigorous and ceaseless pursuit of material and moral development. Washington saw, Bruce argued, that "the negro [sic] must be able to perform his part in the economies of life and must be trained to perform his full share in the world's work. The negro [sic] must be able to perform a white man's task and come up to his ethical standards if he is to render himself worthy of the white man's respect."[53]

Wealth, more than esteem, is what the masses of blacks needed and wanted, and Washington sought to teach them how to attain it. Acknowledging his efforts, many eulogists discussed his attempts at teaching African Americans how to improve their material well-being. Their tributes reflected the importance they believed Washington placed on wealth attainment. Washington, eulogists alleged, told them that they could not expect to improve their economic status quickly. He advocated a long-term plan to achieve prosperity. In a 1900 speech in Dallas, Texas, Washington stated that blacks might "have to struggle for decades and centuries before" they could enjoy financial security. Charles Franklin Thwing, the president of Western Reserve University, recalled Washington making that point. In a tribute in Cleveland, Thwing asserted that Washington understood "that the work he laid out for himself could not be accomplished in a day or a year. He labored for the next generation and the ages to come."[54]

At the tribute in Carnegie Hall, William H. Lewis claimed that Washington told "his people: 'You must own your own lands, you must own your own farms.'" While he structured his advice to help African Americans to improve their material well-being over an extended period, a number of eulogists stipulated that the teachings helped them to increase their financial opportunities within a relatively short time. The *Savannah (GA) Tribune* reported that, at a tribute the Savannah NNBL chapter sponsored, eulogists eloquently expressed their gratitude for Washington's influence "in developing the commercial opportunities of the race."[55]

Assisting black farmers, however, took precedence over businesses. Washington primarily concerned himself with the plight of black agriculturalists and dedicated the majority of the Tuskegee Institute's extension work to help improve the physical and material well-being of this group of mostly landless blacks. As a former farmer from South Carolina, African American attorney Samuel Mitchell asserted in his Flushing, New York, tribute that Washington taught black agrarians simple ways to build wealth. Mitchell said that "Washington taught us to raise pigs. If we raised one pig he taught us the benefit of raising two pigs." Charles G. Medbury, the white pastor of University Church in Des Moines, Iowa, offered a macrocosm assessment of Washington's economic teachings. He alleged that since emancipation Washington had played a leading role in African Americans substantially improving their material well-being. He helped to inspire blacks, declared Medbury, to increase their business houses "from 9,000 to 550,000 and their wealth from $20,000 to $700,000,000." While placing Washington's leadership success in the context of world history, Robert Moton engaged in hyperbole in his Carnegie Hall tribute. "Few men in this world's history," Moton grandiloquently alleged, "have been able to accomplish in so short a period for so large a mass of people what Dr. Washington was able to accomplish."[56]

Eulogists purported that while southern whites permitted Washington to seek his goal, they did not always support his efforts. Washington had to overcome both southern white people's racist resistance and black people's fears to realize his objective. His masterful understanding of southern white men, alleged William H. Lewis, provided Washington with the knowledge he needed to obtain their aid. He "knew the Southern white man," asserted Lewis, "better than the Southern White man knew himself, and knew the sure road to his head and heart." About the anxieties of blacks, the Reverend John F. Waters, the pastor of the Newburg (NY) AMEZ Church, stated that Washington successfully countered the false claim of many Africans that "white people were enemies to the negro [sic] and were adverse" to their advancement. At a tribute in Rochester, New York, the Reverend Lee B. Brown of the Mount Olive Baptist Church professed that Washington had made life easier for blacks since he had "gone out among the enemy and made friends for" them. African Americans generally regarded southern whites as their nemesis. According to President Roosevelt, Washington did not allow that pervasive conviction to prohibit him from courting southern white men. He claimed that Washington realized that these people could, like no other group, provide blacks with what they needed. Thus Washington, proclaimed Roosevelt, considered the respect of southern white people "the greatest asset he possessed in his work." His success at securing the "confidence of the Southern white man" inspired the Reverend W. B. Suthern of Hartford, Connecticut, to describe Washington in his tribute as "one of the greatest of diplomats."[57]

Eulogists submitted that he used the leeway and assistance that southern whites provided him to embrace all humanity. Thus, he not only helped African Americans, he also aided nonblacks. They told their audiences that his fondness for mankind inspired him to assist all people. In New York, Moton proclaimed that Washington "believed in and respected and loved humanity . . . North, South, black and white, were on is heart and in his program." At the tribute that took place in the chapel of the Tuskegee Institute, President Roosevelt made a similar pronouncement. He maintained that Washington's "aim was to help the white man just exactly [as] . . . it was his aim to help the black man." In Tucson, Arizona, the Reverend A. Binkhorst, a white Congregational minister, supported both Moton's and Roosevelt's' claims when he testified that Washington "had not only been of assistance to the colored race, but to the white race as well, in aiding in the solution of economic problems which confronted it." Poor whites in particular benefited

from the Tuskegee movement, avowed Arthur Thompson, the white pastor
of St. John's Congregational Church in Newburgh, New York. He proclaimed
that Washington "in a measure, but not so direct a degree," also improved
the economic lot of dispossessed whites. E. H. Wright made a more inclusive
allegation. He stated that Washington brought "about better conditions for
the whole country."[58]

In the Yankee Protestant creed, charity is an essential supplement to community service. Eulogists also recognized Washington for his generosity.
His benevolence inspired Episcopal bishop Lawrence to eulogize him as
"a great charitable" man. Washington's impartial philanthropy inspired all
of the speakers at his tribute in Indianapolis to extol his benevolence. The
Indianapolis Freeman newspaper reported that all of eulogists at the tribute
"in some manner voiced the general thought that Mr. Washington's heart
was broader than any race." Washington's generosity extended to all persons,
declared Frank P. Chisholm. Carrying the theme even further at a tribute in
Rochester, New York, Chisholm's Tuskegee Institute colleague, John Thomas,
proclaimed Washington "one [of] the greatest benefactors to mankind."[59]

*   *   *

Although eulogists applauded Washington for his benevolence, they
ignored, downplayed, or defended his perceived public attitude concerning
black people's political rights. After having alleged in his Atlanta Exposition
speech that black people entered freedom "at the top instead of the bottom;
that a seat in Congress or the state legislature was more sought than real
estate," he generally avoided discussing African American political activities,
including voting rights. He did occasionally mention politics in the context
of his program of African American advancement. Washington once stated
in a speech in New Orleans that "I have always advised my race to give
attention to acquiring property, intelligence and character necessary bases
of good citizenship, rather than to mere political agitation." While this and
similar statements generated criticism from some quarters of the African
American community, his eulogists tended to disregard both the utterances
and the denunciations. In stating that Washington "was no compromiser
or opportunist," Celia Parker Woolley, in a eulogy at the Lincoln Center in
Chicago, did hint that detractors criticized him for his failure to advocate
strongly for black people's political rights. At the Varick Memorial AMEZ
Church in New Haven, Aubrey L. Magill, an African American physician,
intimated that critics wrongly condemned Washington. He maintained that
Washington "was criticized because in his work with his people he worked
along the line of least resistance. But he accomplished much."[60]

In their tributes, Charles Alexander and other core members of the Tuskegee movement defended Washington more vigorously. A number of these eulogists offered an economic explanation for Washington's positions. Alexander proclaimed that instead of "seeking political office . . . it would be better for the race to establish itself in material possessions." William Lewis echoed those sentiments, arguing at Carnegie Hall that Washington "saw that the political superstructure of our freedom could not last without a solid economic basis." Washington reasoned that freedom, asserted Lewis, rested on an economic foundation. At the tribute on Howard University's campus, Professor George W. Cook took a different tact when he refuted allegations that Washington urged blacks to avoid politics. Cook stipulated that "Washington never in avowed terms denied the importance of political rights upon the welfare of the colored race." Cook claimed that "there was little hope of immediate restoration of their" political rights. Cook alleged that Washington stressed "sobriety, industry and thrift" as the means for blacks to gain full citizenship stature. Cook provided a much more reasonable explanation than the one that Roscoe C. Simmons, Margaret Washington's nephew, put forth. At a tribute in Louisville, Kentucky, he offered a bizarre interpretation of Washington's position as well as of his motivation for downplaying black political rights. Simmons declared that Washington "advised his race to stay out of politics, but not out of government. That advice any statesman would give to any people. Politics enslaved Ireland."[61]

Although his eulogists failed to make a notable issue of it, Booker T. Washington publicly denounced segregation. He wrote articles deploring public transportation discrimination. He even condemned racial prejudice at the 1898 National Peace Jubilee in Chicago. With President William McKinley on the stage, Washington made this declaration to the largest audience that he would address in his life. The Reverend D. S. Klugh, like most, if not all, of the eulogists, failed to credit Washington for his struggle against segregation and other forms of race bigotry. His tribute incorrectly signified that Washington only attempted to sidestep white racism. Klugh asserted that "Washington knew full well the bias and prejudice of the white south. So he began by preaching Gospel of moral regeneration and industrial salvation for the negro [sic]."[62]

Other eulogists indicated that Washington, without protest, accepted racial discrimination for the masses of black as well as for himself. Although a few core members of the Tuskegee movement knew that he privately lobbied against racist laws and helped to fund court challenges to their implementation, neither they, nor any of his other eulogists, publicly acknowledged those behind-the-scenes efforts. Some of their tributes in fact perpetuated the widely held misconception that Washington did not directly fight white racial bias. Alleging that blacks needed "the good will of the white race," for them to advance, Rabbi Wise proclaimed that Washington "was more concerned about the negro [*sic*] doing justice to himself than to secure justice from the white race." Bishop Lawrence provided questionable evidence in his tribute of Washington that he consented to bigotry. He claimed that throughout the thirty years that Washington rode the trains across America, he always waited "until every white person had been served before he entered" the dining car. "He then went in alone and took his meals with the waiters." During his visits to Boston, he would walk with his bag "not to one of the great hotels," but to one that accommodated a predominately black clientele. Washington "would not go," declared Lawrence, "where those of his race could not go."[63]

Washington's apparent personal acceptance of discrimination, his limited public protest against disfranchisement, and his disparaging agitation for civil rights contributed to a widespread belief that he had helped to lessen racial tensions and had substantially improved relations between races. This perception, however, did not reflect reality. Although lynching had subsided, blacks continued to suffer under an incredible weight of racism. White southerners' seemingly endless attempts at stymieing black people's efforts at self-actualization did not deter eulogists from declaring that Washington's calling included promoting racial harmony. The *Indianapolis Freeman* reported that every eulogy delivered at a memorial in Indianapolis announced that Washington "had been called to bring about a better understanding between the white and colored people." Conveying the same message at a tribute in Detroit, a Mr. Harris praised Washington for "bringing together on a more understanding basis, the white and black race." The Reverend Aaron W. Puller, pastor of Peoples Baptist Church in Boston and a former Tuskegee Institute employee, asserted in his tribute that Washington bound "the white and black races together in" an inconceivable way. Although Washington's motto "was 'peace and harmony,'" alleged the Reverend W. Southern, he "cemented the friendships of the two races as an essential to permanent progress," testified William H. Lewis, at the Hampton Institute, without compromising any principle of human rights. The Reverend H. H. Proctor, the African American pastor of the First Congregational Church in Atlanta, Georgia, further declared Washington the leading proponent of "peace between" the races. And his death, alleged the Reverend Josiah Shible, a white southerner at the Calvary Presbyterian Church in San Francisco, deprived the world of "its greatest harmonizer."[64]

* * *

Perhaps Washington's accomplishments as a racial peacemaker inspired eulogists to compare him to major biblical figures. A few even melodramatically equated Washington with Jesus Christ. An unidentified eulogist at the

St. John AME Church in Nashville declared that Washington "came nearer living the life of the lowly Nazarene than any man with whom I ever came in contact." At a commemoration in Baton Rouge, the Reverend B. Mack Hubbard presented a Christlike memory of Washington. He stated that all people claimed Washington and that he in turn received them. Hubbard asserted that Washington "literally gave his life for others."[65]

Most eulogists chose not to compare Washington to the deity. His alleged success in leading African Americans out of their material and moral wilderness inspired them, like several of his obituary writers, to equate him with Moses. At a memorial that both blacks and whites attended in the Portland (OR) Centenary Methodist Church, E. Thompson, an assistant minister at the local First AME Church, proclaimed Washington "the Moses of practical progress." In Denver, Colorado, George Gross delivered a eulogy in the Shorter AME Church titled "Washington, the Modern Moses." George Gross strongly inferred that the late educator, similar to Moses, had undertaken a God-given task. Mrs. George H. Gibbs, a merchant in Rochester, New York, made that claim explicit. She asserted that Washington, "like Moses, in his heart heard the cry of his people and felt that God had called him to lead them out of the Egypt of incompetence, illiteracy, and unpreparedness into the Canaan of opportunity and recognition." Some eulogists, including Jacob H. Schiff, a member of the Tuskegee Institute Board of Trustees, corrected and perhaps contradicted Gibbs's assessment of both Moses and Washington. Analogous to Moses, asserted Schiff, Washington "had led his race, to the boundary of the promised land." In his tribute, Westminster Reformed Church's minister, J. R. Thompson, similarly asserted that Moses did not lead his people to the promised land. He said that Washington therefore resembled Joshua rather than Moses. Thomas E. Roach, too, pointed it out that Washington "was not a leader like Moses, who led 3,000,000 of the Jews in the flight from Egypt. The pastor of Varick Memorial AMEZ Church in New Haven claimed that Washington, who had come out of slavery and had to cope with segregation, "out stripped" Moses.[66]

Eulogists frequently compared Washington's favorability to more recent historical persons. They equated him with both black and white illustrious individuals. Although none cited William E. B. Du Bois, Joseph P. Peaker, a black civic leader in New Haven, Connecticut, and a few other eulogists equated Washington with well-known African American civil rights leaders. At the Varick Memorial AMEZ Church tribute, Peaker alleged that Washington's work for blacks equated that of Frederick Douglass and William Monroe (Trotter) Travis [sic], an impassioned critic of the late educator. The Reverend D. P. Roberts ranked Washington alongside Douglass and Abraham

Lincoln when he declared that the three of them "apparently were destined by Providence for exalted places for ever lasting [*sic*] fame."[67]

In expressing their assessment of Washington's esteem, some eulogists classified Washington with U.S. presidents. A close political ally of Washington, Charles W. Anderson, determined it politically useful to rank a former president and a current candidate for the office, Theodore Roosevelt, the equal of Washington. In a transparent political maneuver, Anderson, a former federal collector of internal revenue and the leading black politician in New York state, stated in his tribute at St. Mark's Methodist Episcopal Church in New York City that "Theodore Roosevelt and Booker T. Washington were the two greatest men of their time in the white and black races." Samuel Mitchell likewise ranked Washington alongside of Roosevelt as one of the three men who best assisted African Americans. He ranked Lincoln third. For Frank H. Ridgely, a Lincoln University professor, Roosevelt's successor William Howard Taft deserved a ranking beside Washington. Ridgely reasoned that since Washington overcame more obstacles in his lifetime than the former president Taft, he possessed the "greater influence." Choosing to bypass contemporary presidents and enhance Washington's historical significance, Ohio governor Frank B. Wills linked him to George Washington and Abraham Lincoln in his eulogy in Columbus.[68]

Washington's perceived historic national prestige did not inspire a large majority of his eulogists to classify him as anything other than an African American leader. A few eulogists, including the one that Bishop William Lawrence delivered, did not limit Washington to Africa America. Lawrence asserted that Washington "may rightfully be termed a great leader." Likewise, Edwin C. Broome, the white superintendent of schools for East Orange, New Jersey, did not place a racial qualification in his assessment of Washington's leadership. He hyperbolically proclaimed Washington the "great leader of the generation." Others, including Harry Pratt Judson, president of Chicago University, categorized Washington as a leader of black people only. Judson asserted that each person has to act a "part in the drama of life; some are qualified to play the minor, and the more competent must play the Major." Washington played the leading role for African Americans. Rather than an acting analogy, F. F. Irvine used the trope of the frontier to describe Washington's leadership of black people: "Booker T. Washington was the trail blazer . . . the man who blazed the trail which is being followed by his people to higher levels." Connecticut congressman John Q. Tilson acknowledged Washington both as a leader of his race and of mankind when he stated that "Washington was much more than a great leader of the colored race. He tower [*sic*] high among the leaders of all races."[69]

While not all African Americans could become the commander in chief of the race, they could emulate many of Washington's traits, particularly those that manifested his embrace of the Yankee Protestant ethic. Eulogists promoted the perceived transformation that they claimed Washington accelerated and effectively facilitated in the South, especially among its black population. Their tributes in essence served, in part, as instruments to bolster the morale of existing black Yankee Protestant ethic cultural warriors and to recruit additional personnel to their ranks. Tributes, like the ones that the *Savannah (GA) Tribune* claimed to have occurred in Washington, D.C., on a Sunday in November 1915, clearly told audiences to pattern themselves after Washington. It reported that pastors in "practically all of the churches" in the city preached eulogies that extolled Washington "as a leader and example for the living, young and old to follow in the conduct of life." Other preachers at different times in various locations made similar assertions. John F. Waters, the pastor of the AMEZ Church in Newburgh, New York, declared in his tribute "that he would urge the living to emulate the example set and follow" in the footsteps of Washington. Telling his audience that as Washington "has done, so you can do," the Reverend Lee B. Brown called for African Americans in his tribute "to follow in the footsteps of" Washington. To Hampton Institute principal Frissell, it had become a Christian duty for blacks to imitate Washington: "In so far as he followed the Masters each one of you must follow [Washington]."[70]

More frequently than preachers, core members of the Tuskegee movement, especially those employed at the institute, exhorted blacks to continue to follow Washington. Even though they probably deeply believed in Washington and the movement, these employees had an interest in the perpetuation of the institute and its extension works. While African Americans donated both cash and service to the movement, white philanthropists gave substantially more money to it. Hence, core members of the movement unambiguously understood the financial consequences to the movement, school, and themselves if major white philanthropists concluded that blacks had either abandoned or lessened their interest in Washington's ideas. J. Henderson Allston, a member of the NNBL, an organization that Andrew Carnegie and other benefactors had financially supported, declared in a eulogy at the People's Baptist Church in Boston "that the negroes [*sic*] follow Dr. Washington's fundamental doctrine of service for others." Moton seemed to have had a greater interest in black people's morals and views about work. At the Alabama State Teachers' Association meeting, he requested that teachers "follow Dr. Washington in teaching the members of our race the necessity of decent living and the beauty and dignity of labor." Telling his audience about the payoff for following the late Tuskegean, Frank P. Chisholm prophesized that if they "would try to live like Dr. Washington they would fulfill the highest types of manhood and womanhood." Emmett Scott could take for granted that his listeners and the readers of his eulogy understood the rewards for embracing the values that Washington promoted. He commanded the attendees at the annual NNBL convention to "harken to the call" that Washington "sounded for brave, patriotic service; let us press forward, strong and unafraid with patience and firm resolve, with the lessons of his devoted life before us, to advance the cause for which he was willing to live, for which he was willing to work, and finally for which he was willing to die."[71]

Epilogue

Devotees desired permanency. They wanted what Delbert Brunton coveted. Writing from Fullerton, California, Brunton prayed that Booker T. Washington's "memory be kept green, not only among his own people, but among the whole American nation." For the most part, admirers of the late educator did not subscribe to the allegation by Saint Paul, Minnesota, resident W. T. Francis that Americans needed no physical reminder of Washington. Francis maintained optimistically that Washington would "live forever in the hearts of his people." Many other supporters seemed to have realized that without permanent reminders, Americans, even blacks, would over time forget Washington and would stray from the tenets he advocated. Although commemorations acknowledged and praised Washington and highlighted and reinforced the Tuskegee movement, they did not ensure the perpetuation of a desired memory of him. Nor did they guarantee continuation of his movement. Disciples wanted forthcoming generations both to memorialize the late educator and maintain the Tuskegee movement. They sought to transform the ethics of Africa America and even the white South into those the Yankees embraced. Supporters therefore sought additional sites of memory to accompany and reinforce the funeral, obituaries, eulogies, and memorial services. Since blacks constituted almost 30 percent of the region's population, converting a majority of them had to occur in the process of transforming the region into the image of New England.[1]

On the day of Washington's burial, supporters initiated the first of several additional sites of memory. An unidentified attendee utilized the latest media technology to film Washington's funeral services and subsequently showed the recording in public halls. The film showed an overflowing assembly of mostly African American mourners, a railroad boxcar load of flowers and plants, and a dignified serene funeral ritual fit for a commanding warrior. On December 18, 1915, a *Savannah (GA) Tribune* front-page article announced a forthcoming showing. "BOOKER T. WASHINGTON PICTURE AT PEKIN" headlined the article, which announced that a matinée and evening screening of the moving picture would occur on the forthcoming Monday. Noting that the theater would likely "be crowded with friends of the great educator who wish to witness scenes of his funeral," the article promised that the movie would "show the entire principal features of the funeral, the distinguished personages present, etc." A prominent advertisement on the front page of the *Tribune* proclaimed in bold print "Don't Fail to See the Funeral of Booker T. Washington The Great Negro Educator, in Moving Pictures." The ad further noted a special 3 o'clock matinee for children. Promoters of the film sought to inspire adults and children alike to commemorate Washington. Although no known copy of the film exists today, it is conceivable that its images, subtitles, and intertitles inspired individual members of the audiences to join the Tuskegee movement, or, if they already supported it, to continue its culture war. This silent movie possessed the ability to fabricate and buttress a very favorable memory of Washington.[2]

A week prior to the Savannah screening, the Tuskegee Institute Board of Trustees clearly manifested their desire to continue the movement and to perpetuate a preferred memory of Washington. They determined that supporters of Washington would donate thousands, if not millions, of dollars to erect a monument to honor him, preserve the Tuskegee Institute, and continue the movement. Meeting Monday, December 12, 1915, two days after more than four thousand people gathered at the institute for a memorial service in honor of the late educator, the board issued a call for contributions to a $2 million Booker T. Washington Memorial Fund. The public solicitation for the fund asserted that "Tuskegee Institute is Booker T. Washington's monument and his most fitting memorial is the perpetuation of his great work for the benefit of the colored people and the promotion of helpful relations between the races." It furthermore claimed that the school needed donations of "approximately $150,000" per year to cover expense overruns. It claimed that the board did not want to "close this gap so completely as to make the Institute independent of the interest and support of the living" but to decrease it to a manageable sum. Announcing that the board had "received subscriptions of more than $450,000," the appeal reported that transforming part of those pledges into cash depended upon the fund receiving matching donations. They wanted African Americans to contribute $250,000 of the total amount. Some of that money, according to the wishes of the board, would fund the construction of "a suitable memorial" on the institute's campus. The appeal directed African Americans to send their monies to "Emmett J. Scott, Secretary of the Institute" and for other subscribers to send their pledges and funds to either "William G. Willcox Treasurer of the Investment Committee" in New York City or to Warren Logan, the treasurer of the institute.[3]

By June 1917, donations had exceeded $1,000,000. This amount included $20,073 from over twelve thousand African Americans to the memorial fund. Donors, black and white, continued to contribute to the fund for several more years. African Americans eagerly responded to various requests from advocates of the Tuskegee movement. They wrote and distributed appeals, held fund-raising meetings, established memorial committees, and staged an assortment of events. A ten-year-old African American, Russell Gibson, established an association that solicited dimes from the nation's children. Adult supporters of Washington established organizations to collect money for the proposed memorial in approximately 150 towns and cities. Admirers organized committees to solicit monies from around the nation: in western cities such as Los Angeles and Portland, in heartland urban centers like Muskogee (OK) and Kansas City, as well as in southern cities that included Asheville (NC), Louisville, and Tampa. Fund-raising organizations appeared in great U.S. metropolitan areas such as Boston and New York City. Many African American–owned newspapers added to the effort. They solicited funds as well as publicized and congratulated local African American donors. Before the campaign ended, no fewer than a hundred thousand African American men, women, and children from across the nation contributed to the fund, the greatest effort of this sort in the history of black America to that time.[4]

Charles Keck, a renowned white sculptor from New York City, secured the commission from the Tuskegee Institute Board of Trustees to construct the desired memorial. Although Keck had constructed a model of the monument in September 1919, he did not install the actual statue until 1922. A prolific artisan, Keck fashioned several noted sculptures, including a Meriwether Lewis and William Clark monument in Charlottesville, Virginia. While working on the Booker T. Washington monument he also completed a statute of Thomas Jonathan Jackson, better known as Stonewall Jackson, the famous Confederate general, for the city of Charlottesville.[5]

After receiving notification of the completion of the Washington monument, Tuskegee Institute officials responded with a massive advertising campaign that announced the upcoming monument unveiling ceremony. They informed the print media, while sending personal invitations to hundreds of the school's supporters as well as to dozens of nationally recognized celebrities. These news releases and letters informed readers that the long-anticipated dedication of the monument would occur on April 5, the

Tuskegean's birthday, at 2:00 P.M. Moton sent an invitation to E. T. Belsaw, a leading African American physician in Mobile, Alabama, which read in part: "We are expecting you to be present [at the unveiling] and hope that you will bring a large number of friends with you."[6]

People from all over the nation attended the ceremony. On the day of the unveiling event, more persons gathered on the campus than the 8,000 to 12,000 people who had attended Washington's funeral. Both white and black people came to witness the dedication of a memorial that honored the memory of the most influential African American of his era. These persons wanted to take part in one of the most impressive events of their lifetime. A significant number of the African Americans came to see the site of memory that a hundred thousand black people had purchased. African American donors of all ages and statuses could rightly feel that they shared ownership in both the campus and the monument.[7]

For one hour and forty-five minutes, the attendees participated in a well-staged prelude to the unveiling of the monument. They heard the school's orchestra and its choir. They listened to the students sing spirituals. Robert E. Jones, the first black bishop of the Methodist Episcopal Church, led attendees in prayer. E. C. Morris, a former president of the National Baptist Convention, the largest predominately black organization in the nation read scripture to them. The audience heard addresses from George Cleveland Hall, Washington's former personal doctor, and Wallace Buttrick, the executive secretary of the General Education Board and a close associate of John D. Rockefeller.[8]

In an unmistakable effort to display white southern elite support for the institute and the myth of improved race relations in the South, the Tuskegee Institute Board of Trustees persuaded Josephus Daniels to address the attendees. A former prominent North Carolina newspaper editor, he had served as the secretary of the navy in President Woodrow Wilson's administration. Daniels had promoted white only primaries. He had also helped to organize and direct the racist Red Shirt Clubs that violently removed blacks and their supporters from the state's body politic, while he worked as the editor of the most popular newspaper in North Carolina during the late 1890s. In his speech, the first delivered during the ceremony, Daniels used Washington's words to convey that black men received the right to vote before securing an adequate education. He, however, ended his address with the assertion that southern white Democrats sought "to measure out even-handed justice to the people of both races."[9]

A few minutes after 3:45 P.M., Emmett J. Scott unveiled the statue that would become world-renowned. Keck had constructed a monument honoring

Booker T. Washington designed to exist for hundreds if not thousands of years. Keck placed the sculpture of two figures, one of Washington, and one of a kneeling younger African American male, on an eight-foot-tall granite base that included a crescent-shaped bench, or exedra. On the base is inscribed

BOOKER T WASHINGTON
1856–1915
HE LIFTED THE VEIL OF IGNORANCE
FROM THE PEOPLE AND POINTED
THE WAY TO PROGRESS THROUGH
EDUCATION AND INDUSTRY

Keck constructed the sculpture from Roman bronze, an alloy of copper and tin that is ideal for statues because it resists oxidation. The sculpture included an eight-foot-tall statue of a standing Washington clad in a stylishly tailored three-piece suit and dress shoes. Keck sculptured a face of a compassionate but determined person who is seeking to assist. Washington is seemingly looking to the far distance while extending his left arm downward and slightly to its front, with the palm opened. With the right hand, the figure of Washington is in the process of removing a cloth from the face of the kneeling, powerfully built young black man whose right hand is assisting in the uncovering, while his left hand is holding a book with a compass and a carpenter's square. This replica of a young African American is seated on an anvil with a plow, hammer, and pair of blacksmith tongs positioned beside his right leg.[10]

The monument honors Washington while strongly communicating to viewers the eagerness of the black youngster to attain "practical" knowledge and apply it in a systemic or "scientific" method. It expresses several of the Yankee Protestant tenets that Washington often advocated: service, charity, education, and systemic work. A Washington quotation inscribed under the sides of the bronze portion of the monument reinforces this concept: "We shall prosper in proportion as we learn to dignify and glory labor and put brains and skill into the common occupations of life." Several other Washington quotations are engraved on the monument. On the pedestal to the right side of the sculpture is: "I will let no man drag me down so low as to make me hate him." On the left side of the pedestal are the words "There is no defense or security of any of us except in the highest intelligence and development of all." On the back of the base is an inscription that the Tuskegee Institute Board of Trustees commissioned: "This monument is erected by contributions from Negroes in the United States as a loving tribute to the memory of their great leader and benefactor."[11]

Notes

Abbreviations

BTW	Booker T. Washington
BTW1	Louis R. Harlan, *Booker T. Washington: The Making of a Black Leader, 1856–1901* (New York: Oxford University Press, 1972)
BTW2	Louis R. Harlan, *Booker T. Washington: The Wizard of Tuskegee, 1901–1915* (New York: Oxford University Press, 1983)
BTW LOC	Booker T. Washington Papers, Library of Congress
BTW TUA	Booker T. Washington Papers, Tuskegee University Archives, Tuskegee, Alabama
BTW Papers	*The Booker T. Washington Papers, 1856–1915*, ed. Louis R. Harlan et al. (Urbana: University of Illinois Press, 1972–89), 14 vols.
EJS	Emmett Jay Scott
Hampton Clippings	Hampton Institute Peabody Library Clippings, Hampton University Library
MN	microfiche or microfilm number. BTW LOC sources accessed before the LOC completed microfilming are unnumbered.
telg.	telegram (communications not designated as telegrams are letters)
TUA	Tuskegee University Archives, Tuskegee, Alabama

Prologue

    1. *BTW1*, preface, unpaginated; *BTW2*, x. Benjamin Quarles, *The Negro in the Making of America* (New York: Collier, 1964), 171. Lerone Bennett Jr., *Before the Mayflower: A History of the Negro in America, 1619–1964* (Baltimore, Md.: Penguin, 1962), 276.

2. August Meier, "Toward a Reinterpretation of Booker T. Washington," *Journal of Southern History* 22 (May 1957): 220–27, reprinted in August Meier and Elliott Rudwick, eds., *The Black Community in Modern America*, vol. 2 of *The Making of Black America* (New York: Atheneum, 1969), 130. Samuel R. Spencer Jr., *Booker T. Washington and the Negro's Place in American Life* (Boston: Little, Brown, 1955), 196.

3. EJS to William H. Lewis, telg. November 14, 1915, MN 421, BTW LOC. Max Weber, *The Protestant Ethic and the Spirt of Capitalism*, translated by Talcott Parson (North Charleston, S.C.: CreateSpace Independent Publishing, 2010). Ernst Troeltsch, *Protestantism and Progress* (Philadelphia: Fortress Press, 1986); Daniel T. Rodgers, *The Work Ethic in Industrial America: 1850–1920* (Chicago: University of Chicago Press, 1974); and George McKenna, *The Puritan Origins of American Patriotism* (New Haven, Conn.: Yale University Press, 2007). Ron Eyerman and Andrew Jamison, *Social Movements: A Cognitive Approach* (University Park, Pa.: Pennsylvania State University Press, 1991), 161–63. The author borrowed the term *Yankee Protestant* from Gerald Kurland, *Seth Low: The Reformer in an Urban and Industrial Age* (New York: Twayne, 1971), 216.

4. James M. McPherson, *The Abolitionist Legacy: From Reconstruction to the NAACP* (Princeton, N.J.: Princeton University Press, 1975), 161–63. William R. Taylor, *Cavalier and Yankee: The Old South and American National Character* (New York: George Braziller, 1961); David Bertelson, *The Lazy South* (New York: Oxford University Press, 1967). James H. Moorhead, *American Apocalypse: Yankee Protestants and the Civil War, 1860–1869* (New Haven, Conn.: Yale University Press, 1978). C. Vann Woodward, "The Southern Ethnic in a Puritan World," *William and Mary Quarterly*, 3rd series, 25, no. 3 (July 1968): 343–70.

5. John M. Murrin, Paul E. Johnson, James M. McPherson, Gary Gerstile, Emily S. Rosenberg, and Norman L. Rosenberg, *Liberty Equality Power: A History of the American People* (Fort Worth, Tex.: Harcourt Brace, 1996), 408–9, 435–36, 458–59, 474–76, 560–62, and 572–73. James M. McPherson, *Ordeal by Fire: The Civil War and Reconstruction* (New York: Alfred A. Knopf, 1982), 399, 557–58. W. E. B. Du Bois, *Black Reconstruction in America: An Essay Toward a History of the Part Which Black Folk Played in the Attempt to Reconstruct Democracy in America, 1860–1880* (Cleveland, Ohio: World Publishing, 1968), 77–79.

6. Gilson Willetts Ruffners, "Slave Boy and Leader of His Race," *New Voice* 16 (June 1899): 3. *BTW1*, 28–51. *Montgomery (AL) Advertiser*, December 5, 1915; William J. Simmons, *Men of Mark: Eminent, Progressive and Rising* (Cleveland, Ohio: George M. Rewell, 1887), 1027. Edward A. Johnson, *A School History of the Negro Race in America from 1619* (Raleigh, N.C.: Edward A. Johnson, 1893), 177; and Samuel William Bacote, "Booker T. Washington, LLD," in *Who's Who among the Colored Baptists of the United States* (Kansas City, Mo.: Franklin Hudson Publishing, 1913), 19. BTW, *The Story of My Life and Work* (Westport, Conn.: Negro Universities Press, 1969), 52–53.

7. BTW, *Story of My Life and Work*, 55. "The Founding of the Hampton Institute," 55. *The Southern Workman*, June 1878. "General Samuel C. Armstrong," *Old South Leaflets*, 6:126–50 (Boston: Directors of the Old South Work, n.d.), 526 and 533. W. J. Cash, *The Mind of the South* (New York: Vintage Books, 1941), 106–47.

8. Ronald E. Butchart, *Schooling the Freed People: Teaching, Learning, and the Struggle for Black Freedom, 1861–1876* (Chapel Hill: University of North Carolina, 2010), 6–7.

9. "General Samuel C. Armstrong," 521, 522, and 590. Butchart, *Schooling the Freed People*, 120. Donal F. Lindsey, *Indians at Hampton Institute, 1877–1923* (Urbana: University of Illinois Press, 1995), 71.

10. "General Samuel C. Armstrong," 521, 522, 525.

11. Robert Francis Engs, *Freedom's First Generation: Black Hampton, Virginia, 1861–1890* (Philadelphia: University of Pennsylvania Press, 1979), 151. Samuel Chapman Armstrong quoted in James D. Anderson, *The Education of Blacks in the South, 1860–1935* (Chapel Hill: University of North Carolina Press, 1988), 45.

12. "Hampton Catalog-1874–75," *BTW Papers*, 2:36. "General Samuel C. Armstrong," 509 and 513. Engs, *Freedom's First Generation*, 144.

13. *BTW1*, 58–108. *Maine Society of the Sons of the American Revolution* (Portland, Maine: LeFavor-Tower Co., 1903), 130. Mary C. Reynolds, "Rev. S. B. Gregory, D. D., and Rev. G. M. P. King, D. D.," *Baptist Missionary Pioneers Among Negroes, Sketches*, ed. Mary C. Reynolds et al. ([Boston?]: N.p., 1900), 45–47.

14. Robert Russa Moton, *Finding a Way Out: An Autobiography* (Garden City, N.Y.: Doubleday Page & Co., 1921), 144. BTW, *Story of My Life and Work*, 72. Lindsey, *Indians at Hampton Institute, 1877–1923*, 95.

15. *BTW1*, 97. "Hampton Catalog-1874–75," *BTW Papers*, 2:44nn.

16. BTW, *Story of My Life and Work*, 63. *The Vassar Miscellany* (Poughkeepsie, N.Y.: Vassar College, July 1914), 665–66. Michael J. Brodhead, *David J. Brewer: The Life of a Supreme Court Justice, 1837–1910* (Carbondale: Southern Illinois University Press, 1994), 1, 2, and 194.

17. "The Catalog of Tuskegee Normal School," *BTW Papers*, 2:177nn.

18. *Savannah (GA) Press*, November 18, 1915; "Items from the Hampton Institute Student Account Book," *BTW Papers*, 2:22, facing. BTW, *Up from Slavery: An Autobiography* (New York: Dodd, Mead & Co., 1965), 42. BTW, *Story of My Life and Work*, 63. *Southern Workman* 30 (May 1902).

19. Allen Johnston Going, *Bourbon Democracy in Alabama, 1874–1890* (Tuscaloosa: University of Alabama Press, 1992), 92–99 and 215. Roger L. Ransom and Richard Sutch, *One Kind of Freedom: The Economic Consequences of Emancipation* (New York: Cambridge University Press, 1977). Anne Kendrick Walker, *Tuskegee and the Black Belt* (Richmond, Va.: Dietz Press, 1944), 19. Kenneth Marvin Hamilton, "Forty Acres and a Mule: Reconstruction and the Booker T. Washington Era," in *The African American Odyssey*, edited by Debra Newman Ham (Washington, D.C.: Library of Congress, 1998), 67–74, 71 and 73.

20. Hamilton, "Forty Acres and a Mule," 74. *Southern Workman*, September 1881. "The Catalog of Tuskegee Normal School," *BTW Papers*, 2:173nn.

21. Stephen B. Weeks, *History of Public School Education in Alabama* (Westport, Conn.: Negro Universities Press, 1971), 171–72. *New York Tribune*, November 22, 1915, MN 732, BTW LOC; Anson Phelps Stokes, *Tuskegee Institute: The First Fifty Years* (Tuskegee, Ala.: Tuskegee Institute Press, 1931), 89–90. *The Tuskegee Institute Bulletin,*

Annual Report Edition of the Principal and Treasurer (Tuskegee, Ala.: Tuskegee Institute, 1916–17), 5, 33, and 38, TUA.

22. *Southern Workman*, September 1881.

23. Reported course offerings in the annual Tuskegee Institute Catalogs, TUA. BTW, "An Address at a Mass Meeting in Washington, D.C.," November 20, 1891, *BTW Papers*, 3:187. BTW, *Story of My Life and Work*, 97, 310. BTW, *Working with the Hands* (New York: Arnor Press and the *New York Times*, 1969 [1904]), 32, 50, 56, 66, 68, 74, 100, and 130. Clipping from unidentified newspaper, December 1915, MN 422, BTW LOC.

24. Lindsey, *Indians at Hampton Institute, 1877–1923*, 97. BTW to Hollis Burke Frissell, January 23, 1897, *BTW Papers*, 4:256n. *Thirty-Third Annual Catalog, The Tuskegee Normal and Industrial Institute, 1913–1914* (Tuskegee Institute, Ala.: Institute Press, 1914), 32 and 33. Anderson, *Education of Blacks in the South*, 47.

25. Stephanie J. Shaw, *What a Woman Ought to Be and to Do: Black Professional Women Workers during the Jim Crow Era* (Chicago: University of Chicago Press, 1996), 95–97. BTW, "A Speech before the New York Congregational Club," January 16, 1893, *BTW Papers*, 3:281 and 3:283. "Number of Persons Reached thru Tuskegee's Extension Activities, May 1909," MN 692, BTW LOC.

26. "Number of Persons Reached thru Tuskegee's Extension Activities, May 1909." A list of Washington's publications is in "A Bibliography of the Writings of Booker T. Washington," *BTW Papers*, 14:xi–xxvi.

Chapter 1. "A Great Man Fallen"

1. Algernon Brashear Jackson to EJS, n.d., MN 421. W. H. Walcott to EJS, November 19, 1915, MN 421; R. W. Thompson to EJS, November 21, 1915; Louis G. Gregory to Mrs. Booker T. Washington, December 1, 1915; see also J. C. Fremout to EJS, November 16, 1915, MN 420, all in BTW LOC.

2. Edyth Williams to EJS, November 15, 1915, MN 421; Spencer Patterson to EJS, November 1915; both in BTW LOC.

3. EJS to William H. Lewis, telg. November 14, 1915; Associated Press to EJS, telg. November 14, 1915, MN 421, both in BTW LOC.

4. Max Weber, *The Protestant Ethic and the Spirit of Capitalism*, translated by Talcott Parson (North Charleston, S.C.: CreateSpace Independent Publishing Platform, 2010); Ernst Troeltsch, *Protestantism and Progress* (Philadelphia,: Fortress Press, 1986); Daniel T. Rodgers, *The Work Ethic in Industrial America: 1850–1920* (Chicago: University of Chicago Press, 1974); and George McKenna, *The Puritan Origins of American Patriotism* (New Haven, Conn.: Yale University Press, 2007).

5. Colin Woodard, *American Nations: A History of the Eleven Rival Regional Cultures of North America* (New York: Penguin Group, 2011), 173–99. Rodgers, *Work Ethic in Industrial America*, 30–33. James M. McPherson, *The Abolitionist Legacy: From Reconstruction to the NAACP* (Princeton, N.J.: Princeton University Press, 1975), 161–63.

6. McPherson, *Abolitionist Legacy*, 162. W. E. Burghardt Du Bois, "The Talented Tenth," in W. E. B. Du Bois et al., *The Negro Problem: A Series of Articles by Representative Negroes of To-Day* (New York: J. Pott, 1903), 13–19. Du Bois, *The Souls of Black Folk* (New York: Fawcett World Library, 1961), 82.

7. James D. Anderson, *The Education of Blacks in the South, 1860–1935* (Chapel Hill: University of North Carolina Press, 1988), 33–78.

8. "Proceedings of the Triennial Reunion of the Hampton Alumni Association," May 28, 1893, *BTW Papers*, 3:347. *Savannah (GA) Press*, November 18, 1915; and "Items from the Hampton Institute Student Account Book," October 1872–June 1873, *BTW Papers*, 2:22, facing.

9. Emancipation Association Committee to EJS, telg. November 16, 1915; Wade H. Richardson to Warren A. Logan, November 15, 1915, MN 421; G. W. Reed to EJS, telg. November 16, 1915, MN 420; and James E. Kefford to EJS, November 15, 1915, MN 420, all in BTW LOC.

10. E. M. Henderson to EJS, November 16, 1915. For the letter to Margaret Washington, see Allerta E. Allwood et al. to Mrs. Washington, November 27, 1915, MN 420. For letters to EJS, see Jerome B. Peterson to EJS, November 15, 1915, MN 421; Guillermo Kessel to EJS, November 15, 1915, MN 420; Jose A. Manroque to EJS, November 16, 1915, MN 421; and Narciso Nodarsy to EJS, November 17, 1915, MN 421, all in BTW LOC. BTW, *Up from Slavery* (New York: Dodd, Mead, 1965), 170–85. BTW to Gladwin Bouton, May 6, 1915, *BTW Papers*, 13:286–87.

11. Renato Rosald, *Culture and Truth: The Remaking of Social Analysis* (Boston: Beacon Press, 1989); Cerena Scantlebury, *Death, Grief, and Ritual: An Overview of American Attitudes Toward Death* (Salem, Ore.: Willamette University Undergraduate Research Grants Program, 1990). Michael R. Leming and George E. Dickinson, "The Contemporary American Funeral," in *Understanding Dying, Death, and Bereavement*, edited by Michael R. Leming and George E. Dickinson, 5th ed. (Belmont, Calif.: Wadsworth, 2006).

12. Mr. and Mrs. J. Rosamond Johnson to Mrs. Washington, telg. November 14, 1915, MN 420; Hattie B. Sprague et al. to Mrs. Washington, telg. November 14, 1915, MN 421; Mary E. Josenburger to Mrs. Washington, telg. November 15, 1915; Harold Peadbody to Mrs. Washington, November 15, 1915; see also Cordelia A. Atwell to Mrs. Washington, telg. November 15, 1915, MN 420, all in BTW LOC.

13. Lillian V. Ramsey Mines to Mrs. Washington, telg. November 17, 1915; and Clifford L. Miller to Mrs. Washington, November 17, 1915; and Julius Rosenwald to Mrs. Washington, telg. November 14, 1915, MN 421, all in BTW LOC.

14. Lyman Beecher Stowe to EJS, telg. November 14, 1915; R. W. Thompson to EJS, November 14, 1915, MN 421; Charles H. Moore to EJS, November 17, 1915, MN 421; William H. Davis to EJS, telg. November 16, 1915; see also James E. Keford to EJS, November 15, 1915, MN 420, all in BTW LOC.

15. John M. Gandy to Mrs. Washington, telg. November 15, 1915, MN 420, BTW LOC. For information concerning Gandy, see "An Account of Washington's Louisiana

Tour" by William Anthony Aery, June 19, 1915, *BTW Papers*, 3:324n. Cal F. Johnson to Mrs. Washington, telg. November 16, 1915; Henry Plummer Cheatham to Mrs. Washington, telg. November 15, 1915; R. C. Hintone to EJS, November 17, 1915, MN 420, all in BTW LOC.

16. Ninth U.S. Cavalry to Mrs. Washington, telg. November 16, 1915, MN 421; and Wade Hampton et al. to Mrs. Washington, November 16, 1915, MN 420, both in BTW LOC. For information concerning Samuel Joe Brown, see *Who's Who of the Colored Race*, ed. Frank Lincoln Mather (Chicago: Frank Lincoln Mather, 1915), 45. Pauline L. Batties et al. to Mrs. Washington, November 14, 1915; Richard A. Blount to Mrs. Washington, telg. November 16, 1915; H. A. Adams to Mrs. Washington, telg. November 17, 1915; and Hotel Brotherhood U.S.A. to Mrs. Washington, telg. November 16, 1915, MN 420, all in BTW LOC.

17. See an article in the "Christian Union," August 14, 1890, *BTW Papers*, 13:21. S. W. Bacote to EJS, telg. November 14, 1915, MN 420; G. W. Robinson, November 20, 1915; and R. S. Stout to EJS, telg. November 16, 1915, MN 421; S. J. Channell to Mrs. Washington, November 17, 1915, MN 420. See also P. K. Foville to Mrs. Washington, November 16, 1915, telg. MN 421, all in BTW LOC.

18. J. S. Flipper et al. to Mrs. Washington, telg. November 14, 1915; and N. M. Carroll et al. to Mrs. Washington, November 25, 1915; MN 420; J. R. Goss et al. to EJS, telg. November 16, 1915, MN 421; J. S. Scott et al. to Mrs. Washington, November 14, 1915, MN 420; see also William H. Thomas et al. to H. T. Kealing, November 16, 1915, MN 420, all in BTW LOC. Logan to BTW, June 7, 1899, *BTW Papers*, 5:127–30nn.

19. W. D. Wetherford to Logan, telg. November 15, 1915; L. B. Brooks to EJS, November 15, 1915, MN 420; Schloss and Kahn to Mrs. Washington, telg. November 15, 1915, MN 421; E. S. Shannon to Tuskegee Institute, telg. November 15, 1915, MN 421; Andrew Carnegie to Mrs. Washington, telg. November 15, 1915, MN 420, all in BTW LOC. For information concerning Carnegie gifts to BTW, see *BTW2*, 135.

20. Dr. and Mrs. LL. Burwell to Mrs. Washington, telg. November 14, 1915, MN 420; Mr. and Mrs. W. S. Schley to Mrs. Washington, telg. November 14, 1915, MN 421; Asheville Newspaper Association to Mrs. Washington, telg. November 16, 1915; and W. T. Francis to Mrs. Washington, telg. November 14, 1915, MN 420, all in BTW LOC.

21. J. I. Washington to EJS, November 19, 1915, MN 421; Walter R. Nicholson to Mrs. Washington, telg. November 15, 1915, MN 421; and Mary Lou Austin to Mrs. Washington, telg. November 15, 1915, MN 420, both in BTW LOC.

22. Roscoe C. Simmons to EJS, November 20, 1915; Jos L. Jones to Mrs. Washington, telg. November 15, 1915; see also Victoria Clay Haley to Mrs. Washington, telg. November 14, 1915, MN 420; P. S. Lewis et al. to Mrs. Washington, telg. November 16, 1915; MN 421; P. K. Foville to Mrs. Booker T. Washington, telg. November 16, 1915; and Melvin J. Chisum to EJS, November 15, 1915, MN 420, all in BTW LOC.

23. R. C. Huston Jr. to EJS, telg. November 14, 1915, MN 420, BTW LOC. For information concerning Houston, see "An Account of Washington's Tour of Texas," by Horace D. Slatter, October 14, 1911, *BTW Papers*, 11:332. Edwina B. Kruse to Mrs. Washington, telg. November 16, 1915; L. B. Brooks to EJS, November 15, 1915; and

W. C. Chance to Board of Trustees Institute, telg. November 17, 1915, MN 420; and J. W. Tuner to EJS, November 16, 1915, MN 421, all in BTW LOC.

24. Leon F. Litwack, *Trouble in Mind: Black Southerners in the Age of Jim Crow* (New York: Knopf, 1998).

25. Maldwyn Allen Jones, *American Immigration* (Chicago: University of Chicago Press, 1960), 207–46. William G. Jordan, *Black Newspapers and America's War for Democracy, 1914–1920* (Chapel Hill: University of North Carolina Press, 2001), 58–61.

26. William H. Taft to EJS, telg. November 16, 1915, MN 421, BTW LOC.

27. Monroe M. Work to BTW, January 22, 1909. BTW, "The South As An Opening for a Business Career," November 20, 1891; and "Extracts from address delivered," May 19, 1901, all in BTW LOC. "An Abraham Lincoln Memorial Address in Philadelphia," February 14, 1899, *BTW Papers*, 5:32–38.

28. For information concerning the early development of the Tuskegee Institute, see BTW, *Up from Slavery*, 67–124. Paul Monroe, ed., *A Cyclopedia of Education* (New York: Macmillan, 1913), 123–24 and 590–91. James D. Anderson, *The Education of Blacks in the South, 1860–1935* (Chapel Hill: University of North Carolina Press, 1988), 33–78.

29. George W. Clinton et al. to EJS, telg. November 15, 1915, MN 420, BTW LOC.

30. John C. Dancey to EJS, November 16, 1915, MN 420, BTW LOC. For information concerning Dancey, see Timothy Thomas Fortune to BTW, June 1, 1899, *BTW Papers*, 5:122–24nn. Sylvester Russell to EJS, November 14, 1915, MN 421; Stanley Yarnall Jr. to Mrs. Washington, November 17, 1915, MN 420; J. L. Carwin et al. to EJS, November 16, 1915, MN 420, all in BTW LOC.

31. Wade H. Richardson to Logan, November 15, 1915; J. I. Washington et al. to EJS, November 18, 1915, MN 421; B. W. Allen to Mrs. Washington, telg. November 15, 1915, MN 420; and Lewis B. Moore to EJS, November 15, MN 421, all in BTW LOC. Richard W. Thompson to EJS, February 4, 1903, *BTW Papers*, 7:36n.

32. BTW to Jacoby Henry Schiff, September 18, 1909, *BTW Papers*, 10:174–76. *New York Times*, April 28, 1898.

33. Stanley Yarnall Jr. to Mrs. Washington, November 17, 1915; Leslie Pinckney Hill to Mrs. Booker T. Washington, November 18, 1915, MN 420, both in BTW LOC; Ninth U.S. Cavalry to Mrs. Washington, November 16, 1915, MN 421, BTW LOC.

34. Gordon Nelson Armstrong to Tuskegee Faculty, November 15, 1915; Charles R. Frazer et al. to Tuskegee Faculty and Students, telg. November 15, 1915, MN 420, both in BTW LOC.

35. "A Bibliography of the Writings of Booker T. Washington," *BTW Papers*, 1:xi–xxvi. Willis Jackson to EJS, November 22, 1915, MN 420; William B. Reily to Officers of the Institute, November 18, 1915, MN 421; A. L. Cassidy to EJS, November 18, 1911, MN 420, all in BTW LOC.

36. "Principal's Report to the Board of Trustees of the Tuskegee Normal and Industrial Institute 1915," TUA. BTW, "Extracts from an Address before the American Missionary Association," October 19, 1910, *BTW Papers*, 10:406–10. BTW to EJS, March 9, 1914, *BTW Papers*, 12:470–71.

37. David H. Jackson Jr., *Booker Washington and the Struggle against White Suprem-acy: The Southern Educational Tours, 1908–1912* (New York: Palgrave Macmillan, 2008), 2–3. Emmett J. Scott and Lyman Beecher Stowe, *Booker T. Washington: Builder of a Civilization* (Garden City, N.Y.: Doubleday, Page, 1917), 185–221.

38. D. H. Jackson Jr., *Booker Washington and the Struggle against White Supremacy*, 66 and 81. Scott and Stowe, *Booker T. Washington*, 185–221.

39. BTW, "The Closing Address before the National Negro Business League," August 24, 1900, *BTW Papers*, 5:603–5. Scott and Stowe, *Booker T. Washington*, 195–219. "Bibliography of the Writings of Booker T. Washington."

40. Jose A. Manroque to EJS, November 16, 1915, MN 421; and Walter S. Buchanan to Mrs. Washington, telg. November 15, 1915, MN 420, both in BTW LOC. *Tuskegee Student*, March 12, 1907, *BTW Papers* 9:229n. W. H. Ellis to EJS, November 15, 1915, MN 420, BTW LOC. Charles William Anderson to BTW, December 4, 1905, *BTW Papers*, 8:461n. The Students League to Logan, telg. November 16, MN 421, BTW LOC.

41. *Tuskegee Student*, January 5, 1900. Herschel B. Cashin to Mrs. Washington, telg. November 15, 1915, MN 420, BTW LOC. For information concerning Cashin, see BTW to Theodore Roosevelt, January 5, 1906, *BTW Papers*, 6:372n. Eva T. Dean to Mrs. Booker T. Washington, n.d., MN 420; W. H. Mixon to Mrs. Booker T. Washington, telg. November 16, 1915, MN 421, both in BTW LOC. Winfield Henri Mixon to BTW, June 8, 1900, *BTW Papers*, 5:557n.

42. Charles S. Medbury to Mrs. Washington, telg. November 15, 1915, MN 421, BTW LOC. Charles Sanderson Medbury to BTW, September 3, 1912, *BTW Papers*, 12:5n. B. T. Smart to Mrs. Washington, November 19, 1915, MN 421; and Scott Bond to EJS, telg. November 17, 1915, MN 420, both in BTW LOC. BTW to Robert Russa Moton, August 21, 1911, *BTW Papers*, 11:297.

43. J. W. Alstork to Mrs. Washington, November 16, 1915; James M. Curley to Mrs. Washington, November 15, 1915; and Charles H. Albert to EJS, November 15, 1915, MN 420; and Sheadrick B. Turner to EJS, telg. November 15, 1915, all in BTW LOC. For information concerning Turner, see BTW to Theodore Roosevelt, January 13, 1906, *BTW Papers*, 8:502n.

44. James Mitchell et al. to Mrs. Washington, telg. November 16, 1916, MN 421; W. Houston to Mrs. Washington, telg. November 16, 1915; and S. N. Dickerson et al. to Mrs. Washington, telg. November 15, 1915; see also C. J. Chapple et al. to EJS, telg. November 18, 1915, MN 420, all in BTW LOC.

45. Scott and Stowe, *Booker T. Washington*, 321. BTW2, 204. J. Y. Joyner to Mrs. Washington, telg. November 15, 1915, MN 420; Wade H. Richardson to Logan, November 15, 1915, MN 421, both in BTW LOC.

46. W. A. Hunton to EJS, telg. November 14, 1915; Thomas Jesse Jones to Mrs. Washington, telg. November 14, 1915; S. B. McCormick to Mrs. Washington, telg. November 15, 1915, MN 421; Caroline Hazard to Mrs. Washington, telg. November 16, 1915; and Charles W. Fairbanks to EJS, telg. November 14, 1915, MN 420. Isaac N.

Seligman to Mrs. Washington, telg. November 15, 1915, MN 421; William James to Mrs. Washington, telg. November 17, 1915, MN 420, all in BTW LOC. William James to BTW, March 8, 1897, *BTW Papers*, 4:264n. William H. Taft to EJS, telg. November 16, 1915, MN 421, BTW LOC.

47. H. L. Chapman to Mrs. Washington, November 18, 1915; Lewis W. Barney to Mrs. Washington, November 15, 1915; George W. Hays to Mrs. Washington, November 15, 1915; Samuel F. Holman et al. to Mrs. Washington, November 16, 1915, MN 420; A. W. Puller to Mrs. Washington, telg. November 16, 1915, MN 421, all in BTW LOC.

48. Charlotte Hawkins et al. to Mrs. Washington, telg. November 15, 1915, MN 420; A. W. Puller to Mrs. Washington, telg. November 16, 1915, MN 421; A. W. Dewar to EJS, November 15, 1915; F. B. Hooker and T. J. Elliott to EJS, telg. November 15, 1915; and Willis Jackson to EJS, November 22, 1915, MN 420, all in BTW LOC.

49. 2 Samuel 3:38. The other biblical reference to a "great man" is in 2 Kings 5:1.

50. John C. Gilmer to Mrs. Washington, telg. November 14, 1915, MN 420; J. S. Clark to the Tuskegee Institute, telg. November 15, 1915, MN 420; Dr. and Mrs. H. C. Bryant to EJS, telg. November 15, 1915, MN 420, all in BTW LOC.

51. Matthew Anderson to Mrs. Washington, November 15, 1915, MN 420, BTW LOC. For information concerning Anderson, see Matthew Anderson to BTW, September 17, 1902, *BTW Papers*, 6:521n. W. A. Fountain et al. to Mrs. Washington, November 17, 1915, MN 420. Mrs. M. Baranton Tule to Mrs. Washington, telg. November 16, 1915; President and Mrs. W. A. Fountain to Mrs. Washington, telg. November 16, 1915; Susie W. Fountain et al. to Mrs. Washington, telg. November 14, 1915; Pauline L. Batties et al. to Mrs. Washington, November 14, 1915; W. T. Johnson to Mrs. Washington, November 16, 1915, MN 420, all in BTW LOC.

52. ABC Baseball Club to EJS, telg. November 15, 1915; E. Sutcliffe to EJS, telg. November 15, 1915, MN 421. James H. Dillard to EJS, telg. November 15, 1915, MN 420, all in BTW LOC. James Hardy Dillard to BTW, May 31, 1907, *BTW Papers*, 9:285n. W. J. Button to Mrs. Washington, November 27, 1915, MN 420; Leo Strassbunger to EJS, November 16, 1915, MN 421; A. W. Dewar to EJS, November 15, 1915; Julian S. Carr to EJS, telg. November 16, 1915, MN 420, all in BTW LOC.

53. J. B. James to Mrs. Washington, telg. November 15, 1915, MN 420; Clarence E. Woods to Chairman Board Trustees, telg. November 15, 1915, MN 421, all in BTW LOC. *BTW Papers*, 9:513n. *BTW Papers*, 13:329.

54. John D. Rockefeller to Mrs. Washington, telg. November 15, 1915, MN 421; Thomas W. Bicknell to John H. Washington, November 16, 1915, MN 420, both in BTW LOC. James Fowle Baldwin Marshall to BTW, October 18, 1882, *BTW Papers*, 2:209n.

55. James P. Munroe to Mrs. Washington, November 17, 1915, MN 421; Julia P. H. Coleman to Mrs. Washington, telg. November 15, 1915, MN 420; J. S. Flippin et al. to EJS, telg. November 16, 1915, MN 420; Wade H. Richardson to Logan, November 15, 1915, MN 421, all in BTW LOC.

56. Shelby J. Davidson to Mrs. Washington, telg. November 15, 1915, MN 420; W. S. Scarborough to Mrs. Washington, telg. November 15, 1915, MN 421; Kappa Alpha Phi Fraternity to Mrs. Washington, telg. November 15, 1915, MN 420. R. R. Moton to Mrs. Washington, telg. November 15, 1915, MN 421, all in BTW LOC.

57. William C. Lloyd to Mrs. Washington, telg. November 15, 1915, MN 421; William B. Reily to Officers of the Institute, November 18, 1915, MN 421; and John C. Anderson to EJS, November 15, 1915, MN 420, all in BTW LOC.

58. Auburn Ministers Union to EJS, telg. November 15, 1915, MN 420; W. D. Wetherford to Logan, telg. November 15, 1915, MN 421; B. W. Allen to Mrs. Washington, telg. November 15, 1915, MN 420; Emmett O'Neal to Mrs. Washington, telg. November 16, 1915, MN 421, all in BTW LOC.

59. James L. Curtis to Mrs. Washington, telg. November 14, 1915, MN 420; Kelly Miller to Mrs. Washington, telg. November 14, 1915; Hungerford School Trustees et al., telg. November 16, 1915; Edyth Williams to EJS, telg. November 15, 1915, MN 421, all in BTW LOC.

60. W. H. Walcott to EJS, November 19, 1915, MN 421, BTW LOC.

Chapter 2. A Symbol of America

1. *Pittsburgh (PA) Times*, November 15, 1915; *Duluth (MN) Tribune*, November, 15, 1915, MN 732; *Augusta (ME) Journal*, November 15, 1915; *Oregonian* (Portland, OR), November 15, 1915; *Houston (TX) Post*; and *Cleveland (OH) Plain Dealer*, November 16, 1915, MN 732. *Methodist Recorder* (Pittsburgh, PA), April 8, 1916, MN 733, all in BTW LOC.

2. *Newton (NC) News*, November 16, 1915, and *Pueblo (CO) Chieftain*, November 23, 1915, MN 732; *Richmond (VA) Planet*, November 27, 1915; *Freeman (OH) Messenger*, November 15, 1915, MN 422, BTW LOC.

3. Janice Hume, *Obituaries in American Culture* (Jackson: University of Mississippi Press, 2000), and Edward W. Chester, "Lyndon Baines Johnson, American 'King Lear': A Critical Evaluation of His Newspaper Obituaries," *Presidential Studies Quarterly* 21, no. 2 (1991): 319–37.

4. Thomas J. Calloway, "Booker Washington and the Tuskegee Institute," *New England Magazine* 17, no. 2 (October 1897); Calloway, an 1889 Fisk University graduate, worked as an agent for Tuskegee Institute when he wrote the article. For information concerning Calloway, see Thomas Junius Calloway to BTW, October 31, 1891, *BTW Papers*, 3:177nn. Max Bennett Thrasher, "Tuskegee Institute and Its President," *Appleton's Popular Science Monthly* 4 (May 1899): 592–610; Max Bennett Thrasher, *Tuskegee: Its Story and Its Work* (Boston: Small, Maynard & Co., 1900); BTW, "My Life Work at Tuskegee, Alabama," *New York Teachers Magazine*, no. 2 (June 1899): 36–38; and BTW, "Early Life and Struggle for an Education," *Howard's American Magazine* 4 (November 1899): 3–6.

5. Washington first published *The Story of My Life and Work* in book form in 1900, rewriting and serializing it in the *Outlook* that fall. The next year, he published the rewritten articles as the book *Up from Slavery*. Arna Bontemps, *Great Slave*

Narratives (Boston: Beacon Press, 1969), viii. BTW, *Up from Slavery* (New York: Oxford University Press, 1965), 41; *Indianapolis Freeman*, November 20, 1915; *New York Freeman*, May 16, 1885; *Montgomery (AL) Advertiser*, December 5, 1915, MN 732, BTW LOC; *Tuskegee (AL) News*, November 15, 1915, book 53, 2:107–9, Hampton Clippings.

6. For a discussion concerning the historical context of *Up from Slavery* see Botemps, *Great Slave Narratives*; Rebecca Chalmers Barton, *Witness for Freedom* (New York: Harper & Brothers, 1948), 3–17; Donald B. Gibson, "Strategies and Revisions of Self-Representation in Booker T. Washington's Autobiographies," *American Quarterly* 43, no. 3 (September 1993): 372–89; Houston A. Baker Jr., *Long Black Song: Essays in Black American Literature and Culture* (Charlottesville: University Press of Virginia, 1972), 85–95; David Lewis Dudley, "'The Trouble I've Seen': Visions and Revisions of Bondage, Flight, and Freedom in Black American Autobiography" (PhD diss., Louisiana State University, 1988), 6–57. BTW to John A. Hertel, September 22, 1900, *BTW Papers*, 5:643. George Eastman to BTW, January 2, 1902, *BTW Papers*, 6:370; David Page Morehouse to BTW, December 26, 1913, *BTW Papers*, 12:382–83. *BTW2*, 130–31.

7. M. R. Werner, *Julius Rosenwald: The Life of a Practical Humanitarian* (New York: Harper & Brothers, 1939), 114, 123, 125, 131, and 334.

8. BTW, *My Larger Education* (Garden City, N.Y.: Doubleday, Page, 1911). *BTW Papers*, 1:xi–xii. Marquis James, "Booker T. Washington," manuscript, n.d., unnumbered page, TUA. *Natchez (MS) Weekly Herald*, February 19, 1916, MN 733, BTW LOC.

9. James MacGregor Burns, *Leadership* (New York: Harper and Row, 1978), 425.

10. *Rochester (NY) Herald*, November 16, 1915; *Duluth (MN) Tribune*, November 16, 1915; *Pensacola (FL) Journal*, November 18, 1915; *Ansonia (CT) Sentinel*, November 15, 1915; *Daily Oklahoman* (Oklahoma City), 1915, MN 732, BTW LOC; *Rochester (NY) Chronicle* quote reprinted in the *Rochester (NY) Democrat and Chronicle*, December 27, 1915, book 55, 2:113, Hampton Clippings; *Harrisburg (PA) Daily Telegraph* quote reprinted in the *Montgomery (AL) Advertiser*, April 27, 1916, MN 733, BTW LOC.

11. *Cincinnati (OH) Enquirer*, November 20, 1915, MN 422, BTW LOC; *Voice of the People*, December 16, 1915, book 54, 2:99–100, Hampton Clippings; *New York Call*, November 16, 1915, MN 422, BTW LOC; *New York Sun*, November 20, 1915, book 54, 1:66–70, Hampton Clippings; *Pittsburgh (PA) Press*, November 1915, MN 422, BTW LOC; *Indianapolis Recorder*, November 20, 1915, book 54, 2:16; and *East Tennessee News*, November 20, 1915, book 53, 1:94, Hampton Clippings.

12. George W. Forbes, "The Passing of Dr. Booker T. Washington," *AME Review* 32, no. 3 (January 1916): 190–96. Timothy Thomas Fortune, "The Quick and the Dead," *AME Review* 32, no. 4 (April 1916): 247–50.

13. Fortune, "The Quick and the Dead," 50.

14. W. E. B. Du Bois, *Dusk of Dawn* (New York: Schocken Books, 1968), 242–43.

15. *Afro-American Ledger*, November 21, 1915, MN 422, BTW LOC.

16. *The Georgia Baptist*, reprinted in the *Atlanta Independent*, January 15, 1916, MN 733, BTW LOC.

17. Allan H. Spear, *Black Chicago* (Chicago: University of Chicago Press, 1967), 81–82. *Chicago Defender*, December 11, 1915, book 55, 2:100, Hampton Clippings.

18. *Springfield (MA) Republican*, November 18, 1915, book 53, 2:99–101; *Boston Evening Transcript*, November 17, 1915, book 55, 1:45–49, Hampton Clippings. *Boston Transcript*, November 15, 1915; *Pensacola (FL) Journal*, November 18, 1915; *Indianapolis Star*, November 15, 1915; *New York City Press*, November 15, 1915; and *Salt Lake City (UT) News*, November 15, 1915, all in BTW LOC. *New York City Amsterdam News*, November 19, 1915, BTW LOC; *Chicago Defender*, November 20, 1915, book 54, Hampton Clippings; and *St. Louis (MO) Argus*, November 17, 1915, BTW LOC.

19. *BTW Papers*, 6:469. *Boston Evening Transcript*, book 55, 1:45–49, Hampton Clippings; *Richmond (VA) Journal*, November 22, 1915, MN 732; for the second quote see the *New York City Amsterdam News*, November 19, 1915, MN 422, both in BTW LOC. *Harrisburg (PA) Advocate-Verdict*, December 31, 1915, book 54, 2:116, Hampton Clippings. BTW, *Up from Slavery* (New York: Dodd, Mead, 1965), 6.

20. *Richmond (VA) Journal*, November 22, 1915; and *St. Louis (MO) Post-Dispatch*, November 26, 1915, MN 732, both in BTW LOC.

21. *Fort Plain (NY) Register*, November 17, 1915, MN 732, BTW LOC; *New York Sun*, November 15, 1915, book 53, 1:18, Hampton Clippings; and *Allentown (PA) Morning Call*, November 15, 1915, MN 732, BTW LOC. James, "Booker T. Washington," chapter 1, 12, and notes; "First Interview with Emma Meadows, daughter of Biah Ferguson Meadows and First Interview with Active Meadows," unnumbered page, BTW TUA.

22. *Boston Herald*, November 15, 1915, book 53, 1:26–27; *Norfolk (VA) Journal and Guide*, January 1, 1916, book 55, 2:119, both in Hampton Clippings. *London Times*, November 16, 1915, MN 732, BTW LOC.

23. *New Haven (CT) Register*, November 15, 1915, book 53, 1:25, Hampton Clippings; *New York News*, November 27, 1915, MN 422, BTW LOC.

24. *Geneseo (NY) Republican*, November 15, 1915; *Piqua (OH) Call*, November 24, 1915; *Two Rivers (WI) Reporter*, November 19, 1915; *New York Daily Graphic*, November 16, 1915, all in MN 732, BTW LOC. *Indianapolis Freeman*, November 20, 1915. *Montgomery (AL) Advertiser*, December 5, 1915, MN 732; and *Tuskegee Student*, January 22, 1916, MN 422, both in BTW LOC.

25. *Boston (MA) Herald*, November 15, 1915, book 55, 1:21, Hampton Clippings. *Boston Transcript*, November 1, 1915; and article in an unidentified newspaper, November, MN 732; BTW LOC. Richard Price and Sally Price, "Saramaka Onomastics: An Afro-American Naming System," *Ethnology* 11 (October 1972): 341.

26. *Utica (NY) Globe*, November 20, 1915; *Pittsburgh (PA) Presbyterian Banner*, November 18, 1915; *Fort Plain (NY) Register*, November 17, 1915; and an article in an unidentified newspaper, 1915, all in MN 732, BTW LOC. *Boston Transcript*, November 15, 1915, MN 732, BTW LOC; *Indianapolis Freeman*, November 20, 1915; and *New York Sun*, November 15, 1915, book 53, 1:18, Hampton Clippings. Basil Mathews, *Booker T. Washington* (Cambridge, Mass.: Harvard University Press, 1948), 150. Ann S. Joplin, "Old Burrough's Home: Birthplace of Booker T. Washington," November 8,

1937, folder 4225, box 403, series 1.3, GEB, Rockefeller Archive Center. Richard Brent Turner, *Islam in the African-American Experience*, 2nd ed. (Bloomington: Indiana University Press, 2003), xvii.

27. *New York Sun*, November 15, 1915, book 53, 1:18, Hampton Clippings. *Tuskegee (AL) News*, November 15, 1915, book 53, 2:107–9, Hampton Clippings; *Birmingham (AL) Age-Herald*, November 15, 1915, MN 732, BTW LOC.

28. *Afro American Page*, November 1915, book 53, 1:10; *Springfield (MA) Republican*, November 18, 1915, book 53, 1:99–101, both in Hampton Clippings. *Tuskegee Student*, January 22, 1916, MN 422, BTW LOC.

29. *New Age*, November, no year, book 53, 2:122, Hampton Clippings. *Piqua (OH) Call*, November 24, 1915, MN 732, BTW LOC. *Springfield (MA) Republican*, November 18, 1915, book 53, 1:99–101, Hampton Clippings. *Utica (NY) Globe*, November 20, 1915, MN 732, BTW LOC. *Little Rock (AR) Gazette*, November 22, 1915, MN 731; *Brooklyn (NY) Eagle*, November 16, 1915, MN 732, both in BTW LOC.

30. *Springfield (MA) Republican*, November 18, 1915, book 53, 1:99–101, Hampton Clippings.

31. *Portland (ME) Express*, November 18, 1915, MN 732; *Salt Lake City (UT) News*, November 15, 1915, MN 732; and *Philadelphia Bulletin*, November 15, 1915, MN 732, all in BTW LOC. Unidentified Brooklyn (NY) newspaper, November 15, 1915, book 55, 1:32, Hampton Clippings.

32. Reprint of the *Philadelphia Inquirer* article in the *Trenton (NJ) Times*, November 16, 1915, MN 732, BTW LOC. Unidentified Brooklyn (NY) newspaper, November 15, 1915, book 55, 1:32; *Hartford (CT) Courant*, November 15, 1915, book 53, 1:35, both in Hampton Clippings.

33. *Hartford (CT) Courant*, November 15, 1915, book 53, 1:33, Hampton Clippings. Suzanne C. Carson, "Samuel Chapman Armstrong: Missionary to the South" (PhD diss., Johns Hopkins University, 1952), 1. James D. Anderson, *The Education of Blacks in the South, 1860–1935* (Chapel Hill: University of North Carolina Press, 1988), 33–78.

34. *Tuskegee (AL) News*, November 15, 1915, book 53, 2:107–9, Hampton Clippings.

35. *Savannah (GA) Tribune*, November 20, 1915; *Indianapolis Freeman*, November 20, 1915; and the *Afro American Page*, November 1915, book 53, 1:10, Hampton Clippings.

36. *Long Branch (DE) Record*, November 16, MN 732; and *Piqua (OH) Call*, November 24, 1915, MN 732; *Indianapolis Freeman*, December 18, 1915, MN 422;. *Atlanta Independent*, November 12, 1915, MN 422, all in BTW LOC. Unidentified Brooklyn (NY) newspaper, November 15, 1915, book 55, 1:32, Hampton Clippings. *Williamsport (PA) Grit*, November 21, MN 732, BTW LOC.

37. *Los Angeles Examiner*, November 1915, MN 732. BTW, *Washington (D.C.) Bee*, November 20, 1915; and *Duluth (MN) Tribune*, November 16, 1915, all in MN 732, BTW LOC. *Christian Recorder*, November 18, 1915, book 53, 2:96–97, Hampton Clippings. *Mobile (AL) Weekly Press*, November 20, 1915, MN 732; and *Minneapolis (MN) Tribune*, November 16, 1915, MN 731, both in BTW LOC.

38. *Danbury (CT) News*, November 15, 1915, MN 732; and *Sioux City (IA) Tribune*, November 22, 1915, MN 732, both in BTW LOC. Woods Hutchinson, article in the *New York American*, December 10, 1915, book 54, 1:84, Hampton Clippings.

39. *Afro American Page*, November 1915, book 53, 1:10; *New York Evening Mail*, November 15, 1915, book 55, 1:39–40; and *Portland (ME) Express*, November 15, 1915, book 53, 1:27, all in Hampton Clippings. *Birmingham (AL) Age-Herald*, November 15, 1915, MN 732; *Daily Oklahoman* (Oklahoma City), November 16, 1915, MN 732; and *Montgomery (AL) Advertiser*, November 15, 1915, MN 422, all in BTW LOC.

40. *Ocilla (GA) Star*, November 18, 1915, MN 732; *Tennessee News* (Chattanooga), reprinted in the *New Orleans Picayune*, November 30, 1915, MN 422; *St. Louis (MO) Republic*, November 16, 1916, MN 732; *Sentinel* (NY), November 17, 1915, MN 422, all in BTW LOC. *New York News*, November 18, 1915, book 53, 1:5, Hampton Clippings. *Lynn (MA) News*, November 18, 1915, LOC, BTW.

41. *Fresno (CA) Republican*, November 15, 1915, MN 732, BTW LOC; *Chicago Journal*, book 53, 1:30, Hampton Clippings; *Natchez (MS) Weekly Herald*, February 19, 1915; and *Detroit (MI) Journal*, November 16, 1915, both in MN 732, BTW LOC.

42. *Des Moines (IA) Leader*, November 16, 1915, MN 732; *Montgomery (AL) Advertiser*, November 25, 1915, MN 422; *Philadelphia Press*, MN 732; *Chicago American*, November 15, 1915, MN 732, all in BTW LOC. *Buffalo (NY) Enquirer*, November 15, 1915, 1:38, Hampton Clippings.

43. *Tacoma (WA) Ledger*, MN 732; *Little Rock (AR) Gazette*, November 22, 1915, MN 731; *Port Jervis (NY) Gazette*, November 16, 1915; *Buffalo (NY) News*, MN 422, all in BTW LOC.

44. *Hartford (CT) Courant*, November 15, 1915, book 53, 1:35; and *Springfield (MA) Republican*, November 18, 1915, book 53, 2:99–101, Hampton Clippings.

45. *Waterville (ME) News*, November 16, 1915, MN 732, BTW LOC; *National Baptist Union Review*, November 20, 1915, book 54, 1:7–9, Hampton Clippings; *Boston Herald*, November 15, 1915, MN 732; *Jacksonville (FL) Times Union Current*, n.d., MN 731; *Richmond (VA) Planet*, November 27, 1915, all in BTW LOC. *Union Review*, November 20, 1915; *Philadelphia Public Ledger*, November 15, 1915, MN 422, both in BTW LOC.

46. W. E. B. Du Bois, *The Souls of Black Folk*, edited by David W. Blight and Robert Gooding-Williams (Boston: Bedford Books, 1997), 63; *BTW1*, 24. *Springfield (MA) Republican*, November 18, 1915, book 53, 2:99–101, Hampton Clippings. For post-speech responses see *Danbury (CT) News*, November 15, 1915, MN 732, BTW LOC. *New York Sun*, November 15, 1915, book 53, 1:18, Hampton Clippings.

47. *New York News*, November 18, 1915, book 53, 1:3, Hampton Clippings; *Norfolk (VA) Journal and Guide*, November 27, 1915, book 54, 1:64, Hampton Clippings; and *Augusta (ME) Journal*, November 15, 1915, MN 732, BTW LOC. Although many of Washington's contemporary and latter-day critics proclaim that the Tuskegean supported segregation in this September 18, 1895, speech, he did not. Contrary to that ill-conceived interpretation, a thorough reading of his address reveals that he called for civil equality under the law.

48. BTW, "An Address at the National Peace Jubilee," October 16, 1898, *BTW Papers*, 4:490–93.

49. BTW, "An Account of the Boston Riot," July 31, 1903, *BTW Papers*, 7:229–40. BTW, "An Article in the New York World," November 7, 1911, *BTW Papers*, 11:359–62.

50. Leon F. Litwack, *Trouble in Mind* (New York: Alfred A. Knopf, 1998), 217–40.

51. *Savannah (GA) Press*, November 15, 1915, book 55, 1:30, Hampton Clippings; *Burlington (IA) Hawkeye*, November 23, 1915, MN 732; *Dallas (TX) Dispatch*, November 15, 1915, MN 732; *Oklahoman* (Oklahoma City), November 16, 1915, MN 732; *Rochester (NY) Chronicle*, November 28, 1915, MN 732; and *Toledo (OH) Blade*, November 18, 1915, MN 732, all in BTW LOC.

52. *Boston Transcript*, November 15, 1915, MN 732; *San Jose (CA) Herald*, November 16, 1915, MN 732; and *Salt Lake City (UT) News*, November 15, 1915, MN 732, all in BTW LOC. *Savannah (GA) Tribune*, November 27, 1915. *Terre Haute (IN) Star*, November 15, 1915, MN 732; *Genesee (NY) Republican*, November 15, 1915, MN 732, both in BTW LOC.

53. *Kansas City (MO) Times*, November 22, 1915, MN 732, BTW LOC; *New York Age*, November 18, 1915, book 53, 1:62–64, Hampton Clippings; *Boston Transcript*, November 15, 1915, MN 732, BTW LOC.

54. Mansel G. Blackford and K. Austin Kerr, *Business Enterprise in American History* (Boston: Houghton Mifflin, 1990), 188. BTW, *Up from Slavery*. *Waukegan (IL) Gazette*, November 16, 1915, MN 732, BTW LOC.

55. *New York Evening Post* reprinted in *New York Age*, November 18, 1915, book 55, 1:18, Hampton Clippings. *St. Louis (MO) Republic*, November 16, 1915; *Waterville (ME) News*, November 16, 1915, both in MN 732, BTW LOC.

56. *Birmingham (AL) Ledger*, November 15, 1915; *Pensacola (FL) Journal*, November 18, 1915, MN 732; and "A Boy Who Worked," in unidentified newspaper, n.d., MN 422, all in BTW LOC.

57. *Boston Herald*, November 15, 1915, book 55, 1:21, Hampton Clippings; *Wichita (KS) Beacon*, November 15, 1915; MN 732; and *Philadelphia Inquirer* article reprinted in the *Trenton (NJ) Times*, November 16, 1915, MN 732, both in BTW LOC.

58. *Colored Alabamians*, November 20, 1915, MN 422; *Minneapolis (MN) News*, MN 732, both in BTW LOC. Anderson, *Education of Blacks in the South, 1860–1935*, 36–53. *Cleveland (OH) Plain Dealer*, n.d., book 53, 1:67, Hampton Clippings; *Worker*, n.d., MN 732, BTW LOC.

59. Material from the *Brooklyn Daily Eagle* is reprinted in the *New York Age*, November 18, 1915, book 53, 1:92; *Jamaica (West Indies) Times*, November 20, 1915, book 54, 1:28; and *New York Sun*, November 15, 1915, book 53, 1:16, all in Hampton Clippings. *Lonaconing (MD) Advocate*, November 18, 1915, MN 732, BTW LOC.

60. Glenn C. Altschuler, *Race, Ethnicity, and Class in American Social Thought, 1865–1919* (Arlington Heights, Ill.: Harlan Davidson Press, 1982).

61. *Bristol (CT) Press*, November 15, 1915, MN 732, BTW LOC.

62. BTW, *Washington (D.C.) Star*, November 15, 1915, MN 422, BTW LOC. *New York Age*, November 18, 1915, book 53, 1:62–64 and 104–66; and the *Chicago Defender*, November 27, 1915, book 55, 1:89, both in Hampton Clippings.

63. *New York World*, November 16, 1915, book 53, 1:50, Hampton Clippings. *Los Angeles Examiner*, November 29, 1915, MN 422; *Tacoma (WA) News*, November 15, 1915, both in BTW LOC.

64. *Allentown (PA) Morning Call*, November 15, 1915, MN 732; *Kansas City (MO) Star*, November 15, 1915, MN 732, both in BTW LOC.

65. See the *Atlanta (GA) Independent*, November 12, 1915; unidentified Michigan African American newspaper, November 16, 1915, MN 422, both in BTW LOC. *National Baptist Union Review*, November 15, 1915, book 54, 1:7–9, Hampton Clippings.

66. *San Francisco Chronicle*, November 16, 1915, MN 732, BTW LOC. *Baltimore (MD) Commonwealth*, November 15, 1915, book 55, 1:28, Hampton Clippings. *Memphis (TN) Commercial-Appeal* quote reprinted in the *Montgomery (AL) Advertiser*, April 27, 1916, MN 733, BTW LOC.

Chapter 3. "Taps"

1. During his many visits to Tuskegee University, the author has observed and toured the Oaks.

2. Dwight David VanHoy, "The Evolution of Funeral Practices in Grayson and Ashe Counties" (master's thesis, Appalachian State University, 1996), 1; Stanley Newell Fix, "Christian Funerals in Light of American Attitudes Toward Death" (PhD diss., Claremont School of Theology, 1976), 118; James J. Farrell, *Inventing the American Way of Death* (Philadelphia: Temple University Press, 1980), 82; Ian Kuijt, "Place, Death, and the Transmission of Social Memory in Early Agricultural Communities of the Near eastern Pre-Porter Neolithic," in *Social Memory, Identity, and Death: Anthropological Perspectives on Mortuary Rituals*, edited by Meredith S. Chesson (Archeological Papers of the American Anthropological Association, no. 10, 2001), 82; Michael R. Leming and George E. Dickinson, "The Contemporary American Funeral," in *American Death and Burial Custom Derivation from Medieval European Cultures*, edited by George E. Dickinson, Michael R. Leming, and Alan C. Mermann (Guilford, Conn.: Dushkin Publishing, 1994), 161; David G. Mandelbaum, "Social Uses of Funeral Rites," in *The Meaning of Death*, edited by Herman Feifel (New York: McGraw-Hill, 1959), 212; John S. Stephenson, *Death, Grief, and Mourning: Individual and Social Realities* (London: Free Press, 1965), 100–101.

3. *BTW1* and *BTW2*.

4. EJS to BTW, January 19, 1912, *BTW Papers*, 11:459n. J. C. Napier to Mrs. Booker T. Washington, telg. November 15, 1915, MN 421; and EJS to J. C. Napier, telg. November 15, 1915, MN 421, both in BTW LOC. Karla F. C. Holloway, *Passed On: African American Mourning Stories* (Durham, N.C.: Duke University Press, 2003), 15. BTW to Grover Cleveland Thompson, November 21, 1913, *BTW Papers*, 12:343–44. Mrs. Roy Corbitts, who with her husband purchased an undertaking business from Thompson, confirmed Grover's family ties (telephone conversation with the author, January 12, 2006). BTW, *The Future of the American Negro* (New York: Haskell House, 1968), 78–79; and BTW, *The Negro in Business* (Wichita, Kans.: Devore and Sons, 1992), 233.

5. Emmett J. Scott and Lyman Beecher Stowe, *Booker T. Washington: Builder of a Civilization* (Garden City, N.Y.: Doubleday, Page, 1917), 248–71.

6. James J. Farrell, *Inventing the American Way of Death* (Philadelphia: Temple University Press, 1980), 4, 8, and 9.

7. *New York Tribune*, November 17, 1915, book 55, 2:64, Hampton Clippings.

8. Richard P. Taylor, *Death and the Afterlife: A Cultural Encyclopedia* (Santa Barbara, Calif.: ABC-CLIO, 2000), 73 and 118–19. Scott and Stowe, *Booker T. Washington*, vii.

9. Isaac Fisher, "Funeral of Booker T. Washington," *Negro History Bulletin* 48 (March 1985): 13; *New York Sun*, November 18, 1915, book 53, 1:89; and *Times Herald* (no city), November 16, 1915, book 53, 1:56–57, both in Hampton Clippings. *New York Age*, November 18, 1915.

10. Max Bennett Thrasher, *Tuskegee: Its Story and Its Work* (Boston: Small, Maynard, 1901), 47–48.

11. *New York Tribune*, November 17, book 55, 2:64, Hampton Clippings. *New York Sun*, November 18, 1915, book 53, 1:89; *Chicago Defender*, November 27, 1915, book 60, 1:57–60; and *Baltimore Ledger*, November 20, book 54, 1:14–15, all in Hampton Clippings.

12. *Chicago Defender*, November 27, 1915, book 54, 1:57–60, Hampton Clippings. Jack Goody, *The Culture of Flowers* (New York: Cambridge University Press, 1993), passim.

13. *Tuskegee (AL) News*, November 25, 1915, book 53, 2:107–9, Hampton Clippings. William Hicks, "Impressions and Reflections at the Funeral of Dr. Booker T. Washington," n.d., MN 420; James R. Europe to EJS, telg. November 15, 1915, MN 420; J. O. Thomas to EJS, telg. November 16, 1915, MN 421; EJS to L. L. Powell, November 29, 1915, MN 421; *Birmingham (AL) Ledger*, November 16, 1915, MN 732, all in BTW LOC. *New York Tribune*, November 17, 1915, book 55, 2:64; *New York Age*, November 18, 1915, book 55, 1:70, both in Hampton Clippings. *New York Tribune*, November 18, 1915, MN 732, BTW LOC; *Chicago Defender*, November 27, 1915, book 54, 1:57–60, Hampton Clippings.

14. See the several pictures of students acting as honor guards at Washington's funeral in the Booker T. Washington Papers at BTW LOC.

15. *Chicago Defender*, November 20, 1915, book 54, 1:26; *New York Tribune*, November 17, 1915, book 55, 2:64; and *New York Age*, November 18, 1915, book 55, 1:70, all in Hampton Clippings. Isaac Fisher, "An Account of Washington's Funeral," *BTW Papers*, 13:456.

16. *Nashville Globe*, November 19, 1915, and *Birmingham (AL) Ledger*, November 16, 1915, MN 732, both in BTW LOC.

17. EJS to S. G. Elbert, telg. November 15, 1915, MN 420, BTW LOC. Charles William Anderson to BTW, May 30, 1909, *BTW Papers*, 10:127n; *Montgomery (AL) Advertiser*, November 17 and 18, 1915, and *Philadelphia Public Ledger*, November 17, 1915, MN 422; and *Springfield (MA) Republican*, November 16, 1915, MN 732, all in BTW LOC; and *Washington (D.C.) Evening Star*, November 16, 1915, book 53, 1:41–42, Hampton Clippings.

18. *Montgomery (AL) Advertiser*, November 17, 1915, MN 422; *Chicago Defender*, November 27, 1915; and *San Jose (CA) Herald*, November 18, 1915, MN 732, all in BTW LOC.

19. *Atlanta (GA) Independent*, November 20, 1915, book 54, 1:20; *Chicago Defender*, November 27, 1915, book 54, 1:57–60, both in Hampton Clippings. Fisher, "Funeral of Booker T. Washington." Benjamin Quarles, *Frederick Douglass* (New York: Atheneum, 1969), 348–50; and William S. McFeely, *Frederick Douglass* (New York: Norton, 1993), 381–83.

20. Samuel P. Hays, *The Response to Industrialism, 1885–1914* (Chicago: University of Chicago Press, 1971), 48. "Schools Established by Tuskegee," n.d., MN 725, BTW LOC. *National Negro Business League Annual Report, 1915* (Nashville, Tenn.: African Methodist Episcopal Sunday School Union, 1915).

21. *New York World*, November 18, 1915, book 53, 1:90, Hampton Clippings, and *Indianapolis Star*, November 21, 1915, MN 732, BTW LOC. *New York Age*, November 25, 1915. *Springfield (MA) Republican*, November 25, 1915, book 54, 1:47, Hampton Clippings.

22. *Springfield (MA) Republican*, November 25, 1915, book 54, 1:47, Hampton Clippings. Scott and Stowe, *Booker T. Washington*, 329. *Chicago Defender*, November 27, MN 732; *Tuskegee Student News*, November 27; *New York Tribune*, November 18, 1915, MN 732, all in BTW LOC; *New York Tribune*, November 17, book 55, 2:64, Hampton Clippings; unidentified newspaper, n.d., MN 732, BTW LOC.

23. *Springfield (MA) Republican*, November 25, 1915, book 54, 1:47, Hampton Clippings; Fisher, "Funeral of Booker T. Washington."

24. *New York Tribune*, November 17, 1915, book 55, 2:64, Hampton Clippings.

25. *Birmingham (AL) Age-Herald*, November 18, 1915, MN 732, BTW LOC; *Springfield (MA) Republican*, November 25, 1915, book 54, 1:47, Hampton Clippings; *New York Tribune*, November 18, 1915, MN 732, BTW LOC.

26. *Tuskegee Student News*, November 27, 1915, MN 715, BTW LOC. BTW, *Up from Slavery* (New York: Dodd, Mead, 1965), 137. Unidentified newspaper, November 18, 1915, MN 422, and *Birmingham (AL) Age-Herald*, November 18, 1915, MN 732, BTW LOC.

27. Kathleen Marie, "An Analysis of Legitimation for the Institution in Funeral Eulogies for heads of State" (PhD diss., University of Iowa, 1976), 11, 32, and 32. Leroy Bowman, *The American Funeral: A Study in Guilt, Extravagance, and Sublimity* (Washington, D.C.: Public Affairs Press, 1959), 8; Charles O. Jackson, *Death and Social Structure* (Westport, Conn.: Greenwood Press, 1977), 195. *Tuskegee Student News*, November 27, 1915, MN 725, BTW LOC.

28. *Springfield (MA) Republican*, November 25, 1915, book 54, 1:47, Hampton Clippings.

29. *Chicago Defender*, November 27, 1915, MN 732, BTW LOC.

30. Fisher, "Funeral of Booker T. Washington"; Hicks, "Impressions and Reflections at the Funeral of Dr. Booker T. Washington." *New York Tribune*, November 18, 1915, MN 732, BTW LOC; *Atlanta (GA) Independent*, November 20, 1915, book 54, 1:20,

Hampton Clippings; *Tuskegee Student News*, November 27, 1915, MN 715, BTW LOC; *Springfield (MA) Republican*, November 25, 1915, book 54, 1:47, Hampton Clippings; *San Francisco Bulletin*, November 17, 1915; *New York World*, November 18, 1915, book 53, 1:90; and *Chicago Defender*, November 27, 1915, book 54, 1:57–60, both in Hampton Clippings.

31. John W. Work, *American Negro Songs: 230 Folk Songs and Spirituals, Religious and Secular* (Toronto: General Publishing, 1998), 108.

32. "We Shall Walk through the Valley," *The Greenwood Encyclopedia of Black Music Lyrics of the Afro-American Spiritual: A Documentary Collection*, edited by Erskine Peters (Westport, Conn.: Greenwood Press, 1993), 377.

33. Isaac L. Fisher, "Booker Washington and the Negro Spirituals," *Tuskegee Messenger* (Tuskegee Institute), May 9–10, 1931, BTW TUA. Kelly Miller to BTW, December 27, 1909, *BTW Papers*, 10:255–56. "Three News Items on the 1875 Graduation Exercises at Hampton Institute," June 10, 1875, 2:51; "Commencement Day with the Colored Students," June 10, 1875, 2:58; and "Incidents of Indian Life At Hampton," September 1886, all in *BTW Papers*, 2:81–82.

34. *BTW1*, 57; and Work, *American Negro Songs*, 17; Booker T. Washington, "A University Education for Negroes," 10:285. BTW to Samuel Chapman Armstrong, February 4, 1884, 2:247n; and BTW to Robert Hannibal Hamilton, September 23, 1894, all in *BTW Papers*, 3:471–72.

35. "The Bell Street Chapel Calendar," November 1893, 2:379; Arthur Copeland to BTW, May 9, 1912, both in *BTW Papers*, 11:533–34.

36. BTW to Samuel Chapman Armstrong, October 16, 1884, *BTW Papers*, 2:266, and Fisher, "Booker Washington and the Negro Spirituals"; "An Account of Washington's North Carolina Tour," November 12, 1910, *BTW Papers*, 10:463.

37. "An Address on the Twenty-Fifth Anniversary of Tuskegee Institute," April 4, 1906, *BTW Papers*, 8:565. Lyman Abbott, "Snap-Shots of My Contemporaries: Booker T. Washington," *Outlook*, October 5, 1921, 181.

38. "'Negro Education Not a Failure,' Address by Booker T. Washington in the Concert Hall of Madison Square Garden, Lincoln's Birthday, February 12, 1904," box 115, and "Parts of Address Delivered by Booker T. Washington at Hampton Meeting held in Woolsel Hall, Yale University, February 28, 1912," box 118, both in BTW TUA.

39. *Tuskegee Student*, November 27, 1915, 1.

40. John W. Whittaker to BTW, December 12, 1887, *BTW Papers*, 2:396n.

41. Louis F. Benson, *Studies of Familiar Hymns* (Philadelphia: Westminster Press, 1929), 37–38.

42. Hicks, "Impressions and Reflections at the Funeral of Dr. Booker T. Washington."

43. "Imes, George Lake," *Who's Who in Colored America [1930–1931–1932]*, 2nd ed., edited by Thomas Yenser (Brooklyn, N.Y.: Thomas Yenser, 1933), 231; and "Imes, George Lake," *Who's Who in Colored America [1950]*, 7th ed., edited by G. James Fleming and Christian E. Burckel (Yonkers-on-Hudson, N.Y.: Christian E. Burckel & Associates, 1950), 605.

44. 1 Corinthians 15:58.

45. Benson, *Studies of Familiar Hymns*, 85–96 and 126; and Arthur Austin, *The Family Book of Favorite Hymns* (New York: Funk & Wagnalls, 1950), 54.

46. Benson, *Studies of Familiar Hymns*, 85–96 and 126.

47. "The Catalogue of Tuskegee Normal School, 1881–82," *BTW Papers*, 2:177n60.

48. Robert Russa Moton, *Finding a Way Out: An Autobiography* (Garden City, N.Y.: Doubleday, Page, 1921), 195–196. Luke 4:18 and Matthew 11:4–6.

49. Moton, *Finding a Way Out*, 196.

50. John Wesley Work, *Folk Song of the American Negro* (Nashville, Tenn.: Fisk University Press, 1915), 58.

51. *Chicago Defender*, November 27, 1915; *Savannah (GA) Tribune*, December 20, 1915; J. B. T. Marsh, *The Story of the Jubilee Singers* (London: Hodder and Stoughton, 1877), 189.

52. *Tuskegee Student*, November 27, 1915, 2.

53. Ibid., and Work, *Folk Song of the American Negro*, 79–80.

54. "Swing Low, Sweet Chariot," *Greenwood Encyclopedia of Black Music Lyrics of the Afro-American Spiritual*, 193.

55. *Tuskegee Student*, November 27, 1915, 2.

56. Ibid.

57. Gerald Kurland, *Seth Low: The Reformer in an Urban and Industrial Age* (New York: Twayne, 1971), 1–48, 50–81, 140–214, and 215–339.

58. Ibid, 324; and Seth Low to BTW, May 29, 1907, *BTW Papers*, 9:281–84.

59. *Tuskegee Student*, November 27, 1915, 2.

60. William Henry Baldwin Jr. to BTW, April 15, 1900, *BTW Papers*, 5:481n. Diane Ravitch, *The Great School Wars: New York City, 1805–1973; A History of the Public Schools as Battlefield of Social Change* (New York: Basic Books, 1974), 212; Nancy J. Weiss, *The National Urban League, 1910–1914* (New York: Oxford University Press, 1974), 23–24, 41–42, 56, and 158; and Eugene Kinckle Jones to BTW, December 11, 1914, *BTW Papers*, 13:198.

61. *Tuskegee Student*, November 27, 1915, 2.

62. Ibid.

63. Ibid.

64. Ibid.

65. *Newark (NJ) News*, November 16, 1915, MN 732; *Buffalo (NY) News*, November 15, 1915, MN 422; *Savannah (GA) News*, November 16, 1915, MN 732; and *Franklin (PA) Herald*, November 16, 1915, MN 732, all in BTW LOC. L. T. Burbridge et & al to Mrs. Booker T. Washington, telg. November 17, 1915, MN 420, BTW LOC. *New Orleans Picayune*, November 16, 1915, MN 732; and M. C. Runwick to EJS, November 14, 1915, MN 420, both in BTW LOC. *Tuskegee Student*, April 29–May 13, 1922, 1.

66. Joan D. Hedrick, *Harriet Beecher Stowe* (New York: Oxford University Press, 1994), vii, viii, 213, and 231–32; and Winifred E. Wise, *Harriet Beecher Stowe* (New York: G. P. Putnam's, 1965), 174–75 and 183.

67. "Still, Still with Thee," in *Plymouth Collection of Hymns and Tunes, for the Use of Christian Congregations*, edited by Charles Ward and John Zundel (New York: A. S. Barnes & Co., 1856), iii, vii, and 214.

68. Methodist Episcopal Church, *The Hymns and Hymn Writers of the Church*, edited by Wilbur F. Tillett and Charles S. Nutter (Nashville, Tenn.,: Smith and Lamar, 1911), 27.

69. *Chicago Defender*, November 27, 1915, MN 732, BTW LOC; and *Savannah (GA) Tribune*, December 20, 1915.

70. *Atlanta (GA) Independent*, November 20, 1915, MN 732, BTW LOC; *Chicago Defender*, November 2, book 54, 1:20, Hampton Clippings; *Pittsburgh (PA) Presbyterian Banner*, December 15, 1915, MN 732; and *Chicago Defender*, November 27, 1915, MN 732; unidentified newspaper, n.d., MN 732, all in BTW LOC; *New York Tribune*, November 17, 1915, book 55, 2:64, Hampton Clippings.

71. *Atlanta (GA) Independent*, November 20, 1915, MN 732, BTW LOC. *Tuskegee (AL) News*, November 25, 1915, book 53, 2:107–9, Hampton Clippings. Fisher, "Funeral of Booker T. Washington." *Baltimore Ledger*, November 20, 1915, book 54, 1:14–15, Hampton Clippings. Norton, the son of a Presbyterian preacher, would become a founder of the American Can Company after the Civil War. Richard H. Schneider, *Taps: Notes from a Nation's Heart* (New York: Harper Collins, 2002), 3, 8, 10, 11, 15, 31, 38–41, and 93.

72. *Tuskegee (AL) News*, November 25, 1915, book 53, 2:107–9; and *New York Tribune*, November 17, 1915, book 55, 2:64, both in Hampton Clippings. EJS to Alexander E. Manning, November 24, 1915, *BTW Papers*, 13:464.

Chapter 4. *"A Debt of Gratitude"*

1. *Mobile (AL) Weekly Press*, November 20, 1915, MN 732. L. L. Campbell to EJS, telg. November 17, 1915, MN 420, both in BTW LOC.

2. Edward S. Casey, *Remembering: A Phenomenological Study* (Bloomington: Indiana University Press, 1987), 216–57; Genevieve Fabre, "African-American Commemorative Celebrations in the Nineteenth Century," in *History and Memory in African-American Culture*, edited by Genevieve Fabre and Robert O'Meally (New York: Oxford University Press, 1994), 72–91; and Barry Schwartz, *Abraham Lincoln and the Forge of National Memory* (Chicago: University of Chicago Press, 2000), 9–17.

3. David Singleton, *Honor Our Flag: How to Care For, Fly, and Otherwise Respect the Stars and Stripes* (Guilford, Conn.: Globe Pequot Press, 2002), 31–33.

4. *Tucson (AZ) Citizen*, November 16, 1915, MN 732; and *Washington (D.C.) Star*, November 16, 1915, MN 732, both in BTW LOC. Josephine Beall Wilson Bruce to BTW, March 15, 1898, *BTW Papers*, 4:391nn.

5. *Washington Times*, n.d., MN 732; Roscoe C. Bruce to EJS, telg. November 16, 1915, MN 420; *California Eagle* (Los Angeles), November 20, 1915; *Boston Transcript*, November, n.d., 1915, MN 422; *Boston Post*, November 18, 1915, and *Chicago Defender*, November 17, 1915, MN 732, all in BTW LOC.

6. *New York Age*, November 25, 1915. *Newark (NJ) News*, November 16, 1915, MN 732, both in BTW LOC; *Patterson (NJ) Call*, November 17, 1915, book 53, 1:18, Hampton Clippings.

7. *Washington (D.C.) Evening Star*, November 16, 1915, book 53, 1:41–42, Hampton Clippings. *New York Age*, November 18, 1915.

8. *New York Age*, November 18, 1915. John Howard Burrows, "The Necessity of Myth: A History of the National Negro Business League, 1900–1945" (PhD diss., Auburn University, 1977), 99–109. *National Negro Business League Annual Report of the Sixteenth Session and the Fifteenth Anniversary Convention*, NBL Fifteenth Convention (Nashville, Tenn.: African Methodist Episcopal Sunday School Union, 1915), 295–320.

9. *New York Tribune*, November 17, 1915, book 55, 2:64; and *Washington (D.C.) Evening Star*, November 16, 1915, book 53, 1:41–42, both in Hampton Clippings. *New Haven (CT) Courier*, November 16, 1915, MN 732; and unidentified New York newspaper, November 17, 1915, MN 422, both in BTW LOC. *Pittsburgh (PA) Telegraph*, November 19, 1915, MN 732, BTW LOC.

10. *Connecticut Courier* (Hartford), November 16, 1915, MN 732, BTW LOC. "An Open Letter to the People of Great Britain and Europe by William Edward Burghardt Du Bois and Others," October 26, 1910, *BTW Papers*, 10:422–25.

11. *New Haven (CT) Courier*, November 16, 1915, MN 732, BTW LOC.

12. *Augusta (GA) Chronicle*, November 16, 1915; *Savannah (GA) News*, November 16, 1915, MN 732; *Indianapolis News*, November 17, 1915; *Indianapolis News*, November 16, 1915, MN 732, all in BTW LOC. BTW to Robert Sengstacke Abbott, December 19, 1903, *BTW Papers*, 12:277nn; *Chicago Tribune*, November 16, 1915, MN 732, BTW LOC.

13. *Savannah (GA) Tribune*, November 27, 1915; *Fort Smith (AR) American*, November 17, 1915; *Pittsburgh (PA) Telegraph*, November 19, 1915; *Boston Evening Herald*, November 17, 1915; *Jackson (MS) Ledger*, November 18, 1915, MN 732, all in BTW LOC. *Lawrence (KS) World*, November 16, 1915, MN 732, BTW LOC. *New York Tribune*, November 17, book 55, 2:64; *Indianapolis News*, November 17, 1915, book 53, 1:86; *Chicago News*, November 17, 1915, book 53, 1:84, all in Hampton Clippings. C. F. Johnson to EJS, November 16, 1915, MN 420, BTW LOC. *San Antonio (TX) Express*, November 17, 1915, MN 732, BTW LOC. *California Eagle* (Los Angeles), November 20, 1915.

14. *New York News*, November 18, 1915, book 53, 1:4, Hampton Clippings. *Chicago News*, November 17, 1915, MN 732, BTW LOC.

15. *Tuskegee (AL) News*, book 53, 2:107–9; *Springfield (MA) Republican*, book 54, 1:47; *Chicago Defender*, November 27, 1915, book 54, 1:57–60, all in Hampton Clippings. *Tuskegee Student News*, November 27, 1915.

16. L. L. Campbell to EJS, telg. November 17, 1915, MN 420, BTW LOC. "An Account of Washington's Tour of Texas by Horace D. Slatter," October 14, 1911, *BTW Papers*, 11:342nn. *Vicksburg (MS) Herald*, November 21, 1915, MN 720. *Memphis (TN) Appeal*, November 18, 1915; and *Washington (D.C.) Star*, November 16, 1915, MN 732, all in BTW LOC.

17. *Washington (D.C.) Star*, November 16, 1915, MN 732. Clipping from unidentified newspaper, n.d., attached to a letter from R. W. Thompson to EJS, November 21, 1915, MN 421. Roscoe C. Bruce to EJS, November 16, 1915, telg. MN 420, all in BTW LOC. *Indianapolis News*, November 17, 1915, book 53, 1:86, Hampton Clippings.

18. *Evansville (IN) News*, November 18, 1915; *Nashville (TN) Banner*, November 17, 1915; *Fort Smith (AR) American*, November 16, 1915, MN 732. W. L. D. Johnson et al. to Mrs. Booker T. Washington, telg. November 16, 1915; and C. F. Johnson to EJS, telg. November 16, 1915; C. B. Johnson to EJS, telg. November 18, 1915, MN 420; and J. D. Martin to EJS, telg. November 16, 1915, MN 421. *Chicago Defender*, November 26, 1915; and *Wheeling (WV) Register*, November 18, 1915, MN 732, all in BTW LOC.

19. *Topeka (KS) Capital*, November 18, 1915, MN 732, BTW LOC. *Topeka (KS) Daily Capital*: 1913; June 5, 1914; July 3, 1918, and August 16, 1932, MN 5403, vertical file, Kansas State Historical Library, Topeka. *New York Times*, February 22, 1914.

20. James K. Mercer, *Ohio Legislative History 1909-1913* (Columbus, Ohio: Edward T. Miller Co., 1913), 197. *Columbus (OH) Journal*, November 16, 1915, MN 732.

21. Robert E. Jones to EJS, telg. November 15, 1915, MN 10; and L. T. Burbridge et al. to Mrs. Booker T. Washington, telg. November 17, 1915, MN 420, both in BTW LOC.

22. E. O. Smith to EJS, telg. November 16, 1915, MN 421; *Savannah (GA) Tribune*, November 20, 1915, MN 422; and J. I. Washington et al. to EJS, November 18, 1915, MN 421, all in BTW LOC. *New York Age*, November 25, 1915.

23. *Kansas City (MO) Post*, November 16, 1915, MN 732, BTW LOC; and Nancy H. Burkett et al., eds., *Black Biographical Dictionaries 1790-1950*, microfiche addenda (Alexandria, Va.: Chadwyck-Healy, 1987), MN 156, 72.

24. *Wheeling (WV) Register*, November 18, 1915; and *Wheeling (WV) Intelligencer*, November 18, 1915, MN 732, both in BTW LOC. Wilbur F. Tillett and Charles S. Nutter, eds., *The Hymns and Hymn Writers of the Church* (Nashville, Tenn.: N.p., 1911), 327 and 32. Theron Brown and Hezekish Butterworth, *Story of the Hymns and Tunes* (New York: American Tract Society, 1907), 534-38. Louis F. Benson, *Studies of Familiar Hymns* (Philadelphia: Westminster Press, 1929), 85-96 and 126, and Arthur Austin, *The Family Book of Favorite Hymns* (New York: Funk & Wagnall's, 1950), 54.

25. *Wheeling (WV) Register*, November 18, 1915; and *Wheeling (WV) Intelligencer*, MN 732, both in BTW LOC. *Black Biographical Dictionaries 1790-1950*, MN 138, 176; and MN 293, 81.

26. *Muskogee (OK) Democrat*, November 16, 1915, MN 732, BTW LOC. *Who Was Who in America with World Notables*, vol. 5, *1965-1973* (Chicago: Marquis Who's Who, 1973), 490.

27. *Muskogee (OK) Democrat*, November 16, 1915, MN 732, BTW LOC.

28. *Montgomery (AL) Advertiser*, November 18, 1915, MN 422; *Asheville (NC) Citizen*, November 18, 1915; and *Birmingham (AL) Age Herald*, MN 732; all in BTW LOC.

29. Louis R. Harlan, *Booker T. Washington* (New York: Oxford University Press, 1972), 109-33. *New York Age*, November 25, 1916.

30. *Petersburg (VA) Colored Virginian*, book 54, 1:11, Hampton Clippings. Luscious Edwards, telephone conversation with the author, January 25, 2009.

31. *Savannah (GA) Press*, November 15, MN 732, BTW LOC. James Sullivan Clarkson to BTW, February 7, 1896, *BTW Papers*, 4:114-15nn.

32. *Montgomery (AL) Advertiser*, November 16, 1915, MN 422, BTW LOC. William B. Paterson to BTW, January 5, 1887, *BTW Papers*, 2:319–20nn.

33. Paul Finkelman, chief ed., *Encyclopedia of African American History, 1896 to the Present: From the Age of Segregation to the Twenty-First Century* (New York: Oxford University Press, 2009), 1:357. Darlene Clark Hine et al., eds., *Black Women in America: An Historical Encyclopedia* (Brooklyn, N.Y.: Carlson Publishing, 1993), 1:60.

34. Finkelman, *Encyclopedia of African American History, 1896 to the Present*, 1:357. Timothy Thomas Fortune to BTW, March 2, 1899, 5:50nn, *BTW Papers*; and Roscoe Conkling Bruce to BTW, February 22, 1902, 6:410nn, *BTW Papers*.

35. *Philadelphia Public Ledger*, November 1915. Leslie Pinckney Hill to Mrs. Booker T. Washington, November 18, 1915, MN 420, both in BTW LOC.

36. "Announcement: 1911–1912: Topeka Industrial and Educational Institute" (Topeka, Kans.: State Printing Office, 1911), 2–3, Spencer Research Library, University of Kansas. *A Book of Information about Kansas Vocational School Topeka, Kansas* (Topeka: Kansas Vocational School, 1942), 3. Thomas C. Cox, *Black Topeka Kansas: 1865–1915* (Baton Rouge: Louisiana State University Press, 1982), 152–53.

37. Cox, *Black Topeka Kansas*, 153 and 201. *Topeka (KS) Capital*, February 2, 1912. *Topeka (KS) Plaindealer*, November 26, 1915. "Announcement," 2. *BTW Papers*, 49nn.

38. Cox, *Black Topeka Kansas*, 153. "Announcement," 2.

39. *Topeka (KS) Plaindealer*, November 26, 1915.

40. Ibid.

41. Ibid.

42. James D. Anderson, *The Education of Blacks in the South, 1860–1935* (Chapel Hill: University of North Carolina Press, 1988), 238–40.

43. William H. Kampschmidt, "Why the Evangelical Lutheran Church Established and Maintains a College for Negroes?" *Journal of Negro Education* 29, no. 3 (summer 1960): 299–306. *Lutheran Pioneer*, January 1916, MN 738, BTW LOC.

44. *Austin (TX) Statesman*, November 15, 1915, MN 732, BTW LOC. J. J. Lane, *History of Education in Texas*, U.S. Bureau of Education Circular of Information No. 2, 1903, edited by Herbert B. Adams, no. 35 (Washington, D.C.: Government Printing Office, 1903), 119–21; Anderson, *Education of Blacks in the South, 1860–1935*, 135.

45. *Boston Post*, November 18, 1915; *Middletown (NY) Press*, November 19, 1915; *Harrisburg (PA) Star-Independent*, November 18, 1915; *Pittsburgh (PA) Times*, November 18, 1915; *Norfolk (VA) Pilot*, November 18, 1915; *Savannah (GA) Press*, November 15, 1915, MN 732. *New York Age*, November 25, 1915. *Knoxville (TN) Sentinel*, November 18, 1915; *Fort Smith (AR) Record*, November 16, 1915; *Chicago Defender*, November 26, 1915; *Mobile (AL) Weekly Press*, November 20, 1915, MN 732; C. J. Chapple et al. to EJS, telg. November 18, 1915, MN 420. *New York Age*, November 25, 1915. L. T. Burbridge & et al. to Mrs. Booker T. Washington, telg. November 17, 1915, MN 420, all in BTW LOC. *Chicago Defender* seemed to have confused the Big Zion AMEZ Church in Mobile, Alabama, with the Mount Zion AME Church in Pensacola, Florida.

46. *Chicago Tribune*, November 18, 1915; *Lawrence (KS) World*, November 17, 1915; *San Antonio (TX) Express*, November 17, 1915, MN 732; *California Eagle* (Los Angeles), November 20, 1915; *Tacoma (WA) News*, November 17, 1916, MN 732, all in BTW LOC.

47. *Black Biographical Dictionaries 1790–1950*, MN 283, 102. *Fort Smith (AR) Record*, November 16, 1915, MN 732, BTW LOC. Delilah L. Beasley, *The Negro Trail Blazers of California* (New York: Negro Universities Press, 1969), 255. Hine, *Black Women in America*, 93.

48. Gunnar Myrdal, with the assistance of Richard Sterner and Arnold Rose, *An American Dilemma: The Negro Problem and Modern Democracy*, 9th ed. (New York: Harper & Brothers, 1944), 726–27, 739–741, 742–44. *Tacoma (WA) News*, November 17, 1916; and *Harrisburg (PA) Star-Independent*, November 18, 1915, MN 732, both in BTW LOC.

49. *Boston Evening Herald*, November 17, 1915, MN 732, BTW LOC; and *Black Biographical Dictionaries 1790–1950*, MN 53, 663–64. On George B. Howard, see *Pittsburgh (PA) Times*, November 16, 1915, MN 732, BTW LOC, and *Black Biographical Dictionaries 1790–1950*, MN 177, 251; and MN 209, 272. BTW and William M. Reed studied together to become lawyers. *Norfolk (VA) Pilot*, November 18, 1915, MN 732. *Savannah (GA) News*, November 16, 1915, MN 732; and *Black Biographical Dictionaries 1790–1950*, MN 151, 196. C. J. Capple & et al to EJS, telg. November 18, 1915, MN 420; and *San Antonio (TX) Express*, November 17, 1915, MN 732, all in BTW LOC.

50. Robert E. Jones to EJS, telg. November 19, 1915, MN 10, BTW LOC.

51. Robert Elijah Jones to BTW, June 1909, *BTW Papers*, 10:130nn; EJS to BTW, June 21, 1903, *BTW Papers*, 7:181nn; Frank Lincoln Mather, ed. *Who's Who of the Colored Race* (Chicago: N.p., 1915), 1:172–73.

52. *Savannah (GA) Press*, November 15, 1915; *Savannah (GA) News*, November 16, 1915; *New Orleans States*, November 16, 1915; *Fort Smith (AR) Record*, November 16, 1915; *Lawrence (KS) World*, November 16, 1915; *San Antonio (TX) Express*, November 17, 1915; *Tacoma (WA) Ledger*, November 17, 1915, MN 732, all in BTW LOC.

53. John M. Murrin et al., *Liberty, Equality, Power: A History of the American People* (New York: Harcourt Brace, 1996), 606. *Norfolk (VA) Pilot*, November 18, 1915; *Knoxville (TN) Sentinel*, November 1915, MN 732; W. Houston to Mrs. Booker T. Washington, telg. MN 420; *Lawrence (KS) World*, November 16, 1916; *Fort Smith (AR) Record*, November 16, 1915; and *Tacoma (WA) Ledger*, November 17, 1915, MN 732, all in BTW LOC.

54. *San Antonio (TX) Express*, November 15, 1915, MN 732; C. J. Chapple & et al. to EJS, telg. n.d., MN 420; and *Savannah (GA) News*, November 16, 1915, MN 732, all in BTW LOC.

55. *San Antonio (TX) Express*, November 17, 1915; and *Brooklyn (NY) Eagle*, November 15, 1915, MN 732; L. T. Burbridge et al. to Mrs. Booker T. Washington, telg. November 17, 1915, MN 420; *Norfolk (VA) Pilot*, November 18, 1915; and *Knoxville*

(TN) Sentinel, November, no year, MN 732. *New York Age,* November 25, 1915. *Chicago Defender,* November 26, 1915, MN 732, all in BTW LOC.

56. *Mobile (AL) Weekly Press,* November 20, 1915; and *Harrisburg (PA) Star-Independent,* November 18, 1915, MN 732, BTW LOC. *Black Biographical Dictionaries 1790–1950,* MN 212, 82f; MN 213, 61; MN 235, 478; MN 281, 37.

57. *Norfolk (VA) Pilot,* November 18, 1915, MN 732, BTW LOC. Although some African Americans received postprimary education in the North, reflecting the location of the vast majority of blacks, a much larger number of them took their training in the South. James D. Anderson, *The Education of Blacks in the South, 1868–1935* (Chapel Hill: University of North Carolina Press, 1988), 4–32, 110–47 and 186–278. *Lawrence (KS) Gazette,* November 17, 1915; *Boston Evening Herald,* November 17, 1915; *Tacoma (WA) Ledger,* MN 732, all in BTW LOC. *Black Biographical Dictionaries 1790–1950,* MN 49, 451; MN 53, 663–64; and MN 283, 102.

58. *Mobile (AL) Weekly Press,* November 20, 1915, MN 732, BTW LOC. *New York Age,* November 25, 1915. Tillett and Nutter, *Hymns and Hymn Writers of the Church,* 387.

59. *Knoxville (TN) Sentinel,* November 1915; reprint of *New Orleans Times* in unidentified newspaper, November 24, 1915; *Savannah (GA) News,* November 15, 1915; and *Tacoma (WA) Ledger,* November 17, 1915, MN 732. *New York Age,* November 25, 1915, all in BTW LOC.

60. *New York Age,* November 25, 1915; and *Norfolk (VA) Pilot,* November 18, 1915, MN 732, both in BTW LOC. Writers born on one of the British Islands wrote the vast majority of the hymns performed at the various Washington memorials. Tillett and Nutter, *Hymns and Hymn Writers of the Church,* 241, 278, 387, and 392; and Brown and Butterworth, *Story of the Hymns and Tunes,* 223, 425–26, 499.

61. *New York Age,* November 25, 1915; and *Norfolk (VA) Pilot,* November 25, 1915, MN 732, both in BTW LOC.

62. James P. Moore Jr., *One Nation under God: The History of Prayer in America* (New York: Doubleday, 2005), xvi–xvii. *Lawrence (KS) World,* November 16, 1916; and *Norfolk (VA) Pilot,* November 18, 1915, MN 732. *New York Age,* November 25, 1915, all in BTW LOC. Matthew 6:6 states that "when thou prayest, enter into thy closet, and when thou has shut thy door, pray to thy Father which is in secret."

63. John 8:32 and 2 Timothy 3:16. Rea McDonnell, *Prayer Pilgrimage Through Scripture* (New York: Paulist Press, 1984), 1. Clayton J. Schmit, *Public Reading of Scripture* (Nashville, Tenn.: Abingdon Press, 2002), 9–10. Richard F. Ward, *Reading Scripture Aloud* (Nashville, Tenn.: Discipleship Resources, 1989), 3–7. *Harrisburg (PA) Star-Independent,* November 18, 1915; and *Mobile (AL) Weekly Press,* November 20, 1915, MN 732. *New York Age,* November 25, 1915, all in BTW LOC.

64. *New York Age,* November 25, 1915. *Pittsburgh (PA) Times,* November 18, 1915; and *Savannah (GA) News,* November 16, 1915, MN 732. See also *Mobile (AL) Weekly Press,* November 20, 1915, MN 732. *New York Age,* November 25, 1915. *Harrisburg (PA) Star-Independent,* November 18, 1915; *Knoxville (TN) Sentinel,* November 1915; *Norfolk (VA) Pilot,* November 18, 1915; all in BTW LOC.

65. *New York Age*, November 25, 1915. *Memphis (TN) Scimitar*, November 16, 1915; *Memphis (TN) Appeal*, November 17 and 18, 1915, MN 732, all in BTW LOC. *Black Biographical Dictionaries 1790–1950*, MN 115, 55; MN 207, 45; and MN 279, 94.

66. *Memphis (TN) Scimitar*, November 16, 1915; *Memphis (TN) Appeal*, November 17 and 18, 1915, MN 732, both in BTW LOC. *New York Age*, November 25, 1915.

67. *Memphis (TN) Appeal*, November 18, 1915. *Black Biographical Dictionaries 1790–1950*, MN 115, 248.

68. *Memphis (TN) Appeal*, November 18, 1915. Eugene Levy, *James Weldon Johnson: Black Leader Black Voice* (Chicago: University of Chicago Press, 1973), 71–73.

69. *New York Age*, November 25, 1915, and the *Memphis (TN) Appeal*, November 18, 1915. R. Nathaniel Dett, ed., *Religious Folk-Songs of the Negro: As Sung at Hampton Institute* (Hampton, Va.: Hampton Institute, 1927), 124; and Erskin Peters, ed., *Lyrics of the Afro-American Spiritual: A Documentary Collection* (Westport, Conn.: Greenwood Press, 1999), 6 and 7.

70. *Memphis (TN) Appeal*, November 18, 1915; *New York Age*, November 25, 1915; and *Black Biographical Dictionaries 1790–1950*, MN 293, 149; MN 115, 143, 258, and 265; MN 281, 109.

71. *New York Age*, November 25, 1915; *Black Biographical Dictionaries 1790–1950*, MN 146, 120; MN 281, 109; MN 100, 754; and MN 101, 238. Five of the most prominent members of the Memphis Business League constituted the committee that wrote the resolutions. It included T. H. Hayes, an undertaker, and owners of the black-owned Solvent Savings Bank and Trust; R. R. Church Jr., a noted black civil rights leader, Republican politician, and the son of R. R. Church Sr.; B. M. Roddy; T. O. Fuller; and A. F. Ward. *Memphis Appeal*, November 18, 1915; Carroll Ban West et al., eds., *The Tennessee Encyclopedia of History and Culture* (Nashville: Tennessee Historical Society, 1998), 861, 160–61.

72. Federation of Colored Organization to Family of BTW, resolution, November 14, 1915; Essex County Colored Democratic Club et al. to EJS, resolution, November 15, 1915; and Students of the State University of Iowa, to Tuskegee Institute, resolution, November 16, 1915. See also Negro Employees of Los Angeles to Tuskegee Industrial Institute, resolution, November 17, 1915; Superintendent and teachers of Sheridan County, North Dakota to Wife and Family of the late BTW and His Race, resolution, November 17, 1915; Colored School and the Colored Citizens of Calvert, Texas to EJS, resolution, November 18, 1915; Woman's Convention, Auxiliary to the General Missionary Convention of Georgia to Mrs. Booker T. Washington, resolution, November 17, 1915; Alpha Physical Culture Club of New York City to Family of BTW, resolution, November 17, 1915; and Elks Westminster Lodge to Family of BTW, resolution, November 17, 1915, all in MN 423, BTW LOC.

73. E. O. Smith to EJS, resolution, November 17, 1915; Colored Citizens of Xenia to Family of BTW, resolution, November 17, 1915; Elks Westminster Lodge to Family of BTW, resolution, November 17, 1915; Negro Employees of Los Angeles to Tuskegee Industrial Institute, resolution, November 17, 1915; and Committee of Alabamans to Mrs. BTW, resolution, November 17, 1915, all in MN 423, BTW LOC.

74. First Baptist Church of Little Rock, Arkansas, to the Family of BTW, resolution, November 17, 1915, MN 423, BTW LOC.

Chapter 5. *"Sermon Tonight on Booker T. Washington"*

1. Quotes from *San Francisco Bulletin*, November 17, 1915.

2. *Boston Daily Globe*, January 31, 1916, MN 733, BTW LOC. Gregory Bond, "The Strange Career of William Henry Lewis," in *Out of the Shadows*, edited by David K. Wiggins (Fayetteville: University of Arkansas University Press, 2006), 49–50.

3. Clarence G. Contee Sr., "William Henry Lewis," in *Dictionary of American Negro Biography*, edited by Rayford W. Logan and Michael R. Winston (New York: W. W. Norton, 1982), 396–97. Bond, "Strange Career of William Henry Lewis," 40–49.

4. Stephen R. Fox, *The Guardian of Boston: William Monroe Trotter* (New York: Atheneum, 1971), 44–45. Bond, "Strange Career of William Henry Lewis," 50–51. Theodore Roosevelt to William Henry Lewis, July 26, 1900, *The Letters of Theodore Roosevelt*, edited by Elting Morrison (Cambridge, Mass.: Harvard University Press, 1951), 2:1364–65.

5. Fox, *Guardian of Boston*, 44–45. William Edward Burghardt Du Bois to BTW, September 24, 1895, *BTW Papers*, 4:26. Emmett J. Scott and Lyman Beecher Stowe, *Booker T. Washington: Builder of a Civilization* (Garden City, N.Y.: Doubleday, Page, 1917), 316. William Henry Lewis to BTW, October 14, 1901, *BTW Papers*, 6:242.

6. Fox, *Guardian of Boston*, 46. Contee, "William Henry Lewis," 396. *Springfield (MA) Republican*, November 24, 1909, *BTW Papers*, 10:226. *Boston Transcript*, November 12, 1910, *BTW Papers*, 10:455–568. BTW, "An Article in the American Magazine," June 1913, *BTW Papers*, 12:223–26.

7. William A. Farris, *The African Abroad or His Evolution in Western Civilization* (New York: Johnson Reprint Co., 1913), 2:797–98. *Boston Daily Globe*, January 31, 1916, MN 733, BTW LOC.

8. *Dallas Morning News*, November 22, 1915. *Waco (TX) Times Herald*, November 22, 1915, MN 732, both in BTW LOC. EJS to the editor of the *Montgomery (AL) Advertiser*, September 6, 1905, 8:353nn. Charles Waddell Chesnutt to BTW, October 3, 1903, 7:320–21nn, both in *BTW Papers*. Robert J. Norrell, *Up from History: The Life of Booker T. Washington* (Cambridge, Mass.: Harvard University Press, 2009), 5, 317, 323, and 326.

9. *California Eagle* (Los Angeles), December 4, 1915. *Stockton (CA) Independent*, December 3, 1915; *Minneapolis (MN) Tribune*, November 28, 1915; and *Dayton (OH) News*, November 27, 1915, MN 732; *Christian Recorder*, November 20, 1915; and *New York Herald*, February 12, 1916, MN 422; *New York News*, January 13, 1916, MN 733, all in BTW LOC.

10. *Austin (TX) Statesman*, November 15, 1915, MN 732. *New York Age*, November 25, 1915. *Lutheran Pioneer*, January 1916, MN 738; *Washington (D.C.) Star*, November 16, 1915, all in BTW LOC.

11. *Kansas City (MO) Times*, November 15, 1915; *Savannah (GA) Press*, November 18, 1915, MN 732; *New York Age* January 27, 1916, MN 422. *Topeka (KS) Plaindealer*,

November 26, 1915. *New York Age*, November 25, 1916. *Montgomery (AL) Advertiser*, December 13, 1915, MN 422, all in BTW LOC.

12. James Earl Russell to BTW, May 4, 1901, *BTW Papers*, 6:104–5. BTW, "The South as an Opening for a Business Career," April 20, 1888, box 133, BTW TUA. David Nasaw, *Schooled to Order: A Social History of Public Schooling in the United States* (New York: Oxford University Press, 1979), 131.

13. Joel Spring, *The American School, 1642–1985: Varieties of Historical Interpretation of the Foundations and Development of American Education* (New York: Longman, 1986), 166–67. *Schenectady (NY) Star*, December 9, 1915, MN 732; and *Buffalo (NY) Express*, December 4, 1915, MN 422, both in BTW LOC. *Trenton (NJ) Times*, December 15, 1915, book 55, 2:100, Hampton Clippings. *South Norwalk (CT) Sentinel*, January 22, 1916, MN 734. *Evansville (IN) News*, November 18, 1915; *Kansas City (MO) Times*, November 15, 1915; *St. Louis (MO) Chronicle Star*, November 16, 1915, MN 732. *Tuskegee Student*, February 19, 1916. *Birmingham (AL) Ledger*, November 16, 1915, MN 732, all in BTW LOC.

14. *Lima (OH) Gazette*, November 16, 1915; *New York Age*, December 9, 1915, MN 732; L. T. Burbridge et al. to Mrs. Booker T. Washington, telg. November 17, 1915, MN 420. *New York Age*, November 25, 1915. *Nashville (TN) Banner*, November 17, 1915, MN 732; C. F. Johnson to EJS, telg. November 16, 1915, MN 420; unidentified newspaper, n.d., MN 422; C. B. Johnson to EJS, telg. November 18, 1915, MN 420; *Vicksburg (MS) Herald*, November 21, 1915, all in BTW LOC. See also Gerald L. Gutek, *Education in the United States: An Historical Perspective* (Englewood Cliffs, N.J.: Prentice-Hall, 1986), 116–17. Nasaw, *Schooled to Order*, 29–65. R. Freeman Butts and Lawrence A. Cremin, *A History of Education in American Culture* (New York: Holt, Rinehart and Winston, 1953), 197–98.

15. *Malden (MA) News*, December 28, 1915, MN 732. Unidentified Springfield (MA) newspaper, 1916, MN 733. *Topeka (KS) Journal*, November 16, 1915, MN 732. *Tuskegee Student*, February 19, 1916, all in BTW LOC. David Edwin Harrell Jr. et al., *Unto a Good Land: A History of the American People* (Grand Rapids, Mich.: William B. Eerdmans, 2005), 648–49. Thomas Winter, *Making Men, Making Class: The YMCA and Workingmen, 1877–1920* (Chicago: University of Chicago Press, 2002), 31–46. C. Howard Hopkins, *History of the YMCA in North America* (New York: Association Press, 1951), 214–15, 227–39, 335–39, and 472–81.

16. Henry McFarland, "An Account of a Speech in Washington, D.C," April 7, 1894, 3:397–402. BTW, "A Sunday Evening Talk," May 26, 1901, 6:125–26.

17. *Chicago Defender*, December 4, 1915, MN 422; and unidentified Yonkers (NY) newspaper, December 2, 1915, MN 732, both in BTW LOC. Elizabeth Wilson, *Fifty Years of Association Work among Young Women 1866–1916* (New York: National Board of the Young Women's Christian Associations of the United States of America, 1916), 23 and 19. Nancy Marie Robertson, *Christian Sisterhood, Race Relations, and the YWCA, 1906–1946* (Urbana: University of Illinois Press, 2007), 47 and 187n73. Judith Weisenfeld, *African American Women and Christian Activism: New York's Black YWCA, 1905–1945* (Cambridge, Mass.: Harvard University Press, 1997), 47.

BTW to Bettie G. Cox Francis, April 21, 1904, *BTW Papers*, 7:482–83n. BTW, *The Story of My Life and Work* (Westport, Conn.: Negro Universities Press, 1969), 172. Nina Mjagkij, *Light in the Darkness: African Americans and the YMCA, 1852–1946* (Lexington: University Press of Kentucky, 1994), 5.

18. *New Orleans American*, November 13, 1915; *Buffalo (NY) News*, January 15, 1916, MN 732; and *New York Times*, November 21, 1915, MN 732. *New York Times*, December 13, 1915, all in BTW LOC. Louis R. Harlan, *Booker T. Washington in Perspective: Essays of Louis R. Harlan*, edited by Raymond W. Smock (Jackson: University Press of Mississippi, 1988), 152–63.

19. *Waterville (ME) Sentinel*, November 20, 1915; *Bridgeton (NJ) Pioneer*, December 9, 1915; *Richmond (IN) Palladium*, December 6, 1915; *Minneapolis (MN) Trip*, November 17, 1915; *Davenport (IA) Times*, December 20, 1915, MN 732; *New York Age*, 1916, MN 422; *Fort Smith (AR) American*, November 17, 1915; and *Pueblo (CO) Chieftain*, December 5, 1915, MN 732. Unidentified New York newspaper, November 17, 1915, MN 422, all in BTW LOC.

20. *Boston Record*, November 17, 1915; *Cleveland (OH) Leader*, November 16, 1915, MN 732. *New Orleans Star*, December 14, 1915; *New York American*, November 20, 1915, MN 732; *Philadelphia Record*, December 6, 1915, MN 422; unidentified newspaper, February 1916, MN 733, all in BTW LOC.

21. *Kansas City (MO) Times*, November 15, 1915; *Minneapolis (MN) Trip*, November 15, 1915; *Newark (NJ) Star*, November 16, 1915; and *Lima (OH) Gazette*, November 16, 1915, MN 732. *Los Angeles (CA) Times*, December 3, 1915, MN 732; *San Francisco Examiner*, January 2, 1916, MN 733; *Kansas City (MO) Post*, February 10, 1916; and *Hamilton (OH) Journal*, March 1, 1916, MN 734. *Tucson Providence Bulletin*, April 1, 1916, MN 734, *Arizona Citizen* (Tucson), April 6, 1916; *Springfield (OH) Morning Sun*, April 7, 1916; *Montgomery (AL) Advertiser*, April 10, 1916; *Providence (RI) Tribune*, December 11, 1915; and *Kansas City (MO) Journal*, November 21, 1915, MN 733. *New York Age*, November 18, 1915. *Chicago Defender*, November 17, 1915, all in BTW LOC.

22. *Fort Smith (AR) American*, November 17, 1915, MN 732, BTW LOC. "Mrs. Mame Stewart Josenberger" [Mary E. Josenburger], *National Cyclopedia of the Colored Race*, edited by Clement Richardson (Montgomery, Ala.: National Publishing, 1919), 1:99. Nancy H. Burkett et al., eds., *Black Biographical Dictionaries 1790–1950*, microfiche addenda (Alexandria, Va.: Chadwyck-Healy, 1987), MR 75, 165.

23. "Mrs. Mame Stewart Josenberger" [Mary E. Josenburger], 99. William A. Pinkerton, "A Report of Pinkerton's National Detective Agency," November 14, 1905, *BTW Papers*, 8:439nn.

24. *Chicago Defender*, November 20, 1915. *New York Times*, August 5, 1994. Mark Harris, *Historical Dictionary of Unitarians Universalism* (Lanham, Md.: Scarecrow Press, 2004), 530–53. The first quote is by Philip Jackson, "Black Charity in Progressive Era Chicago," *Social Service Review* 52, no. 3 (September 1978): 410. Samuel Laing Williams to EJS, July 10, 1905, *BTW Papers*, 8:325. Samuel Laing Williams to EJS, October 22, 1906, *BTW Papers*, 9:102.

25. *New York City Evening Sun*, November 20, 1915, MN 732, BTW LOC. *New York Times*, February 1, 1923.

26. *Who Was Who in America*, vol. 1, *1897–1942* (Chicago: A. N. Marquis Co., 1843), 213. *New York Times*, February 1, 1923. Charles William Anderson to William Howard Taft, March 24, 1911, 11:37–38; and William Howard Taft to BTW, March 12, 1911, 11:10, both in *BTW Papers*.

27. *New York Age*, December 2, 1915, MN 732, BTW LOC. *New York Times*, April 16, 1946, and May, 1, 1955. "The Reminiscences of William Jay Schieffelin (February 1949)," 10, 12, 18, 21, 23, 35, 51, 75, 87, and 96, Oral History Collection of Columbia University.

28. *Kansas City (MO) Post*, February 10, 1916, MN 734, BTW LOC. *Outlook* 88, no. 17 (April 25, 1908), and 88, no. 1 (December 4, 1909). *Rochester (NY) Express*, January 11, 1916, MN 734, 1916, BTW LOC. *New York Times*, June 19, 1922. Unidentified Los Angeles newspaper, November 28, 1915, MN 732, BTW LOC. *Los Angeles Times*, May 8, 2005.

29. *Albany (NY) Times Union*, December 9, 1915, MN 732, BTW LOC. *New York Times*, March 8, 1940. BTW to John Huston Finley, September 28, 1890, 5:222; James Hardy Dillard to BTW, May 30, 1907, 9:284–85nn; and EJS to BTW, January 12, 1910, all in *BTW Papers*, 10:261–63.

30. *Milwaukee (WI) Sentinel*, December 1, 1915, MN 732, BTW LOC. *New York Times*, November 18, 1920.

31. *Albany (NY) Times Union*, December 9, 1915. "A News Item in the Washington Post," March 23, 1911, 11:31 and 11:32n; Seth Low to Edward Morse Shepard, March 27, 1911, 11:45; and "An Article in the New York World," November 7, 1911, 11:361; BTW to Charles Seymour Whitman, November 5, 1914, 13:164, all in *BTW Papers*. *New York Times*, March 30, 1947.

32. *New York Times*, March 31, 1923.

33. Ibid. Gerald Edwin Ridinger, "The Political Career of Frank B. Willis" (Ph. D. dissertation, Ohio State University, 1957), 100–101.

34. *New York Times*, December 31, 1915. "Hammond, Winfield Scott," *The National Cyclopedia of American Biography* (New York: James T. White & Co., 1910), 16:99.

35. *Providence (RI) Bulletin*, April 1, 1916, MN 734, BTW LOC. Emmet O'Neal to BTW, February 17, 1913, 12:117; BTW to Lawrence Fraser Abbott, May 27, 1911, 11:171–72; Emmet O'Neal, November 25, 1914, 13:186–87; Thomas Jesse Jones, November 25, 1914, 13:188–89; BTW to Cleveland Hoadley Dodge, January 6, 1915, 13:215–16, all in *BTW Papers*.

36. *New York City Age*, December 2, 1915, MN 732, BTW LOC. Norrell, *Up from History*, 385–86. *BTW2*, 295–96. William Howard Taft to BTW, March 21, 1921, *BTW Papers*, 11:10.

37. *New York Tribune*, December 13, 1915, book 55, 2:106; and *Memphis (TN) Commercial Appeal*, December 12, 1915, book 54, 1:89, both in Hampton Clippings. *BTW1*, 305, 307–24; and William Henry Baldwin Jr. to BTW, September 18, 1901, 6:211; and Theodore Roosevelt, "An Address by Theodore Roosevelt," October 24, 1905, 8:428–21, all in *BTW Papers*.

38. BTW to Theodore Roosevelt, March 9, 1909, 10:21; Oswald Garrison Villard to BTW, August 5, 1912, 11:575–76; and BTW to William Henry Lewis, January 20, 1913, 12:105–6; Theodore Roosevelt to Julius Rosenwald, December 15, 1915, 13:480–81, all in *BTW Papers*.

39. *San Francisco Bulletin*, January 4, 1916, MN 734, BTW LOC. *San Francisco Chronicle*, May 17, 1957. *New York Times*, May 17, 1957.

40. *Springfield (OH) Morning Sun*, April 7, 1916, MN 733, BTW LOC. Josiah Morrow, "Joseph W. O'Neall," *The History of Warren County, Ohio*, part 5, *Biographical Sketches* (Chicago: W. H. Beers Co., 1882), 767–68. *Elyria (OH) Evening Telegram*, April 6, 1915.

41. *Minneapolis (MN) News*, November 22, 1915, MN 732, BTW LOC. *Minnesota News-Tribune* (Duluth), April, 4, 1915. *New Haven (CT) Register*, February 28, 1884. *Springfield (MA) Republican*, April 7, 1922. *Outlook*, April 26, 1922, 679.

42. Unidentified Los Angeles newspaper, November 28, 1915, MN 732, BTW LOC. *Pittsburgh (PA) Press*, February 2, 1931. *Riverside (CA) Daily Press*, February 9, 1931; and March 31, 1931. *Trenton (NJ) Evening Times*, February 9, 1931. John Willis Baer to BTW, June 21, 1901, 6:157, 163; "A Memorandum on Washington's Itinerary," February 20, 1914, 12:448–50n, both in *BTW Papers*.

43. *Cleveland (OH) Leader*, November 16, 1915, MN 732, BTW LOC. *Albuquerque Journal*, August 28, 1915. *Cleveland (OH) Plain Dealer*, March 31, 1903; March 31, 1910; August 8, 1929; April 29, 1912; and May 26, 1941.

44. *Newark (NJ) News*, December 9, 1915, MN 732, BTW LOC. BTW to Samuel Chapman Armstrong, March 15, 1890, 3:36–37, *BTW Papers*. *Daily Princetonia* 57, no. 105 (October 5, 1932): 1.

45. *Springfield (MA) Republic*, December 10, 1915, MN 732, BTW LOC. *Black Biographical Dictionaries 1790–1950*, MN 116, 63–75; MN 235, 187.

46. *Augusta (GA) Chronicle*, December 5, 1915, MN 732, BTW LOC. *Savannah (GA) Tribune*, August 4 and 8, 1921. *Savannah (GA) Tribune*, August 23, 1921. *Washington (D.C.) Bee*, August 20, 1921. *Black Biographical Dictionaries 1790–1950*, MN 14, 43–46; MN 52, 1:683–88. Iain H. Murray, *The Forgotten Spurgeon* (Edinburgh, U.K.: Banner of Truth Trust, 1966), 12. An internationally renowned London Baptist theologian, Charles Spurgeon, pastored to the largest single Christian congregation in the world. Arnold Dallimore, *Spurgeon* (Chicago: Moody Press, 1984), 97.

47. *Black Biographical Dictionaries 1790–1950*, MN 14, 43–46; and MN 52, 1:683–88. *Washington (D.C.) Bee*, August 20, 1921. Ralph E. Luker, *The Social Gospel in Black and White: American Racial Reform, 1885–1912* (Chapel Hill: University of North Carolina Press, 1991), 180.

48. August Meier, *Negro Thought in America, 1880–1915* (Ann Arbor: University of Michigan Press, 1966), 222 and 224. "Summary of the Proceeding of the Conference at Carnegie Hall," January 6, 7, and 8, 1904, 7:384–87; and BTW to Robert Russa Moton, May 23, 1911, 11:166–67, both in *BTW Papers*.

49. *New York Age*, December 2, 1915, MN 732, BTW LOC. *Black Biographical Dictionaries 1790–1950*, MN 230, 214–19; and MN 247, 340. Timothy Thomas Fortune to BTW, June 1, 1899, 5:122–23n, *BTW Papers*.

50. BTW, "To the Editor of the New York Freeman," June 7, 1887, 2:357; Alexander Walters to BTW, February 16, 1903, 7:79–89; and BTW to EJS, January 16, 1914, 12:417–18, all in *BTW Papers*. Shawn Leigh Alexander, *An Army of Lions: The Civil Rights Struggle before the NAACP* (Philadelphia: University of Pennsylvania Press, 2012).

51. *Lima (OH) Gazette*, November 16, 1915, MN 732, BTW LOC. *Indianapolis Freeman*, August 22, 1903; April 16, 1904; February 11, 1905; February 1, 1908; March 28, 1908; September 4, 1912; and August 7, 1915.

52. *Springfield (OH) Morning Sun*, April 7, 1916, MN 733, BTW LOC. Curry perceived the tribute as a fund-raising event for his school. *Oregonian* (Portland, OR), July 19, 1908. David A. Gerber, *Black Ohio and the Color Line, 1860–1915* (Urbana: University of Illinois Press, 1976), 394–95. *Black Biographical Dictionaries 1790–1950*, MN 7, 58; and MN 281, 50–51. *Indianapolis Freeman*, January 14, 1893, May 1, 1997, and October 1, 1904. *Cleveland (OH) Gazette*, July 25, 1891, and June 22, 1907. *Lexington (KY) Herald*, July 17 and 18, 1908.

53. *Kansas City (MO) Journal*, November 21, 1915, MN 732, BTW LOC. *Black Biographical Dictionaries 1790–1950*, MN 235, 484.

54. *Albany (NY) Journal*, December 16, 1915; *Milwaukee (WI) Sentinel*, December 1, 1915; *Pasadena (CA) News*, November 27, 1915; and *San Francisco Examiner*, November 21, 1915, MN 732, all in BTW LOC. Chicago *Defender*, November 20, 1905. *Riverside (CA) Daily Press*, August 22, 1903. *San Jose (CA) Evening News*, August 9 and 11, 1900.

55. *Detroit (MI) Press*, April 2, 1916. *Black Biographical Dictionaries 1790–1950*, MN 45, 491–93; and MN 143, 182. John Hope Franklin, "John Roy Lynch," in Logan and Winston, *Dictionary of American Negro Biography*, 407–9.

56. Franklin, "John Roy Lynch." *Black Biographical Dictionaries 1790–1950*, MN 45, 491–93; and MN 143, 182.

57. BTW, *Up from Slavery* (New York: Dodd, Mead, 1965), 139. BTW to John Roy Lynch, March 14, 1888, *BTW Papers*, 2:420–21. John Hope Franklin, ed., *Reminiscences of an Active Life: The Autobiography of John Roy Lynce* (Chicago: University of Chicago Press, 1970), 369, 494, and 495.

58. *New York Post*, November 20, 1915, MN 732; *Montgomery (AL) Journal*, January 10, 1916, MN 734; unidentified newspaper, n.d., MN 422, all in BTW LOC. Robert C. Hayden, "Garrett A. Morgan," in Logan and Winston, *Dictionary of American Negro Biography*, 453. *Detroit (MI) Press*, April 2, 1916, MN 733, BTW LOC.

59. *McKeesport (PA) News*, November 17, 1916; and *Vicksburg (MS) Herald*, November 21, 1915, MN 732, both in BTW LOC. *California Eagle* (Los Angeles), November 20, 1915. *Stockton (CA) Independent*, December 3, 1915, MN 732, BTW LOC. *Chicago Defender*, November 27, 1915. *Rochester (NY) Herald*, January 11, 1916, MN 734; *Indianapolis (IN) Star*, December 12, 1915; *Los Angeles Times*, December 3, 1915; and *Chicago Defender*, November 26, 1915, MN 732, all in BTW LOC.

60. *Los Angeles Evening Herald*, May 10, 1916, MN 734, BTW LOC.

61. *Malden (MA) News*, December 28, 1915; *Los Angeles Times*, December 3, 1915; unidentified Newburgh (NY) newspaper, November 22, 1915, MN 732; and *New York*

News, January 13, 1916, MN 733. In Boston "Several hundred negroes [*sic*] attended a memorial service in the People's Baptist Church." *Boston Record*, November 17, 1915, MN 732. *Richmond (IN) Palladium*, December 6, 1915, MN 732, all in BTW LOC.

62. Unidentified Denver (CO) newspaper, November 1916, MN 422, BTW LOC. *Philadelphia Inquirer*, December 8, 1915, book 55, 2:103, Hampton Clippings. *Philadelphia Record*, December 6, 1915, MN 422; *Portland (OR) Telegram*, November 22, 1915; and *Cleveland (OH) Plain Dealer*, November 22, 1915, MN 732, all in BTW LOC. *Indianapolis Freeman*, November 27, 1915. *Indianapolis Star*, December 12, 1915, MN 732, both in BTW LOC. *Memphis (TN) Commercial Appeal*, December 12, 1915, book 54, 1:89, Hampton Clippings. Unidentified newspaper, February 1916, MN 733; *New York Herald*, February 12, 1916; and *Chicago Defender*, December 4, 1915, MN 422; and *Los Angeles Times*, December 3, 1915, MN 732, all in BTW LOC.

Chapter 6. Gone but Not Forgotten

1. Historians, and indeed most other scholars, have generally neglected the properties, purpose, and power of eulogies. On the other hand, rhetoricians have produced the most comprehensive and helpful analysis of these orators. Karen A. Foss, "John Lennon and the Advisory Function of Eulogies," *Central States Speech Journal* 34 (1983): 127, 141, 187, 189, and 192. John F. Davidson, "An Analysis of Selected Eulogies of the Twentieth Century in Light of the Theories of the Classical Rhetoricians" (PhD diss., Bradley University, 1970), 1, 2, 6, 10, 14, 94, 95, and 96. Kathleen Marie German, "An Analysis of Legitimation for the Institution in Funeral Eulogies for Heads of State" (PhD diss., University of Iowa, 1976), 27–28. Paul C. Brownlow and Beth Davis, "A Certainty of Honor, the Eulogies of Ada Stevenson," *Central States Speech Journal* 25 (1974). Steven R. Goldzwig and Patricia A. Sullivan, "Post-Assassination Newspaper Editorial Eulogies: Analysis and Assessment," *Western Journal of Communication* 59, no. 2 (1999): 127 and 141.

2. Davidson, "Analysis of Selected Eulogies of the Twentieth Century," 6. Goldzwig and Sullivan, "Post-Assassination Newspaper Editorial Eulogies," 134.

3. For a discussion concerning affects, see Melissa Gregg and Gregory J. Seigworth, eds., *The Affect Theory Reader* (Durham, N.C.: Duke University Press, 2010). *Montgomery (AL) Journal*, January 10, 1916, MN 734; *New York Age*, 1916, MN 422; *Rochester (NY) Times*, January 12, 1916, and *Rochester (NY) Union-Advertiser*, January 12, 1916, MN 734, all in BTW LOC. *Rochester (NY) Democrat and Chronicle*, January 13, 1916, book 55, 2:124, Hampton Clippings.

4. C. F. Johnson to EJS, telg. November 16, 1915, MN 420; *New York City News*, November 20, 1915; *West Chester (PA) Daily Local News*, November 28, 1915, MN 732, all in BTW LOC. *Redlands (CA) Daily Facts*, December 1, 1915. Unidentified Newburgh (NY) newspaper, November 22, 1915, MN 732, both in BTW LOC.

5. Alexander Stein, "Music, Mourning, and Consolation," *Journal of the American Psychoanalytic* 52, no. 783 (2004): 790, 792, 800, 807, and 808. Robert James Branham and Stephen J. Hartnett, *Sweet Freedom's Song: "My Country 'Tis of Thee" and Democracy in America* (New York: Oxford University Press, 2002), 53–54.

6. *Newark (NJ) News*, December 9, 1915, MN 732; *Flushing (NY) Journal*, March 10, 1918, MN 734; *Dayton (OH) News*, November 27, 1915, MN 732; *Montgomery (AL) Advertiser*, December 13, 1915, MN 422; and *Indianapolis (IN) Freeman*, December 18, 1915, MN 422, all in BTW LOC.

7. *Redlands (CA) Daily Facts*, 1915, MN 732; *Rochester (NY) Chronicle*, February 5, 1916, MN 734, both in BTW LOC. William W. Austin, *"Susanna," "Jeanie," and "The Old Folks At Home": The Songs of Stephen C. Foster from His Time to Ours* (New York: Macmillan, 1975), 223–37. Ken Emerson, *Doo-dah! Stephen Foster and the Rise of American Popular Culture* (New York: Simon & Schuster, 1997), 189–90 and 256–59.

8. *Rochester (NY) Chronicle*, February 5, 1916, MN 734, BTW LOC. Howard L. Sacks and Judith Rose Sacks, *Way up North in Dixie: A Black Family's Claim to the Confederate Anthem* (Washington, D.C.: Smithsonian Institution Press), 3–5. Hans Nathan, *Dan Emmett and the Rise of Early Negro Minstrelsy* (Norman: University of Oklahoma Press, 1962), 268–75.

9. Sacks and Sacks, *Way up North in Dixie*, 160–88. *New York Times*, October 7, 1894.

10. *Trenton (NJ) Times*, February 12, 1916, book 55, 2:115, Hampton Clippings. *Oakland (CA) Sunshine*, March 18, 1916, MN 734, BTW LOC. Annie J. Randall, "A Censorship of Forgetting; Origins and Origin Myths of 'Battle Hymn of the Republic,'" in *Music, Power, and Politics*, edited by Annie J. Randall (New York: Routledge, 2005), 12–16. C. A. Browne, *The Story of Our National Ballads* (New York: Thomas Crowell Company, 1931), 194 and 198. Julia Ward Howe, *Reminiscences, 1819–1899* (New York: Negro University Press, 1899), 273–77.

11. *Trenton (NJ) Times*, February 12, 1916, book 55, 2:115, Hampton Clippings.

12. *Oakland (CA) Sunshine*, March 18, 1916, MN 734, BTW LOC.

13. For examples of tributes that sung "America," see *Redlands (CA) Daily Facts*, December 1, 1915, and unidentified Yonkers (NY) newspaper, December 2, 1915, MN 732, both in BTW LOC. Robert James Branham and Hartnett, *Sweet Freedom's Song*, 15, 37, and 221–28.

14. Branham and Hartnett, *Sweet Freedom's Song*, 210–11.

15. Ibid., 19, 59, 120, 130, 149, 174, 182, 198, 220–28.

16. Alan M. Kraut, *The Huddled Masses: The Immigrant in American Society, 1880–1921* (Arlington Heights, Ill.: Harlan Davidson, 1982), 123–129, 149, 151, and 159. George McKenna, *The Puritan Origins of American Patriotism* (New Haven, Conn.: Yale University Press, 2007), 171–80.

17. *Flushing (NY) Evening Journal*, March 17, 1916, MN 734; *New York Age*, December 9, 1915, MN 732; *New York City Amsterdam News*, December 17, 1915, MN 422; unidentified newspaper, January 1, 1916, MN 734, all in BTW LOC. *Memphis (TN) Commercial Appeal*, December 12, 1915, book 54, 1:89, Hampton Clippings.

18. *Christian Recorder*, November 20, 1915; and *Oak Leaf*, November 28, 1915, MN 422, both in BTW LOC; *Jacksonville Courier*, November 1915, book 54, 1:44, Hampton Clippings. *Savannah (GA) Press*, November 18, 1915, MN 732; and unidentified

periodical, January 1, 1916, MN 732, both in BTW LOC. *Memphis Commercial Appeal*, December 12, 1915, book 54, 1:89, Hampton Clippings.

19. *Oak Leaf*, November 28, 1915, MN 422, BTW LOC. Emmett J. Scott and Lyman Beecher Stowe, *Booker T. Washington: Builder of a Civilization* (Garden City, N.Y.: Doubleday, Page, 1917), 316. *Tucson (AZ) Citizen*, April 10, 1915, MN 733; *Indianapolis Freeman*, December 18, 1915, MN 422; and unidentified Hartford (CT) newspaper, n.d., MN 422, BTW LOC. *Redlands (CA) Daily Facts*, December 1, 1915.

20. Unidentified Hartford (CT) newspaper, n.d., MN 422, BTW LOC. *Newark (NJ) Star*, December 6, 1915, book 54, 1:82, Hampton Clippings. *New Orleans Picayune*, November 30, 1915, MN 732, BTW LOC. William H. Lewis, "Booker T. Washington—A Lover of His Fellow-Men," in *Negro Orators and Their Orations*, edited by Carter G. Woodson (Washington, D.C.: Associated Publishers, 1925), 600. Unidentified Newburgh (NY) newspaper, November 22, 1915, MN 732, BTW LOC. Milan Zafirovski, *The Protestant Ethic and the Spirit of Authoritarianism: Puritanism, Democracy, and Society* (New York: Springer, 2007), 1.

21. *BTW1*, 234–35. Charles William Anderson to BTW, December 11, 1906, *BTW Papers*, 519. *Jacksonville (FL) Courier*, November 1915, book 54, 1:44, Hampton Clippings. Lewis, "Booker T. Washington," 599–600.

22. *BTW1*, 233. *Peoria (IL) Star*, November 29, 1915, MN 732; *Flushing (NY) Evening Journal*, March 17, 1916, both in BTW LOC. Lewis, "Booker T. Washington," 596. *Oak Leaf*, November 28, 1915, MN 422, BTW LOC.

23. *Hartford (CT) Daily Times*, n.d., 422; Lewis, "Booker T. Washington," 599. Undated; *Indianapolis Freeman*, December 18, 1915; unidentified newspaper, n.d., MN 422; and *West Chester (PA) Daily Local News*, MN 732, all in BTW LOC.

24. *Savannah (GA) Press*, November 18, 1915, MN 732; *Hartford (CT) Daily Times*, n.d.; *Christian Recorder*, November 20, 1915; and *Oak Leaf*, November 28, 1915, MN 422, all in BTW LOC. *Southern Workman*, January 1915.

25. *New York City Amsterdam News*, December 17, 1915, book 54, 2:106, Hampton Clippings. *New York Age*, January 27, 1916, MN 734, BTW LOC. Unidentified New Haven (CT) newspaper, November 29, 1915, book 54, 1:74–75; unidentified San Diego (CA) newspaper, December 11, 1915, book 54, 1:85, both in Hampton Clippings. Lewis, "Booker T. Washington," 599.

26. Lewis, "Booker T. Washington," 598. *Milwaukee Living Church*, November 27, 1915; *Los Angeles Herald*, November 24, 1915, and *Waterville (ME) Sentinel*, November 20, 1915, MN 732, all in BTW LOC.

27. *Rochester (NY) Union-Advertiser*, January 12, 1915, MN 734; *Indianapolis Freeman*, December 18, 1915, MN 422, both in BTW LOC. *Redlands (CA) Daily Facts*, December 1, 1915. Unidentified periodical, January 1, 1916, MN 734, BTW LOC.

28. *Redlands (CA) Daily Facts*, December 1, 1915. Unidentified Hartford (CT) newspaper, n.d.; *New York City Amsterdam News*, December 17, 1915; and unidentified newspaper, November 20, 1915, MN 422; *Rochester (NY) Herald*, MN 732; and *Chicago Defender*, December 4, 1915, MN 422, all in BTW LOC.

29. *Norwich (CT) Bulletin*, December 13, 1915; *New York City Post*, November 20, 1915, MN 732, both in BTW LOC.

30. *California Eagle* (Los Angeles), December 4, 1915. Unidentified newspaper, November 20, 1915; *Rochester (NY) Herald*, November 22, 1915; and *Oak Leaf*, November 28, 1915, MN 422, all in BTW LOC.

31. Unidentified, n.d., MN 422, BTW LOC. *Newark (NJ) Star*, December 6, 1915, book 54, 1:82, Hampton Clippings. *Cleveland (OH) Plain Dealer*, November 22, 1915, MN 732; unidentified Hartford (CT) newspaper, n.d.; and *Oak Leaf*, November 28, 1915, MN 422; *Waterville (ME) Sentinel*, November 20, 1915, MN 732, all in BTW LOC.

32. For information concerning labor and conscientiousness, see Daniel T. Rodgers, *The Work Ethic in Industrial America 1850–1920* (Chicago: University of Chicago Press, 1974), 9. *Hartford (CT) Daily Times*, n.d., MN 422, BTW LOC. *Cleveland (OH) Plain Dealer*, November 22, 1915, book 54, 1:38, Hampton Clippings. Lewis, "Booker T. Washington," 800. *Oak Leaf*, November 28, 1915, MN 422, BTW LOC.

33. Unidentified Newburgh (NY) newspaper, November 22, 1915, MN 732; unidentified Detroit journal, n.d., 1916, MN 734, both in BTW LOC.

34. Unidentified Hartford (CT) newspaper, n.d.; and *Oak Leaf*, November 28, 1915, MN 422; *Chattanooga (TN) News*, November 29, 1915, MN 732, all in BTW LOC. *American Baptist*, November 21, 1915, book 55, 1:85, Hampton Clippings. Arnold H. Taylor, "Simmons, William J.," in *Dictionary of American Negro Biography*, edited by Rayford W. Logan and Michael R. Winston (New York: W. W. Norton, 1982), 556–57. *Atlanta (GA) Independent*, September 2, 1916, book 239, 1:12–14, Hampton Clippings.

35. Max Weber, *The Protestant Ethic and the Spirit of Capitalism*, translated by Talcott Parson (North Charleston, S.C.: CreateSpace Independent Publishing Platform, 2010), 78. Ernst Troeltsch, *Protestantism and Progress* (Philadelphia, Pa.: Fortress Press, 1986), 70; *Indianapolis Freeman*, December 18, 1915, MN 422; and *Hartford (CT) Courant*, January 10, 1916, MN 734, both in BTW LOC. Lewis, "Booker T. Washington," 598. *Buffalo (NY) News*, November 23, 1915, MN 732, BTW LOC.

36. Weber, *Protestant Ethic and the Spirit of Capitalism*, 83. Lendol Calder, *Financing the American Dream: A Cultural History of Consumer Credit* (Princeton, N.J.: Princeton University Press, 1999), 89–90; and Paul Langley, *The Everyday Life of Global Finance: Saving and Borrowing in Anglo-America* (New York: Oxford University Press, 2008), 51–52. BTW, *Character Building* (New York: Doubleday, Page, 1902), 267–76; and BTW, *Black-Belt Diamonds: Gems from the Speeches, Addresses, and Talks to Students of Booker T. Washington*, edited by Victoria Earle Matthews (New York: Fortune and Scott, 1898), 39–40, 57, and 86–87. *Chattanooga (TN) News*, November 29, 1915, MN 732, BTW LOC. Lewis, "Booker T. Washington" 599. Unidentified New Haven (CT) newspaper, November 20, 1915, book 54, 1:74; and unidentified San Diego (CA) newspaper, December 11, 1915, book 54, 1:85, both in Hampton Clippings.

37. *Chicago Defender*, November 27, 1915; and *New York City Post*, November 20, 1915, MN 732, both in BTW LOC. Robert R. Moton, "Life of Achievement," in Woodson, *Negro Orators and Their Orations*, 605.

38. John M. Blum et al., *The National Experience: A History of the United States* (New York: Harcourt, Brace & World, 1963), 62–63. David Edwin Harrell Jr. et al., eds. *Unto a Good Land: A History of the American People* (Grand Rapids, Mich.:

William B. Eerdmans, 2005), 107–9 and 776–77. Ronald E. Butchart, *Schooling the Freed People: Teaching, Learning, and the Struggle for Black Freedom, 1861–1876* (Chapel Hill: University of North Carolina Press, 2010), 15 and 149–50. Eric Anderson and Alfred A. Moss Jr., *Dangerous Donations: Northern Philanthropy and Southern Black Education, 1902–1930* (Columbia: University of Missouri Press, 1999), 85–107. Ralph E. Luker, *The Social Gospel in Black and White: American Racial Reform, 1885–1912* (Chapel Hill: University of North Carolina Press), 148–51.

39. *Schenectady (NY) Star*, December 9, 1915; unidentified Newburgh (NY) newspaper, November 22, 1915, MN 732; and *Providence (RI) Bulletin*, April 1, 1916, MN 733, all in BTW LOC.

40. *New York Herald*, December 18, 1915; *Indianapolis Freeman*, December 18, 1915, MN 422; *Detroit (MI) Times*, April 14, 1916; *Montgomery (AL) Advertiser*, April 10, 1916, MN 733, all in BTW LOC.

41. Harrell et al., *Unto a Good Land: A History of the American People*, 777–778. For an example of Washington teaching selected aspects of the Yankee Protestant ethic, see BTW, "A Sunday Evening Talk," November 20, 1898, *BTW Papers*, 4:513–15. BTW, "A Speech before the Philosophian Lyceum of Lincoln University," April 26, 188, *BTW Papers*, 2:439–51.

42. *New York Times*, December 10, 1915, MN 732, BTW LOC. Moton, "Life of Achievement," 604. *Oak Leaf*, November 28, 1915; *Atlanta (GA) Constitution*, November 1915, MN 422; *Trenton (NJ) Times*, MN 731, *Detroit (MI) Times*, April 14, 1916, MN 733, all in BTW LOC.

43. James D. Anderson, *The Education of Blacks in the South, 1860–1935* (Chapel Hill: University of North Carolina Press, 1988), 65–78. Monroe Work to BTW, December 29, 1910, MN 487; and *Oak Leaf*, November 29, 1915, MN 422, both in BTW LOC. Lewis, "Booker T. Washington," 599. *Redlands (CA) Daily Facts*, December 1, 1915. *Montgomery (AL) Advertiser*, December 13, 1915, MN 422, BTW LOC.

44. Lewis, "Booker T. Washington," 599; *Morristown (NJ) Record*, January 10, 1016, MN 734, BTW LOC. *Chicago Defender*, November 27, 1915. *Peoria (IL) Star*, November 29, 1915, MN 732, BTW LOC.

45. *Christian Recorder*, November 20, 1915, MN 422. Unidentified Newburgh (NY) newspaper, November 22, 1915, MN 732, BTW LOC.

46. *Buffalo (NY) News*, January 15, 1916, MN 733; unidentified Newburgh (NY) newspaper, November 22, 1915, MN 32, both in BTW LOC. *Southern Workman*, January 1918. *Harlem (NY) Home News*, November 21, 1915, MN 732, BTW LOC. Unidentified New Haven (CT) newspaper, November 29, 1915, book 54, 1:74–75, Hampton Clippings.

47. BTW, "To the Trustees of the Tuskegee Normal & Ind. Institute," 1909–10; BTW to Seth Low, September 24, 1912, MN 526; Monroe Work to BTW, January 20 and March 1, 1909, MN 475, all in BTW LOC. "Principal's Report to the Board of Trustees of the Tuskegee Normal and Industrial Institute 1909," TUA; for data concerning contacts, see "Number of Persons Reached thru Tuskegee's Extension Activities, May 1909," MN 692, BTW LOC.

48. John Howard Burrows, "The Necessity of Myth: A History of the National Negro Business League 1900–1945" (PhD diss., Auburn University, 1977), 215. Anson Phelps Stokes to BTW, November 24, 1914, *BTW Papers*, 13:182. BTW to Robert Russsa Moton, November 25, 1914, *BTW Papers*, 13:187–86. BTW to James Carroll Napier, January 7, 1915, *BTW Papers*, 13:218. Pheobe Pollitt, "From National Negro Health Week to National Public Health Week," *Journal of Community Health*, December 1996, 2, 3, 5, and 6.

49. BTW to EJS, August 7, 1906, *BTW Papers*, 9:51; BTW to Julius Rosenwald, June 21, 1912, *BTW Papers*, 11:552–54; Anna Thomas Jeanes to BTW, February 25, 1905, *BTW Papers*, 8:201–3nn; BTW to Henry Huddleston Rogers, February 25, 1907, *BTW Papers*, 9:223; Roscoe Conkling Simmons to EJS, January 12, 1904, *BTW Papers*, 8:176–77nn. Mary S. Hoffschwelle, *The Rosenwald Schools of the American South* (Gainesville: University Press of Florida, 2006), xii, 1, and 3.

50. *New York City Post*, November 20, 1915, MN 732, BTW LOC. Moton, "Life of Achievement," 607. Unidentified newspaper, November 18, 1915, book 53, 1.66, Hampton Clippings.

51. *New York City Post*, November 20, 1915, MN 732, BTW LOC. Lewis, "Booker T. Washington," 599. Moton, "Life of Achievement," 602.

52. Unidentified New Haven (CT) newspaper, November 20, 1915, book 54, 1:74, Hampton Clippings. *Providence (RI) Bulletin*, April 1, 1916, MN 734, BTW LOC. *Memphis (TN) Appeal*, December 12, 1915, book 54, 1:89, Hampton Clippings. *Tuskegee Student*, January, 1916. *Chicago Defender*, November 27, 1915. *Christian Recorder*, November 20, 1915, MN 214, all in BTW LOC.

53. Weber, *Protestant Ethic and the Spirit of Capitalism*, 83. *Providence (RI) Bulletin*, April 1, 1916, MN 734; unidentified Milwaukee newspaper, December 13, 1915, MN 422, both in BTW LOC.

54. *Dallas (TX) Morning News*, October 9, 1900. Unidentified newspaper, n.d., MN 422, both in BTW LOC.

55. Lewis, "Booker T. Washington," 599. *Savannah (GA) Tribune*, November 27, 1915.

56. *Flushing (NY) Evening Journal*, March 17, 1916; and *Des Moines (IA) Capital*, November 22, 1915, MN 422, both in BTW LOC. Moton, "Life of Achievement," 602–3.

57. Lewis, "Booker T. Washington," 599. Unidentified Newburgh (NY) newspaper, November 22, 1915, MN 732; *Chicago Defender*, December 4, 1915, MN 422, both in BTW LOC. *Memphis (TN) Commercial Appeal*, December 12, 1915, book 54, 1:89, Hampton Clippings. *Hartford (CT) Daily Times*, n.d., MN 422, BTW LOC.

58. Moton, "Life of Achievement," 603–44. *Tuskegee Student*, January 8, 1916. *Tucson (AZ) Citizen*, April 10, 1916, MN 733; unidentified Newburgh (NY) newspaper, MN 732, all in BTW LOC. *Chicago Defender*, November 27, 1915.

59. *Indianapolis Freeman*, December 18, 1915 MN 422; *Los Angeles Herald*, November 24, 1915, MN 732; *Hartford (CT) Daily Times*, MN 422; and *Rochester (NY) Union-Advertiser*, January 12, MN 734, all in BTW LOC.

60. BTW, *Up from Slavery* (Cornwall, N.Y.: Dodd, Mead, 1965), 130. *New Orleans Daily Picayune*, September 21, 1898, MN 433, BTW LOC. Unidentified Chicago newspaper, November 18, 1915, book 53, 1:66; unidentified New Haven (CT) newspaper, November 20, 1915, book 54, 1:74, both in Hampton Clippings.

61. Unidentified San Diego (CA) newspaper, December 11, 1915, book 54, 1:85, Hampton Clippings. Lewis, "Booker T. Washington," 599. Unidentified newspaper, January 1, 1916, MN 734; *Louisville (KY) Courier Journal*, December 20, 1915, both in BTW LOC.

62. BTW, "An Article in *The New Republic*," September 13, 1915, *BTW Papers*, 13:357. BTW, *The Story of My Life and Work* (New York: Negro Universities Press, 1969), 269–70. Unidentified New Haven (CT) newspaper, November 29, 1915, book 54, 1:74–75, Hampton Clippings. *New York Herald*, December 18, 1915, MN 422, BTW LOC.

63. August Meier, *Negro Thought in America, 1880–1915: Racial Ideologies in the Age of Booker T. Washington* (Ann Arbor: University of Michigan Press, 1963), 109–14. *New York Times*, December 10, 1915; and *Los Angeles Herald*, November 24, 1915, MN 732, both in BTW LOC.

64. Leon F. Litwack, *Trouble in Mind: Black Southerners in the Age of Jim Crow* (New York: Alfred A. Knopf, 1998). *Indianapolis Freeman*, December 18, 1915. *Detroit (MI) Leader*, January 7, 1916, MN 733, both in BTW LOC. *Boston Globe*, November 18, 1915, book 53, 1:118, Hampton Clippings. *Hartford (CT) Daily Times*, n.d., MN 422, BTW LOC. *Southern Workman*, January 1916. *Atlanta (GA) Constitution*, November 1915, MN 422; and *San Francisco Chronicle*, December 13, 1915, MN 732, all in BTW LOC.

65. Unidentified Nashville (TN) newspaper, January 10, 1916, MN 733; and *Oak Leaf*, November 28, 1915, MN 422, both in BTW LOC.

66. *Portland (OR) Journal*, November 22, 1915, MN 732; unidentified Denver (CO) newspaper, November 1915, MN 422; *Rochester (NY) Herald*, November 22, 1915, MN 732, all in BTW LOC. *New York News*, November 25, 1915, book 54, 1:50–51, Hampton Clippings. *New York Age*, November 25, 1915; unidentified Newburgh (NY) journal, November 22, 1915, MN 732; and *New York Age*, December 2, 1915, MN 732, all in BTW LOC.

67. Unidentified New Haven (CT) newspaper, November 20, 1915, book 54, 1:74, Hampton Clippings. *Indianapolis Freeman*, December 18, 1915, MN 422, BTW LOC.

68. *New York Times*, December 10, 1915, MN 732; *Flushing (NY) Evening Journal*, March 17, 1916, MN 734; and *West Chester (PA) Daily Local News*, November 28, 1915, MN 732; and *New York Age*, December 2, 1915, MN 732, all in BTW LOC.

69. *Milwaukee (WI) Living Church*, November 27, 1915; unidentified New Jersey newspaper, December 10, MN 732; *New York Age*, January 27, 1916, MN 734; all in BTW LOC. Unidentified New Haven (CT) newspaper, November 29, 1915, book 54, 1:74–75, Hampton Clippings. *Rochester (NY) Union-Advertiser*, January 12, 1915, MN 734, BTW LOC.

70. *Savannah (GA) Tribune*, November 27, 1915. Unidentified New Burgh (NY) newspaper, November 22, 1915; and *Rochester (NY) Herald*, November 22, 1915, MN 732; and unidentified newspaper, November 20, 1915, MN 422, all in BTW LOC.

71. "Allston, James Henderson," in *Who's Who of the Colored Race: A General Biographical Dictionary of Men and Women of African Descent*, edited by Frank Lincoln Mater (Chicago: Frank Lincoln Mater, 1915), 1:5. *Boston Daily Globe*, November 18, 1915, MN 732, BTW LOC. BTW to Robert A. Franks, December 16, 1908, *BTW Papers*, 9:701. *New York City Amsterdam News*, April 12, 1916, book 55, 2:150, Hampton Clippings. *Hartford (CT) Times*, January 10, 1916, MN 734, BTW LOC. *Atlanta Independent*, September 2, 1916, book 239, 1:12–14, Hampton Clippings.

Epilogue

1. Delbert Brunton to Tuskegee Faculty, November 16, 1915; W. T. Francis to Mrs. Booker T. Washington, telg. November 14, 1915; Delbert Brunton to Tuskegee Faculty, November 16, 1915, MN 420, both in BTW LOC.

2. *Savannah (GA) Tribune*, December 18, 1915.

3. The Booker T. Washington Memorial Fund, n.d., MN 613, BTW LOC.

4. *Thirty-Sixth Annual Report of the Principal and Treasurer Tuskegee Normal and Industrial Institute for the Year Ending May 31, 1917*, TUA, 21. The Booker T. Washington Memorial Fund, n.d., MN 613; *Los Angeles New Age*, June 23, 1916; *Portland (OR) Telegram*, December 4, 1915, MN 732; *Louisville (KY) American Baptist*, March 10, 1916; unidentified Muskogee (OK) newspaper, April, n.d., 1916, all in MN 733; *Kansas City (MO) Advocate*, February 23, 1916; *Asheville (NC) Citizen*, March 26, 1916, MN 734; *Louisville (KY) American Baptist*, March 10, 1916; *Tampa (FL) Tribune*, May 18, 1916, both in MN 733; *Boston Evening Transcript*, April 5, 1916; *New York Age*, May 4, 1916, MN 733, all in BTW LOC. *New York Age*, February 24, 1916, MN 733; *Baltimore Commonwealth*, March 18, 1916, book 55, 2:113, Hampton Clippings. "Programme and Addresses in Connection with Unveiling Exercises of the Booker T. Washington Memorial, Tuskegee Institute Alabama, April 5, 1922," 10, file cabinet, TUA.

5. Robert R. Moton to EJS, September 23, 1919, box 55, Robert R. Moton papers, TUA; William Anthony Aery, "The Booker T. Washington Monument," *Southern Workman* 51, no. 5 (May 1922): 222.

6. Charles Keck to Committee on Booker T. Washington Memorial, July 39, 1919; Moton to E. T. Belsaw, March 22, 1922, box 29, Moton papers, TUA.

7. "Programme and Addresses," 5–7; *New York Age*, April 8, 1916.

8. "Programme and Addresses," 1, 11, 13, and 27.

9. Ibid., 18; J. Morgan Kousser, *The Shaping of Southern Politics: Suffrage Restriction and the Establishment of the One-Party South, 1880–1910* (New Haven, Conn.: Yale University Press, 1974), 76, 189.

10. *Tuskegee Student*, April 29 and May 13, 1922, MN 740, BTW LOC.

11. Aery, "Booker T. Washington Monument," 219–20.

Index

KENNETH M. HAMILTON is an associate professor of nineteenth-century and African American history and the Director of Ethnic Studies at Southern Methodist University. He is the author of *Black Towns and Profit: Promotion and Development in the Trans-Appalachian West, 1877–1917*.

The New Black Studies Series

The University of Illinois Press
is a founding member of the
Association of American University Presses.

Composed in 10.5/13 Minion Pro
by Kirsten Dennison
at the University of Illinois Press
Cover designed by Jim Proefrock
Cover illustration: *Portrait of Booker T. Washington* by
Henry Ossawa Tanner, 1917
Manufactured by Sheridan Books, Inc.

University of Illinois Press
1325 South Oak Street
Champaign, IL 61820-6903
www.press.uillinois.edu